Origins and Consequences of European Crises:

Global Views on Brexit

Peter Lang

Bruxelles · Bern · Berlin · New York · Oxford · Wien

Birte Wassenberg & Noriko Suzuki (eds.)

Origins and Consequences of European Crises:

Global Views on Brexit

Border Studies – Borders and European Integration
Vol. 2

This publication is supported by the Humanities and Social Sciences English-language Scholarly Book Publishing Support Program FY2019 of Waseda University & the Jean Monnet Erasmus + Program of the European Union

With the support of the
Erasmus+ Programme
of the European Union

This publication has been peer reviewed.

No part of this book may be reproduced in any form, by print, photocopy, microfilm or any other means, without prior written permission from the publisher. All rights reserved.

© P.I.E. PETER LANG s.a.
Éditions scientifiques internationales
Brussels, 2020
1 avenue Maurice, B-1050 Bruxelles, Belgium
brussels@peterlang.com ; www.peterlang.com

ISBN 978-2-8076-1539-7
ePDF 978-2-8076-1540-3
Epub 978-2-8076-1541-0
Mobi 978-2-8076-1542-7

ISSN 2736-2450
DOI 10.3726/b17294
D/2020/5678/42

Bibliographic information published by "Die Deutsche Nationalbibliothek". "Die Deutsche National Bibliothek" lists this publication in the "Deutsche Nationalbibliografie"; detailed bibliographic data is available on the Internet at <http://dnb.de>.

Contents

Introduction 9
BIRTE WASSENBERG

PART 1: BREXIT AS A HISTORICAL AND POLITICAL PROCESS

Brexit, World War II Memory, and the Rhetoric of Appeasement ... 23
STEPHANIE BARCZEWSKI

Brexit as a Result of European Struggles over the UK's Financial
Sector 45
DAISUKE IKEMOTO

The Undemocratic Effects of a Referendum: One of the Many
Paradoxes of Brexit. A Legal Perspective 65
FRÉDÉRIQUE BERROD

PART 2: THE SOCIAL CONSEQUENCES OF BREXIT

The Right to Family Reunification after Brexit: The Impossible
Status Quo 89
AUDE BOUVERESSE

Brexit and Its Impact on the Integration of Migrants in the UK 105
SEIKO OYAMA

Effects of Brexit on UK Nationals Living in France 121
NORIKO SUZUKI

PART 3: THE ECONOMIC AND LEGAL CONSEQUENCES OF BREXIT

The "Real" Costs of Brexit 143
EMMANUEL BRUNET-JAILLY

From Opting Out to Brexit in the Area of Freedom,
Security and Justice 161
CATHERINE HAGUENAU-MOIZARD

PART 4: THE (GEO-)POLITICAL CONSEQUENCES OF BREXIT

The Consequences of Brexit for the Island of Ireland
'Deal or No Deal' 173
RUTH TAILLON

Brexit's Territorial Externalities 195
JEREMY SACRAMENTO & JAUME CASTAN PINOS

European Union-Japan Relations in the Shadow of Brexit 215
KEN MASUJIMA

About the Authors 223

Series « Borders and European Integration » 227
Series Editors 227
Scientific Board... 228

Introduction

BIRTE WASSENBERG

Since the vote of the British people in the referendum on 26 June 2016, when 52 % opted to leave and 48 % to remain in the European Union (EU), the European agenda has been dominated by the question how to organize the British exit, the so-called Brexit. There have been three years of passionate debates and negotiations preceding the final date of departure of the United Kingdom (UK) from the EU on 31 January 2020. In general, these debates were marked more by emotions than by facts and figures, mainly because Brexit had come as a shock for many people on both sides of the Channel. Indeed, almost sixty years after the signature of the Treaty of Rome in 1957 creating the European Community (EC), it was the first time in history that a Member State had decided to leave the Union.

But from a historical perspective, the British decision does not come as a total surprise.[1] Since their entry into the EC in 1972, the British have contested a lot of decisions in Brussels and have negotiated numerous advantages, for example regarding their budget contribution, as well as opting outs, such as for the Monetary Union or for the Common Security and Justice Affairs pillar. In fact, the UK has shown a considerable mistrust of the Community from the start, as the first referendum on membership on 5 June 1975 shows, where only 64.5 % had voted in favour of the EC.[2] Political scientists have even developed the very concept

---

[1] Ludlow, N. P., *Dealing with Britain: The Six and the First UK Application to the EEC*, Cambridge, Cambridge University Press, 1997.
[2] Usherwood, S., "Margeret Thatcher and British Opposition to European Integration: Saint or Sinner?", in Gainar, M., Libera, M. (eds.), *Contre l'Europe? Anti-européisme, euroscepticisme et alter-européisme dans la construction européenne de 1945 à nos jours*. Vol. 2. *Acteurs institutionnels, milieux politiques et société civile*, Stuttgart, Steiner, 2013, pp. 75–87.

of Euroscepticism by identifying it as a British phenomenon entering the political arena in the 1980s, notably with Margaret Thatcher's rejection of the EC.[3] Her contestation of the British budgetary contribution, known under the slogan "I want my money back" back or her famous Bruges speech in 1988 when she openly and massively criticized the EC, have constituted crucial moments when resistance to Europe has marked the process of European integration.[4]

Despite this "historical" British Euroscepticism, the Brexit issue has stirred a highly emotional debate in the UK, not so much on the question of why and how to leave or to remain in the EU, but rather because of the way how this question was approached by the Brexiteers. The policy style was new: aggressive, populist and not only critical of the EU, but straightforwardly anti-European, an attitude which Aleks Szerbiak and Paul Taggart would define as "hard Euroscepticism", i.e. as the rejection of the principle underlying European integration itself.[5] Before the Brexit referendum, this trend in British politics was already palpable; during the 2014 European Parliament (EP) elections, where the new United Kingdom Independence Party (UKIP), under the leadership of Nigel Farage, attained an unprecedented success. They obtained the highest national party score with 26.77 %, i.e. 24 seats in the EP by focusing their campaign on the need to recover British sovereignty and on the EU as the principle culprit of uncontrollable immigration.[6] Nigel Farage's anti-European positions were already based on advocating the UK's withdrawal from the EU and the EP elections could therefore be regarded as a kind of "dress rehearsal" for the "leave" campaign of the 2016 referendum. They also led to Brexit being put as a priority on the national political

---

[3] Kopecky, P., Mudde, C., "The two sides of Euroscepticism: party positions on European integration in East Central Europe", *European Union Politics*, vol. 3/3, 2002, pp. 297–326.

[4] Spiering, M., "British Euroscepticism", in Harmsen, R., Spiering, M. (eds.), *Euroscepticism: party politics, national identity and European integration*, Amsterdam, Rodopi, 2004, pp. 127–150.

[5] Szczerbiak, A. Taggart, P., *Opposing Europe? The comparative party politics of Euroscepticism. Comparative and theoretical perspective*, Oxford, Oxford University Press, 2008.

[6] Tournier-Sol, K., "The 2014 Elections to the European Parliament in the UK: The United Kingdom Independence Party (UKIP) and the British National Party (BNP)", in Moreau, P., Wassenberg, B. (eds.), *European Integration and New Anti-Europeanism I, The 2014 European Election and the Rise of Euroscepticism in Western Europe*, Stuttgart, Steiner, 2016, pp. 99–113.

agenda. As UKIP was able to attract voters from all established political parties, its success pushed David Cameron to organize the referendum on UK's EU membership in June 2016.[7] The Brexiteer campaign for the "leave" vote took up the same populist policy style as practiced during the European elections, Nigel Farage being backed up by political figures such as Boris Johnson, then Mayor of London, who propagated hate speech against the EU as the origin of all problems in the UK: migration, loss of national sovereignty, etc.

But the debates on Brexit were not only highly emotional during the referendum campaign. They stayed passionate afterwards, also because it took much longer to actually organize the procedure to leave than it had initially been foreseen by the Brexiteers.[8] After the pro-leave result, it took nine months, until 29 March 2017, for Theresa May to submit the Art. 50 which enabled the UK to negotiate an agreement in order to leave the EU two years later, on 29 March 2019. The chronology of events thereafter resembled more a political thriller that an orderly exit process.[9] During the negotiations with the EU, it became more and more apparent that leaving the Union was more difficult than estimated; not only because of the juridical challenge of how to unravel the *acquis communautaire*, i.e. all the legal regulations that the UK had transposed into its national law since 1973, but also because leaving the customs union suddenly revealed unexpected political problems. Thus, both Scotland and Northern Ireland had voted pro-remain and this triggered off new tendencies towards secessionism or, in the case of Northern Ireland, even of possible re-unification with the Republic of Ireland.[10] Especially for Northern Ireland, Brexit had huge economic and (geo-)political implications, because a "hard" border with Ireland could threaten the peace process under way since the 1998 Good Friday Agreement. Thus,

---

[7] Wassenberg, B., "Euroscepticism at the EP elections in 2014: Reflection of the Different Patterns of Opposition to the EU?", in Costa, O. (ed.), *The European Parliament in Times of EU crisis. Dynamics and Transformations*, Cham, Palgrave, 2019, p. 282.

[8] Mathieu, C., Sterdyniak, H. "Brexit: une sortie impossible?", *L'Économie européenne*, 2019, pp. 60–74.

[9] O'Rourke, K., *A Short History of Brexit. From Brentry to Backstop*, London, Pelican Books, 2019.

[10] See article by Murphy, M., "Brexit and the Irish Case" and by Keating, M., "Brexit and Scotland", in Diamond, P., Nedergaard, P., Rosamond, B., *The Routledge Handbook of the Politics of Brexit*, Abingdon, Routledge, 2018.

negotiations were continuously blocked by the question of the so-called backstop-solution for Northern Ireland, which the EU defended as a possibility for Northern Ireland to remain in the European single market and the customs union, thus shifting the UK border to the Irish Sea – a solution heavily opposed by the British Government.

Therefore, from an initial debate on the principle of Brexit, the discussions quickly moved on to the options of a "soft" or a "hard" Brexit, or, put differently, to a Brexit with a "deal" or a "no-deal" Brexit. This increased the emotional debate both in the UK and in the EU. For many representatives of the economic sector, for British citizens living in the EU and for EU citizens living in the UK, a "no-deal" outcome would have caused immense problems.[11] This explains, why an agreement on the withdrawal of the UK from the EU was only reached on 14 November 2018 by Prime Minister Theresa May – an agreement which contained the backstop solution for Northern Ireland. However, the political thriller had then only started: the draft agreement was rejected three times by the House of Commons on 15 January 2019, on 12 March 2019 and on 29 March 2019, so that Theresa May had to resign from office.[12] The deadline of Brexit also had to be extended twice, first from 29 March 2019 to 12 April 2019 to allow for the British Parliament to ratify the initial Brexit withdrawal agreement; and then, after its failure, a second time until 31 October 2019. Elected Prime Minister in July 2019, Boris Johnson insisted until the very end of the negotiations that he would rather have a "no deal" than a bad deal. Johnson vowed to pull the UK out of the EU before the end of this second deadline. He did not hesitate in August 2019 to ask for a prorogation of Parliament in order to be able to pass the withdrawal deal, an attempt which was crushed by the ruling of the British Court, which identified this as an act contrary to the very principles of democracy.[13]

By summer 2019, the Brexit issue had reached the dimension of a paradoxical, almost absurd situation with very peculiar characteristics affecting not only the relationship between the UK and the EU, but also internal British politics: the political system in the UK suffered from

---

[11] Morgan, J., Patomäki, H., *Brexit and the Political Economy of Fragmentation. Things Fall Apart*, London, Routledge, 2017.

[12] Adam, R. G., "Brexit bedeutet Brexit – Theresa May und die Quadratur des Kreises", in Adam, R. G., *Brexit, eine Bilanz*, Heidelberg, Springer, 2020, pp. 161–249.

[13] Klein, J., "Brexit", in *Europa von A-Z*, Heidelberg, Springer, 2020, pp. 1–6.

a damaged image, for the tergiversations, parliamentary deadlocks and paralysis of Westminster had shaken the prestige of the "oldest" established European democracy. The EU suffered from the renewed extensions of deadlines causing damage to its image as a Community which is supposed to unite and not to divide the European family. Following the delay of Brexit, the UK had to formally take part in the EP elections in June 2019. It was an ironic situation that those who were supposed to leave were legally obliged to send Members of European Parliament (MEPs) to Strasbourg, due to the failure to reach an agreement on Brexit in time. It was even more ironic that the majority of the new MEPs were indeed "Brexiteers", with the Brexit party gaining 30.5 % of votes and 29 out of 73 seats.[14] The rise of anti-Europeanism was painfully illustrated during the opening session of the Parliament, when these MEPs turned their backs in disregard of the European anthem being played.[15] The peak of irony in the Brexit thriller was reached on 19 October when Boris Johnson was forced by a vote of the British Parliament to ask for a third extension until 31 January 2020, although he had vowed not to do so. He therefore sent a letter to the EU demanding this extension that he did not sign and which, he claimed, was not "his" letter.[16] The Brexit thriller only ended after the convocation of a General Election in the UK on 12 December 2019 which granted Boris Johnson the necessary majority for the acceptance of the revised withdrawal deal by the Westminster Parliament, so that it could be signed on 24 January 2020.[17] The exit day took place on 31 January 2020 and the Withdrawal Agreement entered into force on 1 February 2020. It was however not the end of the Brexit process, as the UK still has to negotiate a second deal for the future relationship with the EU, which should formally be reached until the end of the transition period on 31 December 2020, but which may

---

[14] https://europarl.europa.eu/election-results-2019/en/national-results/united-kingdom/2019-2024/ (2.4.2020).

[15] "European Parliament opens amid protest and discord", *BBC News*, 2 July 2019, https://www.bbc.com/news/world-europe-48838498 (2.4.2020).

[16] Malnick, E., "Boris Johnson refuses to sign Brexit extension request and instead sends photocopy, saying: 'This is not my letter, it's Parliament's'", *The Telegraph*, 19.10.2019.

[17] Agreement on the Withdrawal of the UK of Great Britain and Northern Ireland form the EU and the European Atomic Energy Community, 25.11.2018, https://www.gov.uk/government/publications/withdrawal-agreement-and-political-declaration (2.4.2020).

lead to a second thriller with scenarios of a "deal" or a "no deal", with extensions of deadlines, etc.

Having related the mere chronology of events in the course of Brexit, it is not surprising to see that a lot of analyses have been put forward to explain the British referendum result, mainly from the perspective of political sociology, looking at the "leave" or "remain" vote according to geographical criteria or with regard to different categories of the population. However, there has been less research so far on the deeper roots of Brexit as a historical and political process and its development from the start of the referendum campaign until the end of the negotiations between the UK and the EU, nor on its possible social, economic, legal and (geo-)political consequences. In order to examine the origins and consequences of Brexit, this publication develops two original perspectives. On the one hand, it has taken a pluridisciplinary approach comparing the point of views of sociologists, political scientists, legal experts and historians. On the other hand, it has adopted a global approach by comparing the analyses of Japanese, Canadian, American and European researchers. These "Global Views on Brexit" regroup the contributions to an international Conference on "The Consequences of Brexit" organised on 6–7 December 2018 in Strasbourg, in the framework of the Jean Monnet project on Crises in European Border Regions supported by the Erasmus+ Programme of the European Union (EU) for the period from 2018–2020. The publication is also supported by the Humanities and Social Sciences English-language Scholarly Book Publishing Support Program FY2019 of Waseda University in Japan.

In the first part on "Brexit as a historical and political process", the historian Stephanie Barczewski from Clemson University (US) starts by exploring "Brexit, World War II Memory and the Rhetoric of Appeasement". This article focuses on the British memory of World War II and its invocation during the Brexit referendum campaign in 2016. First, it shows that this memory differs sharply from war memory on the European continent and that this contrast has played an important role in determining Britain's less-than-enthusiastic attitude towards the EU. Most obviously, Britain emerged victorious from the war, which meant that its collective memory diverged from that of defeated nations, Germany in particular. For the British, the objective of a lasting peace therefore meant less and their interest in European unification was more purely economic, so that they have been less convinced of the need to share sovereignty. Second, the article demonstrates that appeasement has been used during the Brexit campaign as a political defamation, a comparison to Neville Chamberlain being one of the most devastating critiques a political leader can face. It was employed extensively by both sides, either to denounce the benevolent position of pro-remainers towards the EU or the incapacity of Brexiteers to defend a hardliner course for the exit strategy.

Daisuke Ikemoto from Meiji Gakuin University in Japan then analyses Brexit from a more economically orientated perspective. In his article on "Brexit as a Result of European Struggles over the UK's Financial Sector", the International Relations specialist reveals major economic reasons behind Brexit. Thus, the tension across the Channel was caused by the fact that the euro-zone tried to tackle the economic crisis with further integration including more regulations on the financial sector, of which the UK was not in favour. The Cameron Government faced more and more difficulties in defending the City of London from the EU's regulations, so that the referendum was partly an attempt to win otherwise unobtainable concessions from the rest of the EU. According to his analysis, Brexit was therefore not just a popular backlash against economic globalization, but a considerable part of the UK's establishment was also dissatisfied with "over-regulation" by the EU. Brexit was a result of this unique combination of the rise of populistic movement against the EU and strong anti-EU feelings among the political elites.

Frédérique Berrod, Professor in Law at Sciences Po Strasbourg then follows by illustrating, from a legal perspective, "The Undemocratic Effects of a Referendum" as "One of the Many Paradoxes of Brexit". She argues that Brexit caused certain breeches of democratic principles. Thus, the referendum was transformed by Theresa May's UK Government into a mandate for the Executive to use Art. 50 to notify its intention to withdraw from the EU without any consultation of the Parliament. When the Withdrawal Agreement was then put before the House of Commons several times without being able to gain a majority, the democratic limits of Brexit became even more apparent. According to Frédérique Berrod, one of the paradoxes of the British referendum was also that the democratic decision of the UK had mandatory consequences for 27 Member States which had no say whatsoever of the decision to leave the EU. Finally, she shows that, when Boris Johnson decided to use the traditional suspension of the Parliament to prevent any parliamentary attempts to influence the Brexit deal, this undemocratic act was struck down by the Supreme Court in order to re-establish the democratic legitimacy of the House of Commons. However, as the House of Commons was not capable of finding even a slight majority in favour of any solution, this allowed Boris Johnson to claim that Westminster was in itself "undemocratic"; giving him the right to dissolve the House of Commons by calling for new elections – another paradox in the Brexit story.

The social consequences of Brexit were dealt with in the second part of the publication. In her article on "The Right to Family Reunification after Brexit: the Impossible Status Quo", Aude Bouveresse, professor in Law at the University of Strasbourg, assesses how Brexit threatens the respect of fundamental rights by focussing on the right to family reunification. She claims that, since the interest of family reunification is guaranteed by EU law, Brexit risks causing a weakening of the normative and jurisdictional guarantees surrounding the right to family reunification in the UK. Even though a consensus had emerged from the beginning of the Brexit negotiations on maintaining acquired rights for UK citizens living in the EU and for EU citizens living in the UK, according to her, the prevailing and persistent uncertainty already represented a violation of fundamental rights. Aude Bouveresse argues that the status quo is actually impossible to defend as the legal and normative guarantees attached to the protection of the right to family reunification after Brexit cannot be regarded as equivalent. However, this fundamental right directly affects the lives of citizens involved in European mobility and in this perspective, Brexit cannot be summarized as a deal that would be just harmful to politicians and economic operators.

From a political and sociological point of view, two contributions thereafter assess more in depth the social consequences of Brexit. They both focus on migrants. Seiko Oyama, Political Scientist at the Tokai University in Japan, deals with "Brexit and its Impact on the Integration of Migrants in the UK". She starts by emphasizing that, although the competence on migration policies lies with the Member States, the EU has established many measures and financial tools in order to support the integration of migrants. As the UK has benefited both from policy coordination (multi-actor networks, European semester, etc.) and EU funds so far, migrants in the UK risk losing many benefits after Brexit unless the British Government replaces the EU tools with equivalent national measures. The high risk of poverty and social exclusion of migrants means that the UK needs to develop new comprehensive policies for migrant integration, but without support by the EU, Seiko Oyama believes it will be difficult for local authorities to cope in the future. Noriko Suzuki, Sociologist at the Waseda University in Tokyo then draws our attention to the "Effects of Brexit on UK Nationals Living in France". Indeed, the 1.3 million UK nationals residing in other EU countries, who have been enjoying EU privileges, fear the consequences of Brexit because they will lose their status as EU citizens: they can no longer live nor work in other EU countries freely, unless they obtain proper permissions as non-EU citizens are required to do. Based on a series of interviews conducted with British residents in France, she reveals that many of them are frustrated because they could not even vote for the referendum, having lost their voting rights after a long residence period of overseas. They feel that they could not decide on their own future and in the context of Brexit, they are therefore concerned not only about losing their political rights as EU citizens but also their political rights as British nationals. As a result of Brexit, a significant number of them therefore are trying to maintain their political rights in their resident community in various ways including acquiring the nationality of their resident country.

In the third part of the publication, the economic and legal consequences of Brexit are examined. Emmanuel Brunet-Jailly, Professor in Public Policy at the University of Victoria in Canada, evaluates "The "Real" Costs of Brexit". He reminds us that, during the Brexit campaign, many officials and parts of the public had objected to what they considered to be the excessive UK contribution to the EU annual budget. However, soon after the vote it became clear that there were wide disagreements regarding the "real" cost of the EU membership to the UK public purse. According to his analysis, the Brexiteers have exaggerated the "real" costs of membership because the UK was the only EU Member State with a rebate. They have underscored the "real" costs of Brexit, which, including the settlement bill as well as new necessary custom infrastructures and policies may well exceed 100 billion euros and they have overestimated annual savings on EU membership which will not happen because trading internationally has also a cost, whether it is being part of a free trade agreement or being outside a free trade agreement. In sum, he estimates that economic uncertainties and custom borders will make the economic costs of Brexit very high for the foreseeable future in the UK.

Catherine Haguenau-Moizard, Professor in Law at University of Strasbourg, then turns to the legal consequences of Brexit. In her article on "From Opting out to Brexit in the Area of Freedom, Security and

Justice", she shows that the UK had benefited from a very favourable partly in and partly out position in the EU Treaty framework of the Area of Freedom, Security and Justice, which it will lose following Brexit. Indeed, when the Lisbon Treaty was adopted, the British Government managed to obtain a right to opt out and re-opt in concerning many measures of the area of freedom, security and justice, especially with regard to cooperation on criminal matters and the fight against drugs trafficking. They got for example, access to the Schengen Information System and could take part in the exchange of data on visas, without being member of the Schengen area. According to Catherine Haguenau-Moizard, the British were basically able to pick and choose what they wanted. She maintains that they should have been satisfied by their special status and that Brexit will only make cooperation more difficult as they will now have to use the conventions of the Council of Europe or specific bilateral agreements and the fight against crime will not be as efficient. Shifting from the special status to the position of a third country therefore seems particularly irrational.

When moving to the fourth part of the publication on the (geo-) political consequences of Brexit, other types of consequences are put forward. Ruth Taillon, former Director of the Centre for Cross Border Studies based in Ireland/Northern Ireland reveals the possible damage of Brexit for the peace process on the island of Ireland. In her article on "The Consequences of Brexit for the Island of Ireland: ('Deal or No Deal')" she relates how the "special circumstances" of Northern Ireland and the land border between Ireland and Northern Ireland have become central issues of the Brexit negotiations. In order to keep the Good Friday Agreement intact, it was crucial that there would be no return to the borders of the past so that the peace process in Northern Ireland can be pursued. The possibility of a "no-deal" was therefore a direct threat to this peace process and an unacceptable cost of Brexit. Thus, the Withdrawal Agreement finally contains a special arrangement which includes a single customs territory covering the EU and Northern Ireland. According to Ruth Taillon, this "backstop" solution was the only deal ultimately possible, because without it, there would have been no Withdrawal Agreement and with no Withdrawal Agreement there can be no transition period to allow for an orderly exit. Taking the examples of Northern Ireland, of Scotland and of Gibraltar, Jeremy Sacramento, independent researcher, and Jaume Castan Pinos, Associate Professor in International Politics at the University of Southern Denmark, also identify important (geo-)

political consequences of Brexit, which they define as "externalities". In their article on "Brexit's Territorial Externalities", they show that Brexit has been overshadowed by a certain number of territorial questions which did not immediately come to the surface during the referendum campaign and at the beginning of the negotiations with the EU. These territorial externalities concern Spain's claim over Gibraltar, the Irish border, including the possibility of Irish reunification, and Scotland's pursuit of independence and are inextricably linked to Brexit. According to the two researchers, these three territorial externalities of Brexit risk, apart from altering Britain's relationship with the world, to invariably change the character of the UK itself because they have the potential to seriously compromise the UK's territorial integrity. They have been "an elephant in the room" throughout the Brexit process and it is likely that they will both continue to impinge on the Brexit process, and ultimately challenge the makeup of the UK itself.

Finally, the International Relations specialist Ken Masujima from Kobe University examines the consequences of Brexit on the UK's and the EU's external relations with Japan. In his article on "European Union-Japan Relations in the Shadow of Brexit", he claims that the relations between the EU and Japan have been strongly influenced by the UK and that Brexit will cause serious damage for all parties involved. He argues that, since the accession of the UK to the EU in 1973, the UK has served as the most important gateway to the EU for Japanese government and corporations: the UK received the largest share of Japan's investment in the EU, facilitated contact with the EU as mediator and served as an agent of ideological affinity within the EU. The cost of Brexit for Japan is therefore expected to be felt particularly in those policy domains where the UK has played important roles. Thus, in economic and social policy fields, liberal positions represented by the UK will be lessened. In foreign and defence policy, NATO oriented positions advocated by the UK will be diminished. After Brexit, Ken Masujima believes that for Japan, no other Member State in the EU will be able to completely fill the void left by Brexit in order to assume the roles played by the UK. He therefore expects that the UK will continue to be counted on by Japan, even for a reduced indirect influence from outside that the UK could have on the EU after Brexit.

PART 1

BREXIT AS A HISTORICAL AND POLITICAL PROCESS

Brexit, World War II Memory, and the Rhetoric of Appeasement

STEPHANIE BARCZEWSKI

In August 2016, two months after the Brexit referendum, the historian David Reynolds published an essay in the *New Statesman* about the "special place" of the world wars in "Britain's Brexit-shaped national memory". Reynolds discussed how the mass casualties of the First World War had produced a "passion for appeasement" as the best response to increasing German aggression in the 1930s. But when Hitler invaded Poland in September 1939, "that all changed", as the view of war as national tragedy was supplanted by a new narrative of national heroism, with Britain, the Empire and (eventually) the United States standing together to achieve victory in a "good war" against Nazi evil. Reynolds concluded with an assessment of how this narrative continues to influence British national identity in the present:

> In Britain we are preoccupied – some would say obsessed – with our national memory of the two world wars. The headline slogans of that memory-story are clear. 1914–18: over there in Mud and Blood, sacrificing the Lost Generation to win only the Lost Peace. 1939–45: over here, Our Finest Hour, Alone in 1940. Then victory, won in tandem with the English-Speaking Peoples. Two wars enshrined in ways that serve to distance us from mainland Europe – even though both narratives are highly selective. Across the Channel, however, the story is very different. After 1945 the French and Germans, who had been killing each other for three centuries, managed to kick the habit. Not only were they reconciled but they moved on into what the founding father of the European Economic Community... Yet European integration has not exerted much attraction in the "United Kingdom". As a country we have been at the very most "reluctant Europeans"; after all, no other member of the EU has held two referendums in four decades on whether to get out. And no one else has actually voted to do so... The referendums... reflect what might be called the "Channel of the Mind" between Us and Them, a great divide that

was deepened by our nationalist narratives of 1914–18 and 1939–45. This, in turn, fed into the Brexit vote of 23 June [2016].[1]

Here, Reynolds acknowledged that there was a relationship between the place of the Second World War in British memory and the outcome of Brexit referendum held in June 2016. Many pro-Brexit Britons felt that Churchill's characterization of the Second World War as Britain's "finest hour" was accurate, and that the nation had slipped in global power and prestige ever since. One of the causes of this decline were Britain's decades of concessions to the European Union (EU). For them, the message of 1940 was simple: going it alone was the best course of action. The idea of Britain "standing alone" was thus a very powerful rhetorical weapon in the context of a debate that revolved at a fundamental level around British sovereignty.

As Reynolds demonstrated, World War II remains a touchstone of European politics, not only in Britain but throughout Europe. Politicians from many countries concur that the war was an unmitigated catastrophe, so much so that present-day political rhetoric and action must be constantly vigilant in order to avoid a recurrence. Christian Karner and Bram Mertens observe:

> World War II continues to be a prominent, near ubiquitous point of reference not only across Europe but also across the political spectrum: while the Left and Right of course differ enormously in their respective motivations for invoking World War II, and in the political effects achieved thereby, they appear to share – their defining ideological differences and mutual opposition notwithstanding – a basic consciousness of the enduring legacies, relevance and trauma of this most murderous and destructive of historical ruptures.[2]

Foremost among these efforts to avoid a recurrence of such a destructive conflict has been European unification, which has from the end of the war onwards been seen as a means of securing a lasting peace. The sole alternative to a unified Europe was, in the eyes of its acolytes, and in the words of Mark Mazower, "the chaos of a continent plunged back into the

---

[1] Reynolds, D., "Long Shadows of Old Wars", *New Statesman*, 17.8.2016 (9.5.2019).
[2] Karner, C., Mertens, B., "Introduction: Memories and Analogies of World War II", in Karner C., Mertens B. (eds.), *The Uses and Abuses of Memory: Interpreting World War II in Contemporary European Politics*, New Brunswick and London, Transaction, 2013, p. 2.

national rivalries of the past".[3] If Europe has a collective memory, then the EU is its embodiment. "It is not simply starry-eyed pro-European propaganda to say that the European Union was constructed as a result of the memory of the war", writes Jan-Werner Müller.[4]

At the same time as it functions as a motivating force behind it, however, the continued prominence of the Second World War in European memory threatens to undermine European unity, as it is extremely difficult for it to serve as the source material for a unified European memory. The war divided European nations into allies, enemies and neutrals, and ultimately into winners and losers. However noble its ideals, the European project thus has its limitations, as the economic advantages of the Common Market have struggled to overcome the allure of nationalism and cultural distinctiveness. Lucy Noakes and Juliet Pattinson note that, although in recent decades the numerous acts of commemoration and memorialization related to the war attempt to "assert a continuity between a rapidly changing present and a shared past", they at the same time become "sites of struggle" due to "the difficult and contested status of much of what is being 'remembered'."[5] Accordingly, national historical narratives have survived, and indeed flourished, alongside, and often in opposition to, the dream of European unity. Karner and Mertens continue, "National memories… tend to internally divide any potentially emerging European framework of remembrance."[6]

What, then, of the British case specifically? The British use of historical and national mythologies tends to differ from that of continental countries. For the British, it is difficult to use these mythologies to construct an ideal of the nation as based on a united sense of its people, because Britain is a plural and hybrid nation in terms of its ethnic composition, as is manifested most obviously in the Anglo-Celtic division between England and Scotland, Wales and Ireland. In Britain, the use of these mythologies

---

[3] Mazower, M., *Dark Continent: Europe's Twentieth Century*, New York, Vintage, 2000, p. 399.
[4] Müller, J. W., "On 'European Memory': Some Conceptual and Normative Remarks", in Pakier, M., Stråth, B. (eds.), *A European Memory?: Contested Histories and Politics of Remembrance*, Oxford and New York, Berghahn Books, 2010, p. 30.
[5] Noakes, L., Pattinson, J., "Introduction: 'Keep Calm and Carry On': The Cultural Memory of the Second World War in Britain", in Noakes, L., Pattinson, J. (eds.), *British Cultural Memory and the Second World War*, London, Bloomsbury, 2014, p. 2.
[6] Karner, C., Mertens, B., "Introduction", *op. cit.*, p. 8.

has generally promoted the construction of individual Anglo-Saxon or Celtic identities, while British national identity relies upon narratives that are non-folk-based but instead focus upon the construction of a shared past, present and future. We might think about Francophobia in the 18th century or the use of the British Empire as a unifying force in the 19th century.[7] In the 20th and 21rst, the Second World War has functioned in much the same way: as a narrative reifying a sense of national greatness that was manifested in strength and moral superiority. It also, in a manner that is very relevant to current Brexit-era politics, used the strategy of defining an "Other" in order to encourage national unity. And not just the German (and Italian) foes: from 1939 to 1945, the entire European continent became an "Other" full of hostile enemies and unreliable allies. Not surprisingly given this prevalent cultural attitude, Brexiteering politicians continually invoked the war during the run-up to the 2016 referendum, they referred frequently to the "Battle for Britain" and blasted music from *The Great Escape* from their buses as they campaigned for Leave.

Britain thus stands largely outside the continental debates about wartime history and its meaning in and for the present. The maintenance of a continuous national narrative from the pre- to post-war eras was deeply problematic for nations that had suffered such catastrophic political and military failures as Germany, Italy and France, adding allure to the possibility of overlaying national history with a European one. Britain, however, wanted continuity: it saw itself as having no apology to make for perpetration, collaboration or the moral failure of its political leaders. If European integration helped some countries gain distance from their difficult pasts, Britain had no need, or desire, to do this: they wanted to emphasize the heroism of their wartime conduct instead. Elsewhere, there has been a general trajectory of initial avoidance of the national failures of the Second World War, which many nations accomplished by emphasizing the resistance of their populations to the Nazis, followed in more recent decades by increased focus on the realities of collaboration. Britain, however, has never be part of this shared collective history, or this shared retreat from nationalism, whatever balance of reality and myth underlies it. As Stefan Berger writes, "One outcome of Britain's unique experience was to set British memories apart from of continental

---

[7] For the former, see Colley, L., *Britons: Forging the Nation 1707–1837*, New Haven and London, Yale University Press, 1992.

Europeans, creating a strong mental barrier against a common European memory of the war."[8]

Rare among European nations, Britain's memory of the Second World War has remained largely unaltered in the seventy-two years since 1945; it remains dominated by heroism and a sense of national unity in the face of hardship. This contrast has played an important role in determining Britain's attitude towards the EU, which has consistently been less enthusiastic than that of its continental counterparts. As a government white paper that discussed the prospect of Britain's entry into the European Common Market in 1971 proclaimed, "Our physical assets and our economy... suffered less disastrously than those of other western European countries as a result of the war: nor did we suffer the shock of invasion. We were thus less immediately conscious of the need for us to become part of the unity in Europe."[9] For the British, therefore, the objective of a lasting peace meant less; their interest in European unification was more predominantly economic, and they were less convinced of the need to share sovereignty. As Fintan O'Toole recently observed in the *Guardian*, "England had no deep imaginative commitment to the European project. As an idea, the EU had a distinctly weak grip on English allegiance. It was always understood by most people as a more or less grudging concession to reality, a matter for resigned acceptance rather than joyous embrace."[10]

The ghosts of the Second World War continue to haunt British culture. Particularly prevalent is the fear that things might have come out differently. Counter-factual re-imaginings of what would have happened had Britain been defeated by the Nazis began to appear even before the war was over; examples include Douglas Brown and Christopher Serpell's *Loss of Eden* (1940) and H. V. Morton's *I, James Blunt* (1942). More recently, political thrillers such as Len Deighton's *SS-GB* (1978), Robert Harris's *Fatherland* (1992) and C. J. Sansom's *Dominion* (2002) have sold millions of copies by providing fictional depictions of the aftermath of a British surrender to the Nazis; the first two were transformed into films

---

[8] Berger, S., "Remembering the Second World War in Western Europe", in Pakier, M., Stråth, B. (eds.), *op. cit.*, p. 124.
[9] Cited in O'Toole, F., *Heroic Failure: Brexit and the Politics of Pain*, London, Head of Zeus, 2018, p. 53.
[10] O'Toole, F., "The Paranoid Fantasy behind Brexit", *Guardian*, 16.11.2018 (9.5.2019).

for television that garnered millions of viewers.[11] But these "paranoid fantasies", as O'Toole terms them, are more than just the stuff of popular nightmares. They have also influenced diplomacy broadly and relations with the EU specifically. In 1990, instead of welcoming German reunification as the final culmination of the defeat of Nazism, to which Britain had made a major contribution, Margaret Thatcher carried maps of Nazi-dominated Europe in her handbag. "The summer of 1940", writes Catherine Gallagher:

> is a moment at which history and memory seem to stand at odds. Historians concur that a German invasion would have failed, but the widespread memory remains that of a catastrophe that was averted at the last minute... The meaning of the summer of 1940 has continued to be bound up with the question of what defines Britishness during the decades of controversy over EU membership. In the Brexit debate, those in favour of remaining in the EU have framed it as a time when Britain took the lead in a European rescue mission, while the Leavers present it as a moment of defiance against Continental interference.[12]

We might think that the nations that lost World War II would have a more difficult time leaving the past behind. There is an argument, however, that it is the victorious British who have been unable to do so. Otto English recently wrote for Politico:

> Britain's acute case of "the wars", reinforced by an unending diet of books, TV programmes, films and documentaries, goes something like this: In the early 20th century, the peace of a contented and prosperous nation was rudely interrupted by humorless continental ruffians in spiky helmets who didn't know one end of a cricket bat from another. For four long years, noble Tommys single-handedly took on Germany while the French sat around playing accordions and eating *moules*, before our cousins from America turned up and helped us finish the job... The war is ours; our sacrifice, our victory, our sacred relic. It's a simplistic version of events that reduces the vast complexity of war into a navel gazing exercise of good versus evil. It's a story in which we are always good and the dark and foreboding Continent is a source of malevolence and threat.[13]

---

[11] See Rosenfeld, G. D., *The World Hitler Never Made: Alternate History and the Memory of Nazism*, Cambridge, Cambridge University Press, 2005.
[12] Gallagher, C., "Swastikas on the Strand", *Aeon*, 27.3.2019 (9.5.2019).
[13] English, O., "A Churchill History Lesson for Brexit Britain", *Politico*, 14.2.2019 (9.5.2019).

Anti-Europe British politicians have continued to regard the EU not as, as its founders intended, the ultimate refutation of Hitler's project to unite Europe under German domination via conquest, but as a less bloodthirsty rendition of it. "In Britain", notes David Reynolds, "popular attitudes to the European Union are still inextricably bound up with a sense of alienation from the continent, confirmed in 1940, and with widespread suspicion that the EU is simply a peaceful form of German domination."[14]

Invoked by conservative politicians from the time when Britain first contemplated entering the European Economic Community in the 1960s, this idea retains considerable force, as Boris Johnson recognized in May 2016 when he told the *Daily Telegraph* that the EU was an attempt to do by "different methods" what Napoleon and Hitler had attempted, and referred to it as "an act of economic takeover": "The euro has become a means by which superior German productivity is able to gain an absolutely unbeatable advantage over the whole eurozone territory."[15] Unofficial posters for the Leave campaign, meanwhile, called upon British voters to "Halt ze German advance!"

Why are the British so paranoid that the EU will somehow overturn their victory in 1945? When Churchill declared in June 1940 that the decision to stand alone against Nazism would be Britain's "finest hour", he thought that it would mark another triumphal point in the nation's history as a great power. What it became, however, was a last moment of greatness before a swift post-war decline. In 1945, Germany was a political pariah whose economic infrastructure had been massively damaged by Allied bombing, and France was only just beginning to recover from the humiliation of its swift defeat in 1940 and subsequent occupation. Both had nowhere to go but up. Britain, to be sure, could celebrate, but the war was followed by bankruptcy and exhaustion, which accelerated the forces of industrial decay and anti-colonial nationalism that had already been present before the war. Whatever their ambitions from the late 19th century onwards, the Germans had never achieved global power in the way that the British had, and the French had relinquished it at Waterloo. The British, however, still maintained the pretension of great-power

---

[14] Reynolds, D., "World War II and Modern Meanings", *Diplomatic History*, 25, 2001, p. 470.
[15] Ross, T., "Boris Johnson Interview: We Can Be the 'Heroes of Europe' by Voting to Leave", *Telegraph*, 14.5.2016 (9.5.2019).

status in 1945; for them, its surrender was swift and traumatic, and rendered all the more so by the sense that winning the war should have secured it. The British needed an explanation for how they had lost by winning; they had clearly defeated Hitler, but they could not defeat the more insidious enemy of Brussels. In this context, joining the European Community came to be seen by many British politicians as the surrender that Churchill had so heroically prevented in 1940. In the remainder of this chapter, I will explore how this particular aspect of British memory of World War II – in other words, appeasement – has played a direct role in the decision to leave the EU.

Prior to the 1930s, the term "appeasement" was not a negative one in Britain; rather, it referred to a variety of diplomatic strategies used to prevent war and pursue the national interest. Since at least the 18th century, Britain eschewed continental entanglements in order to focus on international and imperial objectives; this meant that appeasement was often a preferred strategy, and its frequent diplomatic deployment played a key role in Britain's avoidance of major military conflict in Europe between the Napoleonic and First World Wars.[16] This strategy failed in 1914, but it was if anything rendered more attractive by the battlefield carnage that ensued.[17]

When the Second World War broke out in 1939, however, critics of appeasement were swift to argue that it could have been prevented by a firmer stance at an earlier date. The failure of appeasement to secure peace brought about a swift condemnation of not only its merits as a policy, but also of the entire decade that had given birth to it. The 1930s were not even over when W. H. Auden penned his damning critique:

I sit in one of the dives
On Fifty-second Street
Uncertain and afraid
As the clever hopes expire
Of a low dishonest decade:

---

[16] Hughes, R. G., *The Postwar Legacy of Appeasement: British Foreign Policy since 1945*, London, Bloomsbury, 2014, p. 3.

[17] See Otte, T. C., *The Foreign Office Mind: The Making of British Foreign Policy, 1865–1914*, Cambridge, Cambridge University Press, 2011; and Steiner, Z., *The Lights that Failed: European International History, 1919–1933*, Oxford, Oxford University Press, 2005.

> Waves of anger and fear
> Circulate over the bright
> And darkened lands of the earth.[18]

"Never can a decade have ended with more dramatic finality than did the 1930s", write John Baxendale and Chris Pawling:

> Sometime between the declaration of war on 3 September 1939 and the climactic events of May 1940 – the fall of Chamberlain, Hitler's blitzkrieg, Dunkirk – a door slammed: life changed utterly – and, many feared or hoped, permanently. Not surprisingly, then, the autopsies on the thirties began early… Within months, a process that usually takes years was well under way, and the thirties were being thoroughly constructed and reconstructed as an object in posterity's imagination.[19]

In this context, appeasement became the prime embodiment of the ineptitude and cravenness of interwar politicians. "The disappointment of the policy was so abrupt, so violent and so massive", writes David Chuter, "that there has scarcely been room for real debate about the settlement itself."[20] Although fears of invasion and defeat dissipated after the Nazis became bogged down in the Soviet Union and the United States entered the war in December 1941, there was no reassessment of appeasement. In 1943, George Orwell excoriated the politicians of the thirties:

> When one thinks of the lies and betrayals of those years, the cynical abandonment of one ally after another, the imbecile optimism of the Tory press, the flat refusal to believe that the dictators meant war, even when they shouted it from the housetops, the inability of the moneyed class to see anything wrong whatever in the concentration camps, ghettoes, massacres and undeclared wars, one is driven to feel that moral decadence played its part as well as mere stupidity. By 1937 or thereabouts it was not possible to be in doubt about the nature of the fascist regimes. But the lords of property had decided that fascism was on their side, and they were willing to swallow the most stinking evils so long as their property remained secure.[21]

---

[18] Auden, W. H., "September 1, 1939", *Another Time*, New York, Random House, 1940.

[19] Baxendale, J., Pawling, C., *Narrating the Thirties: A Decade in the Making: 1930 to the Present*, Houndmills, Basingstoke, and London, Palgrave Macmillan, 1996, p. 116.

[20] Chuter, D., "Munich, or the Blood of Others", in Buffet, C., Heuser, B. (eds.), *Haunted by History: Myths in International Relations*, Providence and Oxford, Berghahn Books, 1998, p. 66.

[21] Orwell, G., *Collected Essays, Journalism and Letters*, London, Secker and Warburg, vol. 2, 1968, p. 366.

Orwell was writing from a left-wing perspective, but the conservative author J. B. Priestley adopted a similar perspective in his wartime writings and radio broadcasts. During and after the war, the 1930s were thus never romanticized or viewed with nostalgia as the years before the First World War had been in the interwar period.

As the war's end came into sight and the public came to focus more on the future, appeasement came to occupy a different place in British political discourse. It was now less a matter of identifying those responsible for an imminent national threat and more a matter of assessing the mistakes of the past in order to determine who should lead the nation in the post-war era. As wartime unity fractured in the face of the very different attitudes to social welfare held by politicians on the left and right, those in the former camp wielded appeasement as a cudgel with which beat the Conservatives. In *Why Not Trust the Tories* (1944), Aneurin Bevin accused the Tories of having "connived at and facilitated the rise of Hitler to power". Attacks on appeasement came not only from the left, however. In *The Gathering Storm* (1947), the first of his six-volume history of the Second World War, Winston Churchill asserted that more vigorous opposition to Hitler at an earlier date would have prevented the war. Significantly influenced by the context of the Cold War and his strong sense that Soviet expansionism must be contained, *The Gathering Storm* was perhaps even more influential than *Guilty Men*. It sold 200,000 copies in two weeks, and forty-two excerpts were serialized in the *Daily Telegraph* over a period of two months.[22] As his biographer Robert Self notes, Chamberlain came "badly out of history... precisely because Churchill wrote that history in order to ensure that his carefully crafted version of the 1930s would be the one which became indelibly etched upon the national consciousness."[23] This view became a key component of the broader interpretation of the 1930s, in which the decade became

> the first act in a three-act drama. First act: shame, failure and betrayal while the people sleep; second act: danger rouses the people, and their sacrifice and moral courage redeems the national shame (and, incidentally, saves the

---

[22] See Reynolds, D., "Churchill's Writing of History: Appeasement, Autobiography and *The Gathering Storm*", *Transactions of the Royal Historical Society*, vol. 11, 2001, pp. 221–247.

[23] Self, R., "Neville Chamberlain and the Long Shadow of the 'Guilty Men'", *Conservative History Journal*, vol. 7, 2008, p. 21.

nation); finale: everyone marches together into the sunlit uplands of a better life for all. As in any well-made narrative, each act draws its meaning from its relation to the others. This is an optimistic narrative, so it needs a negative starting point: the "devil's decade", which sharpens the positive prospect of postwar reconstruction; both together give meaning, practical and moral, to the sacrifices of wartime.[24]

Appeasement was so roundly castigated in the 1940s that it took almost two decades for any serious reassessment to be possible. In the 1960s, however, appeasement revisionism became a scholarly trend, kicked off by A. J. P. Taylor's *The Origins of the Second World War* (1961), in which he argued that Hitler, genocidal maniac though he might have been, had in fact acted in a conventional manner as a foreign-policy strategist and had merely sought opportunistically to pursue Germany's national interest in a manner not dissimilar to that of Bismarck or the nation's political leaders prior to the First World War. In this view, the Second World War was not the product of unique Nazi aggression and evil intent, but rather merely the continuation of the Europe's failure to solve the changing power dynamic that had resulted from Germany's economic and political emergence in the last quarter of the 19th century. The inability to reconcile German national ambition with a balance of power on the continent had led to two massively destructive world wars. From Taylor's perspective, French and especially British diplomats and leaders were guilty of some serious bumbling as they failed to cope with the "German question", but at the same time Chamberlain had followed what he termed a "moral line". In his view, appeasement was a rational and humane policy – its failure was practical, not moral. Nor had its failure be responsible for the war, as Taylor argued that the Second World War had inevitably followed the First and the ham-handed Treaty of Versailles, which had been overly punitive towards Germany.[25]

This was a stunning reversal. In 1938, Taylor had been a fierce critic of appeasement at a time when the policy was broadly popular with both the political establishment and the British public.[26] But hindsight had led

---

[24] Baxendale, J., Pawling, C., *op. cit.*, pp. 117–118.
[25] For a more recent assessment of Taylor's view of appeasement in *The Origins of the Second World War*, see Kennedy, P., Imlay, T., "Appeasement", in Martel, G. (ed.), *The Origins of the Second World War Reconsidered: A. J. P. Taylor and the Historians*, 2nd ed., London and New York, Routledge, 1999, pp. 116–134.
[26] Most famously, in October, a month after the Munich pact was signed, he had warned at an annual dinner celebrating the resistance of a group of Oxford dons to

Taylor to adopt a less condemnatory view, and by the late 1950s he had come to understand that there were sound reasons why so many British political leaders had thought appeasement a policy worth pursuing. His work was crucial in reminding post-war Britons that it had not been carried out by a small group of deluded diplomats in the face of strong public opposition, as much post-war mythology suggested, but rather was a popular policy whose adherents were attempting to deal with complex problems in a rational manner, even if it ultimately failed.

Other historians followed the trail that Taylor had blazed. Too numerous to list individually, these studies generally asserted the primacy of complex internal and imperial factors in leading politicians to pursue appeasement. In other words, instead of focusing on appeasement exclusively as a response to Hitler's aggression, it was interpreted in the context of a variety of domestic, international and imperial pressures. In particular, economic constraints made it the only viable option. It was a sign of how fast the historiographical landscape was shifting that Martin Gilbert, biographer of Churchill and strong critic of appeasement in *The Appeasers* (1963, co-authored with the journalist Richard Gott), only three years later published a reassessment of his views in which he conceded that appeasement was "not a silly or treacherous idea". Gilbert now argued that it was "a noble idea, rooted in Christianity, courage and common sense", even if he still regarded it as having become "unrealistic" by the late 1930s.[27] Appeasement revisionism reached its apex in the 1970s and 1980s, in works by Maurice Cowling and John Charmley.[28]

The appeasement revisionists, however, never succeeded in overturning the popular consensus that appeasement was a moral failure and only its reversal by Churchill had saved the nation from catastrophe. As Rafael Behr writes,

> Britain has unique confidence in its immunity. It flows through the celebration of our resistance to fascism when so much of Europe succumbed.

James II that if Hitler was not resisted more forcefully their present-day successors might find themselves living under a much worse dictatorship.

[27] Gilbert, M., *The Roots of Appeasement*, London, Weidenfeld and Nicolson, 1966, pp. xi and 187.

[28] Cowling, M., *The Impact of Hitler: British Politics and British Policy 1933–1940*, Cambridge, Cambridge University Press, 1975; Charmley, J., *Chamberlain and the Lost Peace*, London, Hodder and Stroughton, 1989; and Charmley, J., *Churchill: The End of Glory*, London, Hodder and Stroughton, 1993.

The Churchillian narrative of the solitary fightback between the fall of Paris and the arrival of American reinforcements – Our Finest Hour – has eclipsed the preceding years, when appeasement was government policy.[29]

In this interpretation, appeasement, which is too well-documented to be erased entirely from historical memory, must be roundly condemned as the most egregious error of judgment in modern British history. Once this error was overcome, Britain resumed its place as a brave, powerful and unified nation, making Hitler's defeat possible. There could be no mercy for "appeasers", as the post-war fates of interwar politicians: Halifax was banished to the American embassy in Washington in 1940, while Anthony Eden was able parlay the credibility he obtained from his resignation as Foreign Secretary in 1938 – ostensibly but not in reality entirely over appeasement – into the leadership of the Conservative Party and ultimately became Prime Minister.

This view of the war was on frequent display in post-war diplomacy, in which invocations of appeasement were, as R. Gerald Hughes has noted, "tailored to contemporary policy imperatives."[30] This does not mean, to be sure, that British politicians abandoned appeasement in practice; Churchill himself pursued a "peace at any price" strategy with Stalin, sacrificing the very nation, Poland, whose sovereignty Britain had gone to war over in 1939. In the Cold-War era, it was easy to recast such conciliatory policies as "pragmatist", since the alternative of nuclear war was unthinkable. Politicians were desperate to avoid the label of "appeaser", which shaped the rhetoric used to convey their policies to the British public, and sometimes influenced their actions as well. In this way, Hughes writes, "a delicate balance between simultaneously avoiding major war and desisting from being seen to engage in appeasement had come about."[31]

For the British, this "delicate balance" failed in 1956, with consequences as catastrophic for the career and political reputation of the Prime Minister as Munich had been for Chamberlain in the 1930s. In order to justify his aggressive actions during the Suez Crisis, Anthony Eden drew on his anti-appeasement stance as Foreign Secretary from 1935 to 1938. This was, in

---

[29] Behr, R., "Remembrance of atrocities won't save us from present dangers", *The Guardian*, 8.11.2016 (12.1.2018).
[30] Hughes, R. G., *op. cit.*, p. 12.
[31] Hughes, R. G., *op. cit.*, p. 35.

many ways, invented history: Eden's reputation as a "man of principle" derived largely from his hardline stance towards – and resignation over – the appeasement of Italy, while he had displayed a more flexible attitude towards, and significantly less interest in, Germany.[32] This more complex reality, however, failed to prevent Eden from being hamstrung by his own past, as well as by the willingness of other British politicians to invoke the ghosts of Munich. His Conservative rivals and Labour opponents alike knew what a powerful weapon the accusation of appeasement was against him. According to his private secretary Evelyn Shuckburgh, in 1953, when Eden was Foreign Minister, Churchill attempted to goad him into a more forceful stance in Egypt by exclaiming that he "never knew... that Munich was situated on the Nile."[33] In August 1956, shortly after Nasser nationalized the Suez Canal, Labour leader Hugh Gaitskell described the situation as "all very familiar. It is exactly the same that we encountered from Mussolini and Hitler in those years before the war."[34] Eden demonstrated that these comparisons had hit home when he told the House of Commons in September 1956 that

> there are those who say that we should not be justified and are not justified in reacting vigorously unless Colonel Nasser commits some further act of aggression. That was the argument used in the 1930s to justify every concession that was made to the dictators. It has not been my experience that dictators are deflected from their purpose because others affect to ignore it. This reluctance to face reality led to the subjugation of Europe and to the Second World War. We must not help reproduce, step by step, the history of the thirties. We must prove ourselves wiser this time.[35]

But when the Americans forced a humiliating British climb-down, Eden's career was finished: anti-appeasement had made him, and then un-made him, something he himself recognized. In a review of a new biography of Neville Chamberlain published in 1961, he observed that "the Munich Agreement left a trauma from which hardly anyone in Britain over forty years of age may hope to be free."[36]

---

[32] See Rose, N., "The Resignation of Anthony Eden", *Historical Journal*, vol. 25/4, 1982, pp. 911–931.
[33] Shuckburgh, E., *Descent to Suez: Diarird 1951–56*, ed. J. Charmley, London, Weidenfeld, 1986, p. 75.
[34] Quoted in Hughes, R. G., *op. cit.*, p. 51.
[35] Quoted in Hughes, R. G., *op. cit.*, pp. 51–52.
[36] Lord Avon, "Man of Munich", *Times Literary Supplement*, 1.12.1961, p. 857.

In the years after Suez, Britain's weakened international position led to conciliatory foreign policies that were labelled "appeasement" by their critics. Harold Macmillan was accused of appeasing the Soviet Union over the Berlin Wall, and similar criticisms were lobbed throughout the Cold War at the American-led and British-supported policy of *détente* by opposition politicians – mostly on the right – looking to score points. During the negotiations over the Helsinki Accords in 1975, the MP Winston Churchill, grandson of the wartime Prime Minister, asserted than in formally acknowledging Soviet domination of Eastern Europe western democracies were "in danger of signing a second Munich agreement". The future Conservative leader Margaret Thatcher later recalled of this era that it was "difficult to see any difference between appeasement and *détente*."[37]

After she became Prime Minister in 1979, Thatcher, an admirer of Churchill who had come of age during the Second World War, would maintain the view that conciliation and appeasement were one and the same thing. In 1982, as British diplomats and military strategists debated how to respond to Argentina's invasion of the Falkland Islands, she repeatedly invoked appeasement as an example of what not to do. In his memoir, the American Secretary of State Alexander Haig described a meeting in which she "rapped sharply on the table top and recalled that this was the table at which Neville Chamberlain sat in 1938 and spoke of the Czechs as a faraway people about whom we know so little."[38] Nor was it the last time that Thatcher invoked appeasement in the context of an international crisis. In September 1990 in reference to Iraq's invasion of Kuwait, she told the House of Commons that "we have bitter memories of the consequences of failing to challenge annexation of small states in the 1930s. We have learned that the time to stop the aggressor is at once."[39]

---

[37] Quoted in Hughes, R. G., *op. cit.*, pp. 86 and 89.

[38] Hughes, R. G., *op. cit.*, p. 93. This bellicose spirit was not limited to right-wing Conservatives. Returning to his "Guilty Men" days, Labour leader Michael Foot was swept up in the opportunity to avoid the missteps of the past and restore Britain's prestige. He adamantly supported British military intervention and later accused those who did not of "simple appeasement". Deputy Labour leader Denis Healey, who tried to convince Foot to take a less strident position, was convinced that Foot saw the situation as "a repetition of the Nazi challenge which Britain had failed to meet in the thirties". Hughes, R. G., *op. cit.*, p. 102.

[39] Hughes, R. G., *op. cit.*, p. 124.

In more recent years, appeasement has continued to haunt British foreign policy. The government's non-confrontational approach to Serbian aggression against Bosnia in 1995 was criticized by Liberal Democrat leader Paddy Ashdown as "redolent of the worst appeasement."[40] John Nott, Thatcher's Defence Secretary during the Falklands War, wrote in the *Times*:

> I am ashamed to say that the British Government, by a huge miscalculation, has been an unwitting accomplice to the destruction of these people. For every Bosnian saved from starvation by the outstanding humanitarian efforts of British troops, thousands have either died, been made homeless or become refugees through a policy of such incompetence and arrogance that it is akin to the appeasement of the Nazis.[41]

When he became Prime Minister in 1997, Tony Blair took a more interventionist stance and repeatedly proved willing to back diplomatic initiatives with military force. In 2002 in reference to Saddam Hussein and his purported possession of weapons of mass destruction, he told the House of Commons that "we know... from our history that diplomacy not backed by the threat of force has never worked with dictators and never will." A few months later, Foreign Secretary Jack Straw declared, "If we fail to back our words with deeds, we follow one of the most catastrophic precedents in history. The descent into war in the 1930s is a searing reminder of the dangers of turning a blind eye whilst international law is subverted by the law of the jungle."[42] Invocations of appeasement thus remain effective rhetorical weapons of political rhetoric in British political culture. In 2010, Paul Kennedy observed that appeasement had become a "powerful term... growing evermore in strength as the decades advance". In contemporary politics, he continued, it had come to take on connotations of

> cowardice, abandoning one's friends and allies, failing to recognize evil in the world – a fool, then – or recognizing evil but then trying to buy it off – a knave. Nothing so alarms a president or a Prime Minister in the western world than to be accused of pursuing policies of appeasement. Better to be accused of stealing from a nunnery, or beating one's family.[43]

---

[40] Hughes, R. G., *op. cit.*, p. 149.
[41] Nott, J., "America Is Right about Bosnia", *Times*, 1.12.1994.
[42] Quoted in Hughes, R. G., *op. cit.*, pp. 165–166.
[43] Kennedy, P., "A Time to Appease", *The National Interest*, vol. 108, 2010, p. 7.

Kennedy's claim is confirmed by the use of appeasement rhetoric in reference to Britain's relations with the evolving project of European unification. In a famous exchange with the BBC's Robin Day after nearly two-thirds of British voters opted to remain in the European Economic Community in a referendum in 1975, the Conservative politician and early Tory Euro-skeptic Enoch Powell compared the moment to the Munich agreement:

> Powell: This is like September 1938. In September, October 1938 I'm sure that, if Neville Chamberlain had gone to the country, he would have swept the country for an act of abnegation. But the very same people, within 12 months, when they saw behind the facade, when they penetrated to the realities, stood up to fight for the continued existence of our nation; and that's what will happen.
> Day: You're saying that this is a kind of Munich?
> Powell: Yes I am
> Day: I see
> Powell: You seem surprised!
> Day: And when do you see our 1940 coming, when we stand alone?
> Powell: Well, let's have our 1939 first, when we decide we have to fight.[44]

Moving forward to the present and the 2016 referendum on Britain's membership in the EU, there were a number of ways in which appeasement was invoked. Leavers were eager to compare David Cameron's efforts to secure reforms from the EU to Chamberlain's dealings with Hitler at Munich. "Mr Cameron will no doubt emerge [from the negotiations with the EU], like Neville Chamberlain, waving a list of half-promises he hopes will be enough to sell to the public," opined the *Sun* in June 2015.[45] Similarly, David Mellor, holder of many cabinet posts under Thatcher and Major, declared in January 2016 that "I feel like voting Out simply because I am not going to be conned by that man, borrowing Chamberlain's overcoat, stumbling down the plane's steps waving a piece of paper, claiming that this is a triumph for Britain."[46]

---

[44] Kellner, P., "EU vote: Enoch Powell's warning from beyond the grave", YouGov, 15.6.2015 (9.5.2019).
[45] "Cam into the Open over EU", *The Sun*, 23.6.2015, p. 8.
[46] Parker, G., Allen, K., "Tories' Uneasy Truce on Europe about to Be Tested", *Financial Times*, 1.2.2016 (9.5.2019).

These comparisons culminated four days before the vote on the 19th of June 2016. That evening, Cameron appeared on the BBC television programme *Question Time*. The audience had been deliberately selected to be split between the pro- and anti-Brexit camps, and Cameron had already been given a tough time by the Leavers when, about half-an-hour into the broadcast, a man in a striped shirt accused him of being a "twenty-first century Neville Chamberlain waving a piece of paper in the air saying to the public this is what I have, I have this promise where a dictatorship in Europe can overrule it". Here, once again, was a Leaver drawing an implicit parallel between Hitler and the governance of the EU – "a dictatorship in Europe" – and invoking the image of Neville Chamberlain on the tarmac of the Heston Aerodrome waving the Munich Agreement – "a piece of paper in the air". Predictably, Cameron was not best pleased. He launched into a fiery response in which he argued that Britain had joined the EU out of its own free will and could leave of its own free will, and had therefore not surrendered its sovereignty to Brussels. He then paused, took a sip of water, and decided that was not finished, and said:

> At my office I sit two yards away from the Cabinet Room where Winston Churchill decided in May 1940 to fight on against Hitler – the best and greatest decision anyone has made in our country. He didn't want to be alone, he wanted to be fighting with the French and with the Poles and with the others but he didn't quit. He didn't quit on Europe, he didn't quit on European democracy, he didn't quit on European freedom. We want to fight for those things today. You can't win, you can't fight, if you are not in the room.[47]

The man's question – and Cameron's response – received massive coverage from the British press the next day.

For their part, Remainers recognized the danger that these kinds of comparisons posed. To reduce the damaging power of the historical analogy, some sought to seize control of it for their cause. For them, it was not the Chamberlain who returned from Munich on the 30th of September 1938 who was relevant, but rather to the Chamberlain of three days earlier, when he had declared in a BBC speech "How horrible, fantastic, incredible it is that we should be digging trenches and trying on gas masks here because of a quarrel in a far-away country between

---

[47] "Question Time", *BBC*, Episode 1293, 19.6.2016.

people of whom we know nothing."[48] On the 16th of June 2019, Neal Ascherson wrote in the *New York Times*:

> Isolation brings out the worst in Britain. And it never works. In the 1930s, a complacent Britain refused to help Spain fight fascism, appeased Hitler and Mussolini, and for too long turned away refugees fleeing persecution. As Czechoslovakia cried out for help, Prime Minister Neville Chamberlain dismissed "a quarrel in a faraway country between people of whom we know nothing". Will a British leader soon speak again about faraway Europe in the same tones? When Britain did admit that it belonged to Europe, after all, it was at the eleventh hour. In 1940, isolation ended in a fight for survival, and complacency gave way to five years of grim determination. During those war years, the Continent was devastated and its nation-states discredited. Thanks to that harsh experience, the British after the war recognized their share of responsibility by supporting the vision of a united Europe. Must Britain learn that painful, costly lesson all over again?[49]

Such efforts, however, were scattered and for the most part limited to more intellectually-minded journalists. They did little to blunt the force of the appeasement rhetoric coming from the other side.

After the vote, as both sides grappled with the implications of Britain's departure from the EU, appeasement rhetoric continued to be deployed. Leave supporters used it to warn against any retreat by the British government as they negotiated the terms of Britain's withdrawal. In announcing his resignation as leader of the United Kingdom Independence Party, Nigel Farage declared that "if we see significant backsliding or weakness, or frankly appeasement from the British government we will certainly say so."[50] Letters comparing any apparent wavering on a hardline stance towards Brexit to appeasement appeared frequently in right-wing British newspapers as the months passed. The most frequent invocations of appeasement in the weeks and months after the referendum, however, came from Remainers who compared Cameron to Chamberlain as a Prime Minister whose historical reputation had been

---

[48] Ratcliffe, S., "Neville Chamberlain 1869–1940: speech at Central Hall, Westminster, 4 April 1940", *Oxford* Essential Quotations, Oxford, Oxford University Press, 2016.

[49] Ascherson, N., "From Great Britain to Little England", *New York Times*, 16.6.2016 (9.5.2019).

[50] Peck, T., "Nigel Farage Has Signed Off with His Most Sinister Speech Yet", *Independent*, 4.7.2018 (9.5.2019).

undone by a colossal mistake. Writing in the *New Statesman*, Dominic Sandbrook asserted:

> Like Chamberlain, Cameron seems destined to be remembered for only one thing. When students answer exam questions about Chamberlain, it's a safe bet that they aren't writing about the Holidays with Pay Act 1938. And when students write about Cameron in the year 2066, they won't be answering questions about intervention in Libya, or gay marriage. They will be writing about Brexit and the lost referendum.[51]

Similarly, Andrew Rawnsley wrote in the *Guardian*:

> David Cameron has just become one of those leaders who will be remembered for a single enormous mistake. Neville Chamberlain had achievements to his name before appeasement. There was more to Anthony Eden than the Suez debacle. Lord North had a career before he lost America. But each of those premiers is defined by their one towering disaster. So it will be with David Cameron, the Prime Minister who accidentally ruptured more than four decades of his country's economic, security and foreign policy by losing the referendum on Europe. That will be the inscription etched deep on his tombstone.[52]

The competition for the legacy of 1940 in the Brexit campaign was thus fierce and bitter. Both sides wanted to be Churchill, and neither wanted to be Chamberlain. But in the end, the Leavers had the easier case to make. It was much more natural fit to depict the Leave campaign as advocating a return to the "Finest Hour" of 1940, when Britain stood alone against the political and military failures of the rest of Europe. In arguing that Britain's future lay alongside Germany and France, the Remainers had a far more difficult argument. Perhaps British memories of the Second World War will eventually come more to congrue with their European counterparts, and the emphasis on "standing alone" in 1940 will begin to dissipate. But if the current political situation is any guide, I would not bet on it. Mere hours after Theresa May announced on the 14th of November 2018 that she had reached a deal on the terms of Britain's exit from the European Union with EU negotiators, the United Kingdom Independence Party issued a statement complaining that "this

---

[51] Sandbrook, D., "How Will History Treat David Cameron?", *New Statesman*, 29.8.2016 (9.5.2019).

[52] Rawnsley, A., "Brexit: A Journey into the Unknown for a Country Never before so Divided", *The Guardian*, 26.6.2016 (9.5.2019).

is a historic betrayal": "Theresa May has made Neville Chamberlain look like Winston Churchill."[53] The accompanying tweet included a picture of Chamberlain holding the Munich Agreement at the Heston Aerodrome, but with his head replaced by May's.

---

[53] https://www.ukip.org/national-ukip-news-item.php?id=128 (9/05/2019).

Brexit as a Result of European Struggles over the UK's Financial Sector

Daisuke Ikemoto

In June 2016, a referendum was held to decide whether the United Kingdom (UK) should leave or remain in the European Union (EU). The British people opted to leave the Union by a small majority of 51.9 % against 48.1 %. A commonly held view regards the EU referendum as Prime Minister David Cameron's response to the rise of the anti-establishment and eurosceptic UK Independence Party (UKIP), as well as the internal division within the Conservative Party over the issue.[1] During the referendum campaign, popular antipathy for the recent rise in immigration as well as concerns over sovereignty played decisive roles by tipping the balance of public opinion in favour of Brexit.[2] Nowhere in the UK was support for Brexit higher than in the declining industrial areas of Northern England.[3] These facts suggest that Brexit was caused by a revolt of pensioners and less well-educated people who felt marginalized during the process of economic globalization.[4] This view is not limited to the world of academia. For instance, Nick Robinson, BBC's political editor, commented shortly after the referendum result was announced that "this is as close to a revolution as we've experienced in my lifetime".[5]

---

[1] For instance, Martill, B., Staiger, U., "Introduction: Brexit and Beyond", in Martill, B., Staiger, U. (eds.), *Brexit and Beyond: Rethinking the Futures of Europe*, London, UCL Press, 2018.

[2] Clarke, D. H., Goodwin, M., Whiteley, P., "Why Britain Voted for Brexit: An Individual Level Analysis of the 2016 Referendum Vote", *Parliamentary Affairs*, vol. 70, 2017, pp. 439–464.

[3] Goodwin, M. J., Heath, O., "The 2016 Referendum, Brexit and the Left Behind: An Aggregate-Level Analysis of the Result", *The Political Quarterly*, vol. 87/3, 2016, pp. 323–332.

[4] *Ibid.*, p. 331.

[5] https://twitter.com/bbcnickrobinson/status/746187739784052736 (13.8.2019).

While these accounts of the referendum are not completely off the mark, this chapter demonstrates that they may have underestimated the contributions made by British elites to the Brexit saga. In particular, the explanation above does not fully consider the fact that British political elites became increasingly concerned with changes within the EU brought about by measures taken to save the single euro currency in the wake of the Eurozone crisis. What is missing when framing the story of a populist revolt against the EU is that concerns among the elites played a vital role in both Cameron's decision to organize an in/out referendum on EU membership and his renegotiation of the UK's status within the EU that preceded the actual referendum campaign.

The tension across the channel was caused by dissimilar approaches. While the Eurozone tried to address its crisis with further integration (including more regulations on the financial sector), the UK did not convert to the euro and the British economy continued to rely heavily on the City of London.[6] The Cameron government faced additional challenges to maintain the UK's influence over economic policymaking among EU members and defend the City of London from the EU's regulations.[7] Since the outbreak of the Eurozone crisis in 2007, both sides clashed over numerous issues, including the Fiscal Compact Treaty, the banking union, financial transaction taxes and, above all, proposed caps on bankers' bonuses.

From its origin, the referendum was an attempt to win otherwise unobtainable concessions on these issues from the EU. It was during the Bloomberg speech that Cameron first promised to hold an in/out EU referendum if the Conservative party won the next general election.[8] However, the Prime Minister never mentioned the word "immigration" in his speech.[9] Instead, his main concern was the responses to the Eurozone

---

[6] According to TheCityUK, *A Practitioner's Guide to Brexit: Exploring Its Consequences and Alternatives to EU membership* (2016), the financial 'industry accounts directly for 11.8 % of UK GDP, employs nearly 2.2 million people and is the nation's largest tax paying sector – contributing 66bn in 2014/2015'.

[7] Thompson, H., "Inevitability and contingency: The political economy of Brexit", *The British Journal of Politics and International Relations*, vol. 19/3, 2017, pp. 434–449.

[8] Cameron, D., "EU speech at Bloomberg", 23.1.2013. https://www.gov.uk/government/speeches/eu-speech-at-bloomberg (15.8.2019).

[9] Evans, G., Menon, A., *Brexit and British Politics*, Cambridge, Polity Press, 2017, p. 20.

crisis by countries using the single currency after they embarked on far-reaching integration regarding macroeconomic policies and banking regulations, thereby driving a fundamental wedge between the Eurozone members and those outside. Assuming that the UK would never adopt the single currency – hence his insistence on Britain's opt-out from the objective of "ever closer union" – Cameron called for a fair solution for both sides and respect for the integrity of the single market. Therefore, although the issue of immigration dominated the referendum campaign, it was not instrumental in Cameron's decision to organize a referendum. Although Cameron supported EU membership, a substantial sector of the Conservative party was dissatisfied with "over-regulation" by the EU and thus supported Brexit in principle.[10] Brexit resulted from this unique combination of anti-EU sentiment among the elites and the rise of the populist movement against the EU.

In this chapter, I first trace how conflicts arose between the UK and the Eurozone countries, particularly France and Germany, over the aforementioned issues: the Fiscal Compact Treaty, the banking union, the financial transaction tax, and the cap on bankers' bonuses. Then I illustrate how the British government attempted to renegotiate the terms of the UK's EU membership during the run up to the referendum campaign. While Cameron obtained only token concessions on the issue of immigration, he negotiated a better deal for the City of London, including a secret agreement to scrap the cap on bankers' bonuses if the UK chose to remain within the EU. I conclude by pointing out that while Brexit (and the election of Donald Trump as US president) forced the world to pay closer attention to the issues of immigration and international trade, unsolved issues such as the reforms of the global financial system and the unequal distribution of income were almost forgotten. One might see only chaos in the Brexit saga and the ongoing situations surrounding Trump, but these phenomena have succinctly redefined the terms of our discourse regarding globalization.

---

[10] According to BBC, 138 Conservative MPs (out of 323) declared their support for Brexit during the referendum campaign. See: "EU vote: Where the cabinet and other MPs stand", *BBC*, 22.6.2016 (25.8.2019).

The Politics of Financial Regulation in the Aftermath of the Crisis

In the United States, the collapse of the real estate boom left a mountain of bad loans and culminated in a major financial crisis in 2007. At first, many Europeans considered this a "fire on the opposite shore", blaming the crisis on the excessive reliance of American capitalism on the financial sector.[11] The impact of the financial crisis, however, soon reached their side of the Atlantic. As major customers of securitized products whose values depended on the repayment of property loans in the United States, a number of European financial institutions recorded huge losses.[12] In addition, housing bubbles in European nations were bursting as well. Some were hit particularly hard, including the UK, Ireland, Greece and Spain where property prices had risen as much or more than in the United States during the boom. The financial health of many European States deteriorated rapidly as they were forced to spend vast amounts of public funds in order to rescue their financial institutions.[13]

To make matters worse, the Social Democratic Party in Greece won the general election in 2009. Shortly thereafter, the new government revealed that its predecessor had misreported the actual size of the country's budget deficit.[14] In reality, Greece had never satisfied the "sound and sustainable finances" condition stipulated in the convergence criteria for acceptance into the single currency group. The long-term interest rate of Greece skyrocketed, making it impossible for the government to issue new bonds. Their only alternative was to ask for international assistance. The crisis soon spread to Portugal, Ireland, and Spain (these affected countries, together with Greece, were soon labelled 'PIGS', based on their acronym), thereby triggering the European sovereign debt crisis. Among EU members, there was a widely held belief that the City of London and the unregulated Anglo American finance market were directly to blame for the Eurozone crisis.[15]

---

[11] Bastasin, C., *Saving Europe: Anatomy of a Dream*, Washington, Brookings Institution Press, 2012, p. 17.
[12] *Ibid.*
[13] *Ibid.*, p. 42.
[14] *Ibid.*, Chapter 5.
[15] *Ibid.*, pp. 18–22.

In May 2010, the EU established the European Financial Stability Mechanism (EFSM) and the European Financial Stability Facility (EFSF) in order to bail out Greece and other affected countries. Nations within the Eurozone also pushed for a long-term solution to the crisis. In exchange for financial assistance, Germany demanded a fiscal compact that would oblige Eurozone countries to maintain balanced budgets and they also insisted that these policies be enshrined into the domestic laws of all Member States. The British government did not oppose the attempt by Eurozone members to save the single currency. Instead, believing that they could block necessary treaty modifications and thus be in a strong negotiating position, Cameron tried to restore British veto power over the EU's financial regulations in exchange for his support for the inclusion of a fiscal compact in the EU basic treaties.[16] However, Nicholas Sarkozy, the President of France at the time, was firmly opposed to this deal, thus leaving Cameron isolated during the European Council meeting held in December 2011. In the end, to circumscribe British opposition, the fiscal compact was written as an intergovernmental treaty. The UK and the Czech Republic did not participate in the European Fiscal Compact.[17]

In June 2012, Eurozone members also reached agreement to establish the banking union, including the Single Supervisory Mechanism (SSM) whereby the European Central Bank would work as the central prudential supervisor of financial institutions in the euro area, as well as the Single Resolution Mechanism (SRM), a central institution for EU banking resolutions. Although the British government supported the banking union and SSM in principle, it did not intend to join the organization. Still, British policymakers were afraid that Eurozone members might first reach agreements on new banking regulations among themselves and then present them to the rest of the EU as a *fait accompli*. To allay British concerns, the European Banking Authority, which had been set up as a single regulatory framework for the entire EU banking sector, would use a dual majority system (a majority of both Eurozone members and non-Eurozone members was required) for its decision-making.[18]

---

[16] "David Cameron defends decision to block EU-wide treaty", *BBC*, 9.12.2011 (16.8.2019).
[17] "EU treaty will not 'place obligations' on UK, says PM", *BBC*, 31.1.2012 (16.8.2019).
[18] Howarth, D., Quaglia, L., "Brexit and the Single European Financial Market", *Journal of Common Market Studies*, vol. 55, Annual Review, 2017, pp. 149–164.

To understand the politics of financial regulation in the aftermath of the global financial crisis and how it was intertwined with the attempts to save the single currency, attention must be paid to the presence of two conflicting political coalitions in the EU.[19] These coalitions first emerged during the completion of the single finance market. While the UK and Northern Europe advocated a market-making approach by emphasising competition and efficiency, France, Italy, Germany (sometimes) and a sector of the European Parliament supported a more interventionist approach. The predominance of the former coalition was reflected in EU financial regulations before the crisis, which emphasised the liberalisation of financial services and open-market access across Europe. However, the outbreak of the global financial crisis strengthened the position of continental European countries and the European Parliament.[20] They took advantage of the situation in order to promote their long-standing priorities as an international agenda.

At first, the G20 became the main forum for international debate related to reforms of the global financial system. However, the EU was not powerful enough to unilaterally achieve its agenda on the global stage. There were no international agreements over measures supported by the continental European countries while opposed by the United States, such as a cap on bankers' bonuses or a Financial Transaction Tax (FTT).[21] President Sarkozy of France and Chancellor Angela Merkel of Germany were willing to let the EU proceed alone even if the United States or any other major country did not support the proposed reforms. This left the UK reeling in an unfavourable position for the upcoming battle over financial regulations within the EU.

Battle over a Cap on Bankers' Bonuses…

In the financial sector, there is a widespread practice that bankers receive a large proportion of their remuneration in the form of performance-based bonuses. These are usually related to the share prices

---

[19] Pagliari, S., "A Wall Around Europe? The European Regulatory Response to the Global Financial Crisis and the Turn in Transatlantic Relations", *Journal of European Integration*, vol. 35/4, 2013, pp. 391–408.

[20] *Ibid.*, p. 398.

[21] *Ibid.*, p. 393.

of the institutions.[22] In the aftermath of the global financial crisis, the banker bonus practice came under fierce attack. It is widely believed that equity-based benefits for bankers led to excessive risk-taking and speculation, thereby becoming one of the contributing factors to the crisis.[23] The EU, led by France and Germany, placed a cap on bankers' bonuses as a cornerstone of their banking regulation reforms in order to avoid excessive risk-taking and the recurrence of any similar financial crisis.[24] Conversely, the British Government was fearful that these regulations might damage the international competitiveness of the City of London and thus did everything possible to block the introduction of a bonus cap.[25] Even after the cap took effect in EU law, British authorities continued their resistance against the implementation of the rule.

Initially, the dispute between the two sides was fought mainly in the forum of the newly created G20. In April 2009, the G20's London summit issued a communique outlining reforms to the global financial system, including risk-taking and the banker's bonus.[26] The EU swiftly published a report featuring various policy recommendations on remuneration.[27] The report emphasised that corporate governance and remuneration schemes should take into account not only the shareholders' interests but also the overall stability of the financial system. In August 2009, France became the first developed country to impose a sector-wide bonus cap on financial institutions. President Sarkozy also appealed to other G20 members to introduce similar regulations, which led to a joint proposal by France and Germany to be introduced at the G20's London meeting of financial ministers and central bank governors in September of that

---

[22] Longjie, L., "The End of Bankers' Bonus Cap: How Will the UK Regulate Bankers' Remuneration after Brexit?", *European Business Law Review*, vol. 27, 2016, pp. 1091–1125.

[23] The Larosière Report, which was published at the request of the European Commission in February 2009, was merely one example to take this view. https://ec.europa.eu/economy_finance/publications/pages/publication14527_en.pdf (25.8.2019).

[24] Longjie, L., *op. cit.*, p. 1095.

[25] *Ibid.*

[26] G20 Communique, "London Summit – Leaders' Statement", London, 2.4.2009 (25.8.2019).

[27] European Commission, Recommendation on remuneration policies in the financial services sector, (2009/384/EC), 30.4.2009.

year.[28] However, the meeting failed to reach consensus on the issue as both the United States and the UK rejected the proposal. Three weeks later, continental Europe and the Anglo American axis clashed again over the same issue during the G20 summit in Pittsburgh.[29]

As the G20 failed to reach agreement on the issue, the battleground moved from the global to the European level. In July 2011, the European Commission published a proposal to revise the Capital Requirement Directive (CRD).[30] In May 2012, the Committee of Economic and Monetary Affairs (ECON) of the European Parliament approved the inclusion of a bonus cap in the revised CRD. According to the committee's proposal, a variable percentage of bankers' pay could not exceed 50 % of total annual remuneration.[31] In August, the European Commission rejected this proposal as too restrictive, and a vote by the European Parliament was delayed until 2013. Not surprisingly, the British government was vehemently opposed to the bonus cap. However, as financial regulations were among the matters to be decided by Qualified Majority Voting (QMV) in the Council of Ministers, the British Government was unable to exercise a veto over the bill.

In February 2013, the European Parliament enacted an amendment that the proportion between variable remuneration and fixed remuneration could be raised to 2:1 upon the approval of shareholders. When the Council of Ministers put the matter to vote in March, the British government was soundly defeated, 26 to 1.[32] Over the next month, the European Parliament finally approved the revised CRD and set January 2014 as its effective date.[33]

Shortly before enactment, the British government brought a case to the European Court of Justice in September 2013, seeking annulment of

---

[28] "France and Germany declare war on bankers' bonuses", *The Guardian*, 1.9.2009 (25.8.2019).
[29] "G20 leaders split over bank bonus curbs", *The Guardian*, 25.9.2009 (25.8.2019).
[30] Longjie, L., *op. cit.*, p. 1094.
[31] The European Parliament, "Bank capital rules: reform to boost risk resilience and lending to the real economy", Brussels, 15.5.2012 (25.8.2019).
[32] "George Osborne is defeated 26 to 1 on EU bonus caps", *The Daily Telegraph*, 5.5.2013 (25.8.2019).
[33] The European Parliament, "Parliament votes reform package to strengthen EU banks", Brussels, 16.4.2013 (25.8.2019).

the regulation.³⁴ The government feared that the cap on bankers' bonuses would weaken the competitiveness of the City of London against other major financial centres, such as New York and Singapore. The British were also concerned that the EU regulation was incompatible with previous reforms implemented in the UK in the aftermath of the global financial crisis.

After the EU *avocat généraux* (advocate generals) expressed the opinion that the bonus cap was compatible with EU law, the British government withdrew its complaint.³⁵ However, the friction between the two sides continued even after the bonus cap became EU law. In the UK, small financial institutions were exempted from the new regulation by the Bank of England and the Financial Conduct Authority (FCA) despite the European Banking Authority's insistence that there should be no exemptions from the bonus cap.³⁶

... and a Financial Transaction Tax

The idea of a Financial Transaction Tax (FFT) first surfaced in 2009 during dialogue related to international diplomacy.³⁷ The proponent of the idea argued that such a tax was necessary to not only recoup money from the financial institutions bailed out by the government in the wake of the global financial crisis but also to curb excessive short-term speculation.³⁸

A number of actors pushed the idea as a subject of discussion for the third meeting of the G20 Summit scheduled for September 2009 in Pittsburgh. Surprisingly, it was first backed by Adair Turner, Chairman of the Financial Services Authority in the UK.³⁹ Next, President Sarkozy

---

[34] "Osborne bats for bankers' bonuses citing risk to City from EU cap", *The Guardian*, 25.9.2013 (25.8.2019).

[35] "George Osborne backs down over EU cap on bankers' bonuses", *The Guardian*, 20.11.2014 (25.8.2019).

[36] Longjie, *op. cit.*, pp. 1106–1107 and p. 1113.

[37] Tsuda, K., "Put Sand in the Wheels of the Market: Political Process of EU Financial Transaction Tax, 2009–2013(1)", *The Hokkaido Law Review*, vol. 66/6, 2016, pp. 101–158 (in Japanese).

[38] Schulmeister, S., "The Struggle over the Financial Transactions Tax: A Politico-Economic Farce", *Revue de l'OFCE*, 2015, pp. 15–55.

[39] "Financial Services Authority chairman backs tax on 'socially useless' banks", *The Guardian*, 27.8.2009. (16.8.2019).

supported the idea of a new global tax on financial transactions.[40] The communique of the Pittsburgh Summit invited the International Monetary Fund (IMF) to examine the idea.[41] In December 2009, Sarkozy and Gordon Brown, Britain's Prime Minister at the time, issued a joint statement appealing for the introduction of a global FTT.[42] In March 2010, the European Parliament passed a resolution which called for an effective FTT.[43] That year also marked the rise of citizen movements advocating the benefits of the so-called Robin Hood Tax.[44]

However, at the Toronto G20 Summit meeting in June 2010, participants failed to reach agreement on the issue.[45] The British Labour Party had recently lost the general election, and the newly-formed Conservative-Liberal coalition opposed the idea on behalf of the UK. Before the Toronto Summit, George Osborne, then Chancellor of the exchequer, expressed his support for a proposal to force financial institutions to contribute to public finance through a bank levy.[46] He was opposed to the introduction of an FTT on the grounds that such a move would simply drive financial transactions to other jurisdictions where the tax was not applied. Thus, a clear chasm was about to emerge between France, Germany, and the EU who supported the introduction of a global FTT on one side, and the United States, the UK, and the IMF who resisted the plan on the other.[47]

After the Toronto meetings, France and Germany were willing to act unilaterally, and they appealed directly to the EU to introduce an FTT.[48] However, the two countries had dissimilar motives.[49] Sarkozy continued to seek possibilities for implementing a global FTT by adding it to the

---

[40] "Sarkozy to press for 'Tobin Tax'", *BBC*, 19.9.2009 (25.8.2019).
[41] G20, "Leaders' Statement, the Pittsburgh Summit", Pittsburgh, 24–25.9.2009 (25.8.2019).
[42] "Brown and Sarkozy move to fund climate aid with global banking tax", *The Guardian*, 11.12.2009 (25.8.2019).
[43] Tsuda, K., *op. cit.*, p. 139.
[44] "'Robin Hood' tax campaign launched", *Reuters*, 10.2.2010 (25.8.2019).
[45] G20, "The G-20 Toronto Summit Declaration", Toronto, 26–27.6.2010 (25.8.2019).
[46] "Budget: Bank levy to raise £8.3bn in four years", *BBC*, 22.6.2010 (25.8.2019).
[47] Tsuda, K., *op. cit.*, p. 143.
[48] "France and Germany push for transaction tax", *The Financial Times*, 9.7.2010 (25.8.2019).
[49] Tsuda, K., *op. cit.*, pp. 59–116.

agenda as host nation of the next G20 Summit to be held in Cannes in November 2011. His decision also accelerated a debate on the tax among EU nations. Germany, in contrast, supported an FTT in order to mitigate the Euro crisis and reconstruct the deficit-ridden finances of Eurozone members.

In June 2011, José Manuel Barroso, then President of the European Commission, proposed the introduction of an FTT as a component of the EU's own resources in the next multi-annual financial framework.[50] In September 2011, the European Commission presented a draft bill outlining an FTT framework.[51] During the meeting of the Economic and Financial Affairs Council (ECOFIN) in November 2011, the bill met strong opposition from Osborne. Sweden was also firmly against any EU-wide FTT. In retort, Wolfgang Schäuble, Germany's Minister of finance, described the issue as a matter of dispute between Eurozone members and those outside.[52] In the next month, Sarkozy and Merkel called for the introduction of an FTT as a countermeasure to the Euro crisis.[53] In May 2012, Francois Hollande beat Sarkozy to become the first Socialist Party President of France since Francois Mitterrand; nevertheless, France continued to support an FTT. Meanwhile, Merkel was being pressured by her political opponents to not turn away from the issue. The Social Democratic and Green parties demanded early passage of the EU's FTT bill in exchange for their support for the ratification of the Financial Compact Treaty.[54] The bill was approved by the European Parliament in May 2012.[55] However, because the FTT was subject to the same legislative procedure as the harmonization of indirect taxation, it required a unanimous decision by the Council of Ministers. As a result,

---

[50] The European Commission, "Investing today for growth tomorrow", IP/11/799, Brussels, 29.6.2010 (25.8.2019).
[51] The European Commission, Proposal for a Council Directive on a common system of financial transaction tax and amending Directive 2008/7/EC, (COM/2011/0594 final), Brussels, 28.9.2011.
[52] Tsuda, K., *op. cit.*, pp. 81–82.
[53] "Eurozone: France and Germany urge common taxes", *BBC*, 7.12.2011 (25.8.2019).
[54] Tsuda, K., *op. cit.*, p. 88.
[55] The European Parliament, "Parliament adopts ambitious approach on financial transaction tax", Brussels, 23.5.2012 (25.8.2019).

ECOFIN had to abandon the introduction of the EU-wide FTT in June.[56]

In October 2012, still resolute in their attempts to introduce an FTT, eleven countries led by France and Germany expressed their intentions to use the "enhanced cooperation procedure". The move was approved by the European Parliament in December and passed by a majority vote of ECOFIN in January 2013 despite abstention by the UK.[57] However, the EU's legislative proposal turned out to be very problematic for the British government as it would impose taxes on both the buyer and the seller of a financial transaction. This provision meant that financial institutions in the UK would be obliged to pay the tax if their counterparts were located in any country participating in the enhanced integration. The British government filed a suit against the plan in the European Court of Justice in April 2013. The Court dismissed the claim one year later on grounds that the enactment of the bill was not complete.[58] In fact, the proposal has been on hold to this day because of differences among the participating countries.

Cameron's Bloomberg Speech

It is fair to say that most literature on Brexit pays only minor attention to the content of Cameron's Bloomberg speech or to the revised terms of the UK's EU membership as renegotiated prior to the referendum. However, to fully understand Brexit from the point of view of British policymakers who considered the EU problematic, these two events must be examined more closely and placed in the context of what happened in the EU during Cameron's premiership.

In his long-anticipated speech, Cameron declared on behalf of the UK that "the European Union is a means to an end – prosperity, stability, and the anchor of freedom and democracy both within Europe and beyond her shores – not an end in itself."[59] Nonetheless, he spoke as the "British

---

[56] Council of the European Union, "Press Release, 3178th Council meeting, Economic and Financial Affairs", Brussels, 22.6.2012 (25.8.2019).

[57] Tsuda, K., *op. cit.*, p. 80.

[58] "Europe rejects UK's financial transaction tax challenge", *BBC*, 30.4.2014 (25.8.2019).

[59] The following quotations are from Cameron, "EU speech at Bloomberg", London, 23.1.2013.

Prime Minister with a positive vision for the future of the European Union... in which Britain wants... to play a committed and active part". According to Cameron, Britain and Europe were confronting three major challenges: "First, the problems in the Eurozone are driving fundamental change in Europe. Second, there is a crisis of European competitiveness... and third, there is a gap between the EU and its citizens which has grown dramatically in recent years". Of all three challenges, the Prime Minister placed more emphasis on the first:

> The Union is changing to fix the currency – and that has profound implications for all of us, whether we are in the single currency or not... [The essential foundation of] the European Union...is the single market rather than the single currency. Those of us outside the euro recognise that those in it are likely to need to make some big institutional changes. By the same token, the members of the Eurozone should accept that we, and indeed all Member States, will have changes that we need to safeguard our interests and strengthen democratic legitimacy... Whatever new arrangements are enacted for the Eurozone, they must work fairly for those inside it and out... Our participation in the single market, and our ability to help set its rules is the principal reason for our membership of the EU. So it is a vital interest for us to protect the integrity and fairness of the single market for all its members. And that is why Britain has been so concerned to promote and defend the single market as the Eurozone crisis rewrites the rules on fiscal coordination and banking union.

As we have already seen what transpired between the UK and the continental European countries over issues such as the cap on bankers' bonuses and the FTT, it is not difficult to imagine what Cameron had in mind when he delivered the Bloomberg speech. Before the global financial crisis, the political coalition in favour of a market-making approach led by the UK was predominant while the EU was engaged in the creation of the single market for financial services. However, the Eurozone crisis changed the balance of power inside the EU. In order to save the single currency, the regulations and taxes which had been advocated by the group supporting a more interventionist approach, albeit unrealistic before the crisis, were either adopted or about to be introduced. To counter this trend, Cameron reiterated his demands for safeguards for Britain's financial sector against these measures throughout his speech.

In other words, the Prime Minister was neither satisfied with the current situation of the EU nor Britain's reduced influence in the organization to the extent that he seemed willing to accept the risks of a major political gamble like a referendum. This interpretation is supported by an article Cameron wrote for the *Daily Telegraph* almost six months prior to the Bloomberg speech. In the article, he argued that "the single currency is driving a process that will see its members take more and more steps towards fuller integration".[60] The question before the UK was "how do we avoid the wrong paths of either accepting status quo meekly or giving up altogether and preparing to leave?"[61] An in/out referendum was not just a device for party political advantages, but also a negotiating tactics to win otherwise unobtainable concessions from the rest of the EU.

The UK's Renegotiation of the Terms of EU Membership (2015–2016)

In the general election of 2015, the Conservative Party unexpectedly won an overall majority in the House of Commons. This result opened a path for an in/out referendum. In November 2015, terms of the UK's EU membership were renegotiated in the following four areas: economic governance, competitiveness, sovereignty, as well as social benefits and free movement.[62] Clearly, the first three areas corresponded to the three challenges identified by Cameron in his Bloomberg speech. By contrast, social benefits and free movement between EU nations were new issues added by the British government at this stage in order to allay the general public's concerns about immigration.

The two parties eventually reached a deal in February 2016, thereby strengthening Britain's special status in the EU. The agreement was to take effect only if the "Remain" campaign won the referendum. The section related to economic governance declared the following: "measures, the purpose of which is to further deepen economic and monetary union, will be voluntary for Member States whose currency is not the euro and will be open to their participation wherever feasible."[63] The relationship

---

[60] Cameron, D., "We need to be clear about the best way of getting what is best for Britain", *Daily Telegraph*, 30.6.2012.
[61] *Ibid*.
[62] Letter from David Cameron to Donald Tusk, "A new settlement for the United Kingdom in a reformed European Union", London, 10.11.2015 (25.8.2019).
[63] European Council meeting, EUCO 1/16, Conclusions, 18–19.2.2016, p. 12.

between the Eurozone members and those outside would be based on the following principles:

Principle 1: "Discrimination between natural or legal persons based on the official currency of the Member State, or…where they are established is prohibited. Legal acts…directly linked to the functioning of the euro area shall respect the internal market…and shall not constitute a barrier to or discrimination in trade between Member States."[64] The purpose of this clause was to ensure that the City of London would not be handicapped by Britain opting out of the single euro currency. In 2009, Christine Lagarde, the French Minister of finance at the time, publicly insisted that the euro-clearing business (for which the City's share was over 40 %) should be located in the Eurozone. In 2011, the European Central Bank called for legislation to oblige clearing houses with more than 5 % share of the market to be based within the euro area. Although the European Court of Justice ruled that the European Central Bank was acting beyond its authority, the conflict left a foul aftertaste for the British government.[65]

Principle 2: "Union law on the banking union conferring upon the European Central Bank, the Single Resolution Board or Union bodies exercising similar functions, authority over credit institutions is applicable only to credit institutions located in Member States whose currency is the euro. The single rulebook is to be applied by all financial institutions in order to ensure the level-playing field within the internal market."[66] This clause confirmed that the UK would not participate in the banking union but would be subject to a single supervisory framework overseen by the European Banking Authority.

Principle 3: "Emergency and crisis measures designed to safeguard the financial stability of the euro area will not entail budgetary responsibility for Member States whose currency is not the euro."[67] In other words, countries outside the Eurozone would not be required to fund euro area bailouts. The background for this clause was the establishment of the EFSM in 2010 to enable the European Commission to provide financial assistance to any EU country experiencing severe difficulties. In order to

---

[64] *Ibid.*, p. 13.
[65] Howarth, D., Quaglia, L., *op. cit.*, p. 153.
[66] European Council meeting, EUCO 1/16, *op. cit.*, p. 13.
[67] *Ibid.*, p. 14.

raise necessary funding, the EFSM issued bonds using the EU budget as collateral. Despite fierce opposition from the British government, the EFSM offered a bridge loan to Greece in 2015, with all of the Eurozone members voting in favour. This clause was inserted to ensure that the British government would be reimbursed for their incurred costs and that a similar exercise would not be repeated.[68]

Principle 4: "The implementation of measures, including the supervision or resolution of financial institutions and markets, and macro-prudential responsibilities, to be taken in view of preserving the financial stability of Member States whose currency is not the euro is, subject to the requirements of group and consolidated supervision and resolution, a matter for their own authorities and own budgetary responsibility."[69] This clause is usually interpreted as the confirmation of the status quo,[70] but it might actually be related to a secret deal between the two sides on the banker's bonus cap (see below).

Principle 5: "The informal meetings of the ministers of the Member States whose currency is the euro…, the Euro Group, shall respect the powers of the Council as an institution upon which the Treaties confer legislative functions and within which Member States coordinate their economic policies."[71] The intention of this clause was to prevent the Euro Group, an informal gathering of financial ministers from the euro area, from making unilateral decisions by themselves and imposing them on the entire EU without British approval.

All told, these agreements on economic governance are generally regarded as the confirmation of the existing law and practice rather than something substantially new.[72] However, it is important to note that the above assurances of the British position outside the Eurozone were to be included in the basic treaties of the EU, thus offering better protection for British interests.[73] Moreover, according to the British media, there was a secret deal between the two sides whereby the UK would be allowed to

---

[68] Howarth, D., Quaglia, L., *op. cit.*, p. 155.
[69] European Council meeting, EUCO 1/16, *op. cit.*, p. 14.
[70] Howarth, D., Quaglia, L., *op. cit.*, p. 156.
[71] European Council meeting, EUCO 1/16, *op. cit.*, p. 14.
[72] Howarth, D., Quaglia, L., *op. cit.*; Craig, P., "Explaining the EU deal: the UK and the eurozone", *Full Fact*, 22.2.2016 (25.8.2019).
[73] European Council meeting, EUCO 1/16, *op. cit.*, p. 15.

lift the cap on bankers' bonuses.[74] (This deal may have been implied in Principle 4 above.) If that was indeed the case, the British government actually obtained substantial concessions from the other EU nations through the renegotiation.

The UK's Future Relationship with the EU

Economic governance of the EU played only a minor part in the referendum campaign. Given the fact that the financial sector was unpopular among the British public, it was not surprising that the British government did not publicize its negotiating success while defending the interests of the City of London. In any case, Cameron resigned as Prime Minister immediately after the result of the referendum was announced. In March 2017, his successor, Theresa May, officially conveyed to the EU the intention to leave the organization in accordance with Art. 50 of the Treaty of the European Union (TEU).

It is natural to criticize Cameron for taking a huge political gamble by calling the in/out referendum. By doing so, he not only ended his political career but also left the City of London in an insecure position. If the UK leaves not only the EU but also its single market, financial institutions in the City will lose the euro-clearing business and the so-called passport that guarantees their access to the European financial market.

Another position, however, is that the priority of the UK should be to ensure that the City of London is not subject to burdensome EU regulations. To many it seems acceptable to lose access to the European market if that is the only way the UK's financial sector can escape from the restrictive shackles of EU laws.[75]

Building on how the financial sector was managed during negotiations regarding the future relationship between the UK and the EU (Table 1), the latter seems to be the position adopted by the British government. Of note, and contrary to the trade of goods where frictionless trade would

---

[74] "There is little to stop the City maintaining its status as Europe's capital market hub", *The Times*, 27.8.2016 (25.8.2019).

[75] For example, Nigel Lawson, who served Prime Minister Margaret Thatcher as the chancellor of the exchequer, supported Brexit on the ground that withdrawing from the EU would save the City of London from Brussels' regulations, including the FTT. See "Ex-chancellor Lord Lawson calls for UK to exit EU", *BBC*, 7.5.2013 (25.8.2019). Lawson became the chairman of the Vote Leave board in February 2016.

Table 1ª

	British demands for the financial sector
May's Lancaster House Speech (Jan 2017)	UK will leave the single market, but should still be able to enjoy maximum access.
Chequer's agreement (July 2018)	Accepts limited access to the single market in exchange for regulatory freedom. Seeks enhanced equivalence with more protection.
Political Declaration (November 2018)	Based on equivalence decisions (Normal third country treatment).

ª This table is based on the following sources: UK Government, "The government's negotiating objectives for exiting the EU: PM speech", London, 17.1.2017 (16.8.2019); HM Government, "The Future Relationship between the United Kingdom and the European Union", London, 12.7.2018 (16.8.2019); European Commission, Political declaration setting out the framework for the future relationship between the European Union and the United Kingdom, CO EUR-PREP 54, Brussels, 22.11.2018 (16.8.2019).

be maintained between the two sides, service trade would be based on equivalence decisions, the same treatment received as any normal third country, such as the United States and Japan. If the EU judges that the UK's regulation is equivalent to that of the EU, the UK will enjoy limited access to the European market.

This outcome resulted from the EU's stance that the UK should not be able to "cherry-pick" only the policies and regulations it prefers from the single market.[76] It also reflects the British government's desire to avoid EU regulations over the City of London at almost any cost. It is highly likely that the British government will try to compensate the loss of access to the European financial market by lowering regulatory demands on its own financial sector.

Conclusion

What does this analysis tell us about the potential impact of Brexit? Judging from the result of the referendum, the majority of the British public was somehow persuaded that the EU, and particularly immigrants from Eastern Europe, were to blame for whatever problems they face. It is important to note that economic globalization is a multifaceted

[76] Shoji, K., *The Brexit Paradox*, Tokyo, Iwanami Shoten, 2019 (in Japanese).

phenomenon. Brexit (and the election of Donald Trump as US president) leaves us preoccupied with issues of immigration and tariffs on international trade. By contrast, we now pay less attention to issues such as reforms of the global financial system and the unequal distribution of income than we did ten years ago. For example, who still remembers the Occupy Wall Street movement? As we have seen, Brexit would most likely allow the City of London to escape from EU financial regulations and taxes. This is an ironical situation given that the current dissatisfaction with globalization throughout the developed world was fuelled by the economic downturn resulting from the global financial crisis for which immigrants played absolutely no part. Although we might only witness chaos in the ongoing Brexit saga and the drama surrounding President Trump, these phenomena succinctly redefined the terms of our discourse on globalization.

The Undemocratic Effects of a Referendum: One of the Many Paradoxes of Brexit. A legal Perspective

Frédérique Berrod

In the referendum campaign in spring 2016, Brexit has been advocated as a means to recover British sovereignty. The option of the Leave has been presented as a necessary step for the UK "to be great again", out of the ambit of European Union (EU) treaties, regulations and directives and out of the jurisdiction and influence of the European Union Court of Justice (ECJ).[1]

The choice of a referendum in a country which has been governed for centuries by the principle of the Parliamentary sovereignty is surprising. It was a promise of the Prime Minister Cameron to give a voice to the People on the UK's membership of the EU, which has been politically contentious ever since the very entry of the UK in the European Community in 1973. From a legal point of view, the referendum is purely consultative and is not subject to any requirement of specific majority. The strategy of Prime Minister Cameron's Cabinet was to use the referendum to reunify the Conservative Party on the question of the place of the UK within the EU. It is worth recalling that the UK has always given a priority to an exclusive economic dimension of the Union and obtained special status not to be constrained by three main achievements of a more political Union: the Charter of Fundamental Rights, the Monetary Union and the Area of Freedom, Security and Justice (encompassing the Schengen Area).

---

[1] Faulconbridge, G., MacLellan, K., " 'I'll make Britain great again', PM Johnson says, echoing Trump", *Reuters*, 25.7.2019 (7.9.2019).

On the 23rd of June 2016, the result of the referendum quite unexpectedly turned out to give a 51.9 % majority for the Leave. Following the provisions of article 50 of the Treaty of the EU (TEU) (the withdrawal procedure laid down by the Treaty), the UK notified its intention to withdraw on the 29th of March 2017, which opened a two-year period to negotiate a deal organizing the withdrawal. A first deal was signed by the EU and Theresa May, Prime Minister at that time, in December 2018. No majority in favour of this deal was possible at the British Parliament before the end of the two-year period. Following the refusal acted by the parliament regarding Prime Minister May's agreement, a first and second delay were asked by the UK and granted by the EU in order to secure a deal before the end of October 2019. Theresa May had to resign from her office after three refusals of Parliament. Boris Johnson has been designated by the Conservative Party to replace her in July 2019.[2]

A new deal has been obtained in September 2019 between Boris Johnson and the EU. The House of Commons showed again its incapacity of finding a majority for anything but a "No deal solution". The Members of Parliament did not manage to find any legal solution to shape the Brexit according to British political priorities. Having obtained three-month delay until the end of January 2020, the UK government promised to stop the exam of the deal. It was considered as a major concession by the Labour Party which accepted the principle of new elections for the 12th of December 2019.

This rough summary of the Brexit saga clearly showed the ambiguous effects of the referendum, which ultimately led to a parliamentary crisis in the UK. The British Supreme Court clearly stated in September 2019 that the oldest democracy in the world was put in danger by Johnson's strategy of "Do or Die Brexit".[3]

The EU has benefited from the Brexit negotiations to build a surprising political block between the 27 Member States. The EU is nevertheless impacted by the blockage imposed by the UK to ratify

---

[2] Berrod, F., "Royaume-Uni, cap sur le Brexit dur!", *The Conversation*, 23.7.2019 (7.9.2019).

[3] Matthews, O., "Now it is really 'Do or Die' for Boris Johnson", *Foreign Policy*, 24.9.2019 (15.10.2019).

the two deals that it has accepted on its part.[4] The EU's democratic legitimacy is contradicted by the British incapacity to decide for any legal organization of Brexit. This is also the result of the wording of article 50 TEU which mixes unilateral decision to withdraw and multilateral negotiations to determine a deal of withdrawal. It seems that the treaty refuses to choose between a sovereign national decision to withdraw and a multilateral protection of the integrity of EU integration process within a withdrawal deal. Last but not least, as soon as Brexit will become a legal reality, the UK will cease to be a Member State to become what the EU calls a 'third country'. A Bilateral agreement can be negotiated to organize the relationships between the UK and the EU. The interaction between national political priorities and EU general interest is therefore too complex to be fully controlled.

This complex procedure was laid down with the idea that a withdrawal was in practice impossible.[5] Brexit shows once again that that all provisions of the EU treaties serve a purpose and can as such be triggered at some point (EU lawyers call it the principle of *effet utile*). This leads to a fundamental question: how far can a sovereign national decision legally impact interconnected States within the EU?

The question will be analysed from the point of view of the EU to assess the "external" impact of the British referendum on the question of "Leave or Remain". The question of the democratic nature of this referendum will be asked in the light of the landmark *Wightman* ruling of the Full Court of European Court of Justice[6]. The undemocratic "internal" effects of the referendum will then be analysed in the framework of the UK parliamentary political regime. The position of the UK Supreme Court will be scrutinized to understand the very specific role played by British Parliament in the Brexit process.

---

[4] The second deal has been signed by the European Council. The European Parliament will ratify after a solution is founded in the British parliament.
[5] Eeckhout, P., Frantziou, E., "Brexit and Article 50 TEU: A Constitutionalist Reading", London, UCL European Institute, 2016.
[6] EU, European Court of Justice (ECJ), Full Court, Andy Wightman and Other vs Secretary of State for Exiting the European Union, (C-621/18), ECLI:EU:C:2018:999, 10.12.2018.

External Effects of the (Un)Democratic Referendum for Brexit

The Question of the Democratic Nature of the 2016 Referendum

The difficulties of the UK since the notification of its intention to withdraw in March 2017 are mainly linked with the question asked for the referendum in 2016. As the referendum is not traditionally used in the UK and knowing the difficulty of asking very technical questions in such a process, the British authorities gave priority to a very simple question: "Should the United Kingdom remain a member of the European Union or leave the European Union?".[7] The objective was to give a voice to the voters and not to the traditional political parties, largely divided on the question of the British membership to the EU.

A bunch of documents was provided for the voters on the British government website on the EU referendum concerning 7 topics (they are entitled: The best of both worlds: the UK's special status in a reformed European Union; Alternatives to membership: possible models for the UK outside the EU; Rights and obligations of EU membership; The UK's cooperation with the EU on justice and home affairs and on foreign policy and security issues; HM Treasury analysis: long-term economic impact of EU membership and the alternatives; HM Treasury analysis: the immediate economic impact of leaving the EU). But the referendum campaign focused on the priority of leaving the EU to recover British sovereignty and be able to decide "alone" on migration policies and the national health system. The questions of leaving the EU and the future relationship between both parties were not debated during the referendum campaign. The campaign for Brexit was mainly focused on the idea that the UK would take back control of its money, laws and borders and Nigel Farage and Boris Johnson even used lies to convince people, as Nigel Farage publicly recognized it on TV the day after the referendum, speaking of its main slogan as errors of the campaign.[8]

---

[7] See the report of the Electoral Commission, "The 2016 EU referendum: Report on the 23 June 2016 referendum on the UK's membership of the European Union", 2016. The report contains important recommendations for improving referendum process.

[8] His declaration is available on https://www.youtube.com/watch?v=cA3XTYfzd1I.

The result of the referendum meant "there was a small but clear majority for the whole of the UK to leave the EU, at some point, by some means, with the country also leaving the single market, the customs union or Euratom, and with some kind of relationship with the EU to follow, or not".[9] All the difficulties of the Brexit 2019 in a nutshell… With this comment, it is easy to understand that the implementation of article 50 TEU just after the vote was a political decision, more precisely the decision of the UK government under the authority of the new Prime Minister Theresa May.

The results of the referendum clearly showed a will of the people to leave the Union; that is why the government decided to make Brexit happen. Even if doubts can be raised on the outcome given the numerous manipulations of the public opinion by Brexiters, let us assume that it was a democratic decision. As it was democratic it must be acknowledged that the decision was representative of a state of the opinion which can, by nature, evolve.[10] A new vote may have changed the majority in favour of a Remain or a different Brexit. The second legal point which is of importance is that the referendum has been used by the executive to prepare a quick withdrawal following the conditions laid down in article 50 TEU, the only provision of the Treaty devoted to a withdrawal. No place was given in the beginning of the process for a second vote on the Brexit after the negotiations with the EU on its content and modalities.

The Effects of the Referendum on the British Decision to Withdraw

The political leadership has been taken by Theresa May, who was designed as Prime Minister after Cameron had resigned the day after the referendum. The result was unexpected by the British authorities as much as by the EU institutions. Nobody contested that a majority of votes was in favour of Brexit. That is why Theresa May advocated for a clear shift

---

[9] Green, A. D., "The tale of the Brexit referendum question", *Financial Times*, 3.8.2017.

[10] It is worth remembering that the results of a second referendum might be different because the composition of the voters has changed in three years, see Kellner, P., "In January 2019 Britain will officially switch from a pro-Brexit to an anti-Brexit country, and this is how we know", *The Independent*, 17.9.2018.

to Global Britain in her *Lancaster Speech*.[11] The doctrine she chose to develop was to regain sovereignty and to look, as she stated "beyond our continent and to the opportunities in the wider world". As a conclusion, she said that "the referendum result was clear. It was legitimate. It was the biggest vote for change this country has ever known. Brexit means Brexit – and we're going to make a success of it".

By this sentence Theresa May transformed the referendum into a mandate for her government to use article 50 TEU and to notify its intention to withdraw from the EU. She considered at that time that article 50 TEU could not be triggered after an agreement given by the Parliament. She even considered in a violent comment that the Members of Parliament "are not standing up for democracy, they're trying to subvert it". This *Lancaster doctrine* was later however contradicted by the UK Supreme Court.[12] It nevertheless clearly showed that Brexit has been decided and managed by the British executive without any consultation of the Parliament. May's priority was also to negotiate the Brexit and the future relationship at the same moment. The EU 27[13] did not accept this methodology and disconnected the two phases of negotiations. Article 50 TEU was interpreted as meaning that the divorce had to be negotiated first. When Brexit will be accepted by the EU and the UK, a second phase would begin, entirely dedicated to the agreement on the future relationship.

To understand what the legal meaning of Brexit is, the EU and the UK determined three preliminary questions: the financial arrangement of divorce, the rights of EU citizens residing or working in the UK and the protection of the Irish border to allow for a collective guarantee of the preservation of the Good Friday Agreement. The deal allowing for Brexit also encompassed provisions for the application of EU law to avoid any legal vacuum. It comprised the negotiation of a period of transition of a

---

[11] The Lancaster House is the seat of the Ministry of Foreign Affairs and of the Commonwealth. A symbolic House for a Speech on Brexit… May, T., "The government's negotiating objectives for exiting the EU: PM speech", London, 17.1.2017.

[12] See details below.

[13] The European Council has been reduced to the 27 remaining Member States to establish and follow the mandate given to Michel Barnier to negotiate first the Brexit (which means the divorce) and second the future relationship. See https://www.consilium.europa.eu/media/24173/15-euco-statement.pdf and https://www.consilium.europa.eu/en/press/press-releases/2017/03/31/tusk-remarks-meeting-muscat-malta/.

maximum of two years after the Brexit during which EU law would still be applicable. A smooth Brexit was organized by the first deal signed in December 2018.

This deal has been refused three times by the House of Commons. This raises an interesting question of democracy concerning the legitimate power to shape the deal for Brexit. Is it only for the Executive power to negotiate with the EU. Even if she has been obliged to accept ratification by the two chambers of Parliament of the decision to notify the intention to withdraw and the deal for the withdrawal as such, Theresa May never took the views of the legislative power in-between. It is logical that the Executive power organises the every-day negotiations during the two-year delay opened by the notification of the intention to withdraw.

There is also a role for the EU. The European Commission has to negotiate an international agreement between the UK and the EU. The Treaty determines that it is the Commission that is responsible for these kinds of international negotiations. President Juncker had chosen a special commissioner entirely devoted to the negotiation – Michel Barnier.[14] The European Parliament has a final say on the outcome of such negotiations, but cannot be implicated throughout the whole process. Hence comes the question: is this procedure sufficiently democratic?

The EU faces the same question concerning the role of European and national parliaments in the signature and the ratification of free-trade agreements with third countries. The regional Parliament of Wallonia has for example threatened not to sign the Comprehensive and Economic Trade Agreement (CETA) between the EU and Canada, considering among other arguments that the CETA had been negotiated for so long that the parliament did not have other choice but to sign the agreement.[15] Not signing would indeed mean undermining the legitimacy of negotiations by the European Commission under the direction of the EU Council. The *Namur Declaration* was issued to tackle the democratic deficit of such a process, advocating for more space and more implication of the European and national (or regional) parliaments in the course of the negotiations and not only at the very end of the process.[16] President Juncker did not totally follow this approach but

---

[14] Berrod, F., Ullestad, A., "Michel Barnier négociateur du Brexit: la Juncker touch", *The Conversation*, 26.8.2016.
[15] See De la Baume, M., "Walloon Parliament rejects CETA deal", *Politico*, 10.10.2016.
[16] Declaration available on the website http://declarationdenamur.eu/.

conceded more transparency of the negotiation process towards the European Parliament.[17] Theresa May did not even apply such a logic and decided to force the UK chambers to ratify the deal after almost two years of negotiations. As a former judge of the German Constitutional Court explained, when a large range of domestic legislation is concerned by an international agreement, such as it is the case with Brexit, it is "unsustainable, from a democratic perspective, to leave those negotiations exclusively in executive hands".[18]

Theresa May had to face a strong opposition in the House of Commons, expressed in three consecutive votes against the deal she had negotiated in Brussels. The opposition was concentrated on one specific mechanism of the deal which was called the *backstop*. The idea behind this modality was to find a mechanism to guarantee that no physical border would be rebuilt on the territory of the island of Ireland. Different solutions were proposed by the European Commission. Northern Ireland could stay aligned with some rules of the EU single market, if another solution wasn't found by the end of the transition period programmed to end in December 2020. That meant that goods coming into Northern Ireland would not need to be checked at the Irish Border because they would meet EU security standards. But controls would not be organised between the UK and the island of Ireland to avoid any fraud into the internal market. The UK refused this solution which would have created a maritime border between the two islands and would have isolated Northern Ireland from the rest of the Kingdom. Theresa May gave priority to another form of backstop. She accepted a temporary single custom territory with the EU, effectively keeping the whole of the UK in the EU customs union – unless – and until – both the EU and the UK agreed that it was no longer necessary in the future Treaty organising their relationship. Maintaining the UK into the EU customs union in case no agreement could be found on the future relationship was considered as a means to safeguard the Irish peace process settled by the Good Friday Agreement.[19] This direct protection of Ireland and Northern Ireland has been considered as too stringent for the British

---

[17] Juncker, J.-C, "State of the Union", European Commission, Brussels, 13.9.2017.
[18] Luebbe Wolff, G., "Democracy, Separation of Powers and International Treaty-Making", Current Legal Problems, *Oxford Journals*, vol. 69/1, 2016, pp. 175–198.
[19] See https://www.consilium.europa.eu/media/32236/15-euco-art50-guidelines-en.pdf.

sovereignty by the Members of Parliament. It must be recalled that the membership of the UK to the EU customs union implies that it is only for the EU to determine commercial external policy, which was obviously an obstacle for getting back British sovereignty.

The impossibility to define any majority on any points at the House of Commons: a deal, no deal, a Brexit, no Brexit… led to refill the debate on the necessity of a second referendum. Scotland pushed for such an option as it has voted for the Remain in June 2016 and did not want to leave the EU as a mechanical consequence of a Brexit. Since 2018, the idea has also been discussed in the House of Lords.[20] Some British politicians defended the option of a second referendum, hoping to obtain a majority for remaining in the EU and avoiding at the same time Scottish independence and ever more political distance between Westminster and Northern Ireland, which might lead to Irish reunification.[21] The legal question was to assess if a second referendum could supersede the results of the first, which was fairly democratic in the sense that the majority of voters had chosen Brexit.[22] Yet, before taking such a decision the legal possibility to revoke a notification of a national intent of withdrawal had to be addressed by the judges.

The EU Legal Framework of a Revocation of the Withdrawal

The European Court of Justice (ECJ) answered in its landmark *Wightmann* judgement to a question for preliminary ruling on the interpretation of article 50 TEU, which was addressed by the Court of Session of Scotland. The case was brought before the Scottish Court by seven members of the Scottish, British and European Parliaments who wished to know if and how a unilateral revocation of the withdrawal decision could be done. The ECJ accepted to answer the question, considering that it was not just a theoretical one but could lead to a possible alternative to "no deal" or "Brexit with a deal", which ought to be known by Members of the British Parliament to determine their votes at the end of the two-year negotiation period.

---

[20] See Coleman, C., "Case for a Referendum on the Outcome of EU Withdrawal Negotiations: Debate on 25 October 2018", House of Lords, London, 19.10.2018.

[21] See 2.3 below.

[22] See Allen Green, D., *op. cit.*

The ECJ chose an answer based on the "constitution" of the EU. The Commission and the Council defended a more institutional approach, considering that any decision to revoke the withdrawal should be confirmed by a mandatory consent of the European Council.[23] The Court said that the decision to withdraw from the constitutional charter of the EU (and all the law derived from it) was a sovereign[24] right of the Member State.[25] This right must be interpreted in a specific context of interconnected Member States within the Union and with the Union. The interpretation is to be understood according to two objectives of article 50 TEU, *i.e.* the right to withdraw and the respect of a procedure designed to allow for a withdrawal in an orderly fashion. The right to revoke must be understood as a parallel of the intention to withdraw, which means that it is a unilateral decision and should be opened as long as the two-year period opened by article 50 TEU was not finished or a deal concluded.[26] To understand this position, the Court indicated the use of a theological interpretation of article 50 TEU according to the very foundation of the EU embodied in the values of democracy and liberty.[27] The consequences of withdrawal on the fundamental status of the European citizens imply that the withdrawal decision is taken on a democratic basis. The referendum is an adequate means as a decision of the national Parliament could also be. The Court also answered on the ground of a decision of withdrawal: all "Member States have freely and voluntary committed themselves to the respect of EU values based on the fundamental premises that each member states shares with all the others" (point 63). As Advocate General Campos Sanchez-Bordona concluded:

> Article 50(1) TEU is, in fact, an important sign of respect for the national identities of the Member States, acknowledging their right to withdraw from the European Union in accordance with their own constitutional requirements. In the same way that a Member State may, at a particular time, consider that its national identity is incompatible with membership of the European Union, there is no reason that that identity (which should not

---

[23] See Benlolo-Carabo, M., "L'arrêt Wightman de la Cour de justice de l'UE. Au nom de 'l'union sans cesse plus étroite'", *Jus Politicum*, 31.1.2019 (7.9.2019).

[24] This word is new in the vocabulary of the ECJ and has been used many times in the judgement.

[25] Point 50.

[26] Point 56.

[27] Point 62.

be understood as an unchanging, fossilised concept) may not become linked to its integration into the European Union.[28]

A decision of withdrawal is triggered when a Member State does not share one or more EU values due to its national evolutions. This was the case for the UK, clearly opposed to an "ever closer Union". As Piet Eeckhout and Eleni Frantziou concluded long before this judgment:

> Provided that there is a new decision not to withdraw that is taken in good faith, the Article 50 clock can be stopped. After all, the goal of the Union is integration, not disintegration.[29]

The *Wightman* decision gave the UK the legal possibility to revoke on its own motion its decision of withdrawal. A second referendum or new elections could then legally determine an alternative to Brexit from the point of view of the ECJ. The Court helped to understand a part of the question asked in the introduction of this paper. A national decision of withdrawal or of revocation of the aforementioned decision can bind the EU institutions as soon as it has been taken on a democratic basis. The 2016 referendum was a democratic decision on the Leave but a second referendum could be organized either on the legal modalities of Brexit negotiated in a deal, or on the possibility to have a no deal for Brexit, or even on the possibility to remain within the Union. The respect of democratic principle was at the heart of the *Wightman* Judgement. It was at the same time at the heart of the political crisis brought up by Brexit in the United Kingdom.

One of the paradoxes of the British referendum was that the democratic decision of the UK had mandatory consequences for 27 Member States which had no say whatsoever of the decision to leave the EU. From a democratic perspective, the British decision took the other EU citizens and Member States by surprise.[30] Such an interpretation can be followed for other referendum: they may result in the disintegration of the EU if they are used to withdraw or to block a European decision (such as the one organised by Victor Orban in

---

[28] Opinion delivered on 4.12.2018, point 131.
[29] Quoted above, p. 41.
[30] Auer, A., "The People have spoken abide? A critical view of EU's dramatic referendum (in)experience", *European Constitutional Law Review*, vol. 12, 2016, pp. 397–408.

Hungary to legitimize its opposition to the EU decision to relocate migrants).[31] This was the sense of the arguments developed by the institutions and Member States before the ECJ. To respect the interests of the 27 Member States and of the EU's political structure, a decision to revoke the intention to withdraw must be taken according to the national constitutional rules and after the approval of the European Council. The ECJ took a different option, probably to give the UK all the legal means to avoid Brexit.

Internal Undemocratic Effects of Brexit

The EU Conditions for a Democratic Withdrawal and the Parliamentary Crisis in the UK

One of the legal questions brought by the MPs at the very beginning of the withdrawal process was the respective role of the UK government and Parliament for the notification of the intention to withdraw. Given the "foreign affairs" dimension of the notification to the European Council provided for by article 50 TEU, the May government considered that it was only for the government to act. The British MPs considered that it was against the sovereignty of Parliament, a key point of the UK constitutional identity. Once again, the conflict on the consequences of Brexit has been decided upon by judges, *i.e.* the UK High Court[32] and the UK Supreme Court[33] in the *Miller* cases. The judges have considered that the Parliament must be given a right of consent to the notification of withdrawal: "as an aspect of the sovereignty of Parliament, it has been established for hundreds of years that the Crown, *i.e.*, the government of the day, cannot by exercise of prerogative powers override legislation enacted by Parliament". The membership of the UK has been introduced in UK law by the 1972 Act of Parliament for EU law to become part of British domestic law. It was therefore for the Parliament to repeal that

---

[31] See an analysis from an Eastern point of view, Krastev, I., *After Europe*, Pennsylvania, Penn Press, 2017.
[32] Miller and Santos v. Secretary of State [2016] EWHC 2768 (Admin).
[33] See the judgment, R (on the application of Miller and another) (Respondents) v Secretary of State for Exiting the European Union (Appellant) [2017] UKSC 5; and Craig, R., "Miller Supreme Court Case Summary", U.K. Const. L. Blog, 26.1.2016.

act and to enact a Withdrawal Act before the government can notify the British intention to withdraw from the EU.

The UK Supreme Court confirmed that judgement and added that the devolved institutions (Scottish Parliament, Northern Irish Parliament and National Assembly for Wales and their executive branches) did not have a veto power or even a say on Brexit as "relations with the EU and foreign affairs matters are reserved to UK Government and parliament, not to devolved institutions". We will see that this position might have serious consequences of the unity of the UK (see below). The democratic dimension of the withdrawal decision of the State was reinforced by this statement. What is striking in the judgement of the Supreme Court is the reference to the very specific context of the Brexit. The majority of the judges considered that:

> Withdrawal makes a fundamental change to the UK's constitutional arrangements, by cutting off the source of EU law. [...] Such a fundamental change [including the removal of existing domestic rights] will be the inevitable effect of the Notice being served. [...] The UK constitution requires such changes to be effected by Parliamentary legislation.

The role of the Parliament was emphasized to guarantee the proper functioning of the British constitution and the rights of British citizens under EU law. The very substance of the autonomy of the EU legal order was the basis for the legal interpretation of the first unilateral phase of the withdrawal procedure laid down in article 50 TEU. The Parliament has jurisdiction to authorise the notification of the intention to withdraw. It is interesting to recall the statement of the *Wightman* case in this respect. In a very short sentence, the ECJ summarized the formal conditions for a democratic withdrawal:

> The revocation of the notification of the intention to withdraw must, first, be submitted to the European Council and, secondly, be unequivocal and unconditional, that is to say that the purpose of that revocation is to confirm the EU membership of the Member State concerned under terms that are unchanged as regard the status as a Member State, and that revocation brings the withdrawal procedure to an end.[34]

---

[34] Point 74 of the ruling.

The Clash between Two Types of Sovereignty

Article 50 TEU distinguishes the first unilateral phase of the withdrawal, sending back to each national constitution for the determination of the responsible authority that is to give the intention to withdraw. That is why the British Parliament has such a prominent role. The ECJ added two other conditions for the beginning or the ending of the second multilateral process of negotiation of the withdrawal article. The notification or its revocation should be unequivocal and unconditional.

According to the *Miller* judgements, the UK government must be authorised by the Parliament to send an intention of withdrawal to the European Council. This implies a majority of the Parliament to support the action of the government concerning the principle of withdrawal. The Withdrawal Act adopted by the UK Parliament added conditions to ratify any Withdrawal Agreement in a democratic manner. The documents and an associated statement have to be published. The UK government became the first in history to be found in contempt of Parliament because of its failure to publish Attorney General Geoffrey Cox's full legal advice to cabinet on the deal negotiated by Theresa May (3rd of December 2018)[35]. The negotiated withdrawal agreement and the framework for the future relationship had to be approved by a resolution of the House of Commons. This explains why Theresa May had to come back before the House of Commons to present and defend her deal in January 2019. She never obtained any majority for the deal and had therefore to resign after having negotiated two delays for Brexit with the 27 EU Member States.

If we remember Theresa May's declaration during her *Lancaster Speech* and Boris Johnson's strategy against the influence of the democratic debate before the Members of Parliament, it is obvious that democracy is a fragile process even in the country in which it has such a long tradition. This shows that there are two contradictory and coexisting conceptions of British sovereignty. The first, that of the legitimacy of the executive power, is dominant in international affairs and the second, that of the legislative power, is necessary when the domestic legal order is impacted by an international agreement. The only way to reconcile these two expressions

---

[35] See Kirkland, C., "Ministers found in contempt of parliament over legal advice – why it matters for Brexit", *The Conversation*, 4.12.2018.

of political legitimacy is to guarantee a constant effort of concentration between both powers. Coordination has never been developed since the notification of the intention to withdraw.

Brexit was in fact an occasion to show the divisions of the British society, put on the public stage within the traditional scene of the Westminster Chamber. The Prime Ministers preferred confrontation to any sort of coordination, dramatizing the need of a deal with the EU and hoping that it would be enough to make a majority of MPs ratify the "organized Brexit" determined between the British government and the European Commission. This seems to have had a totally opposite effect, reinforcing the clash between legitimacy of the government and sovereignty of the Parliament. The option defended by Boris Johnson was clearly to confront without any ambiguity with the House of Commons in September 2019.

He hence decided to extend the traditional suspension of the Chamber in September to five weeks to prevent any parliamentary attempts to influence the deal or even the idea of Brexit. Once again it was for the UK Supreme Court to judge if this decision was against the principle of democracy embedded in the British constitution.[36] The Supreme Court struck down the suspension by a unanimous decision announced by her President. It was a surprising decision putting the judiciary into the turmoil of political passion. Some commentators underlined it was a turning point for the British judges.[37]

The legal reasoning was mainly that extended suspension obstructed Parliament's ability to "carry out its constitutional functions as a legislature and as the body responsible for the supervision of the executive". It was not possible to eliminate the Parliament of the Brexit political game. Lady Hale, President of the Supreme Court declared: "the conduct of government by a Prime Minister and cabinet, collectively responsible and accountable to Parliament, lies at the heart of democracy". Once again the very essence of democracy has been endangered by the strategy of the executive to give legal reality to the 2016 referendum.

---

[36] See Davis, F., "Decision of the Supreme Court on the Prorogation of Parliament", House of Commons Library, 24.9.2019 (10.10.2019); and Clapham, N., "UK Supreme Court: ten years of treading the knife edge between politics and law", *The Conversation*, 30.9.2019.

[37] Landler, M., Mueller, B., "How the UK Supreme Court's Rebuke to Boris Johnson remakes British Law", *New York Times*, 24.9.2019.

The UK supreme judges have strongly contributed to reinforce the democratic legitimacy of the House of Commons, elected by voters. So doing, it was the figure of the representative democracy which has been privileged by the judiciary. The decision taken by the executive and the legislative power to give reality to the results of the 2016 referendum has resulted in a profound crisis in the UK: the House of Commons was not capable of finding even a slight majority in favour of any solution and it was easy to proclaim, as Boris Johnson did, that this chamber was against the People, giving him the opportunity to dissolve the House of Commons by calling for new elections. Due to a reform in 2011, such a decision had to be enacted by a majority of two-third at the House of Commons.[38] After having obtained the guarantee that no "no-deal Brexit" would be decided by the executive, the Labour Party accepted to vote with the Conservatives and Liberal-Democrats and a strong majority voted for the unequivocal decision to convoke general elections on the 12th of December 2019.[39]

Is this profound political crisis due to Brexit or is it just a symptom of profound divisions of British society? Jonathan Coe, the famous British author, gave some keys to understand this question in his novel on Brexit.[40] In the book, during a therapy to save a couple of the crisis deriving from their two opposite votes to the 2016 referendum, the therapist's verdict was: "What's interesting about both of these answers is that neither of you mentioned politics. As if the referendum wasn't about Europe at all. Maybe something much more fundamental and personal was going on. Which is why this might be a difficult problem to resolve". The UK government had decided to give legal effects to a consultative referendum and chose opposing the will of the People to the will of the Members of Parliament as a political strategy. The Parliament felt obliged first to follow the "decision" of Brexit in 2017 and used its power to block any "no deal Brexit", and to refuse to vote for the first negotiated deal. The Members of Parliament have accepted in October 2019 to examine the implementation Act of the second deal negotiated by Johnson in September 2019. No clear majority in favour of the text was foreseen. The examination of the implementation Act may give rise to many

---

[38] See http://www.legislation.gov.uk/ukpga/2011/14/section/2.
[39] See "General Election 2019 timetable", https://www.parliament.uk/about/how/elections-and-voting/general/general-election-2019-timetable/. (2.2.2020).
[40] Coe, J., *Middle England*, London, Penguin Books, 2018.

amendments during the debates at the House of Commons. One of them might even be the organization of a second referendum to "confirm" the content of the deal, *i.e.* the material content of Brexit. Referendum would then be used to "comfort" the choice of the Parliament; a tricky solution regarding the respect of the "sacred" principle of Parliamentary sovereignty promoted by the UK Supreme Court.

The Effects of Brexit on the Unity of the Kingdom

Boris Johnson decided to be the promoter of Brexit "Do or Die" by the end of November 2019. After having ignored European institutions, he managed to negotiate a second deal in September 2019. He got rid of the so-called *Backstop* and took the decision to put the entire UK out of the EU customs union. To avoid reinforcing violent tensions in Northern Ireland, he promised not to impose any control on the Irish border. The EU 27 protected the integrity of the internal market by imposing an EU normative space between Ireland and Northern Ireland. Controls must be organized in the British harbours. The problem arising from this second deal was that, nor Scotland nor the unionists of Northern Ireland[41] were satisfied and feel betrayed by London. For, the 2016 Referendum has been organized for the United Kingdom as a whole. As Allen Green wrote:

> The question mentions the UK – not the constituent home nations, or even Gibraltar. This means there can be no explicit mandate from the terms of the question for, say, Scotland or Northern Ireland to remain. There is no explicit mandate either for Gibraltar to leave, though this would be implicit in the UK leaving. Whatever happens as a result of the question and the referendum result, it would be for the whole of the UK.[42]

This position of the referendum happened to reopen the question of the unity of the UK.

The Supreme Court judges in the *Miller* cases have clearly stated that Brexit was concerning the UK and not the devolved institution. From the very beginning, this was problematic for Scotland and Northern Ireland

---

[41] Especially by the DUP party, the political allies of Theresa May. The DUP does not accept the idea of a maritime border between Northern Ireland and the rest of the UK in the Irish Sea. That is why Theresa May had to negotiate the famous backstop which has been refused by the UK Parliament.

[42] See Allen Green, D., *op. cit.*

because, in these two nations of the Kingdom, the Remainers were a large majority of the voters.[43] Respecting the results of the vote for the whole UK has been a decision which has reinforced the division between some of its constituent nations.

Scottish First Minister Nicola Sturgeon has always defended the political line to stay within the EU, following therefore the very clear results of the referendum in Scotland. This autonomy of devolved institutions has been used to weigh the UK policy decided by the Prime Minister Theresa May. Unless the specific interest of Scotland to remain within the EU was to be satisfied, a referendum of independence from the UK would be organized. The price of Brexit is the division of the Kingdom and the possible secession of Scotland. Nicola Sturgeon never changed her strategy, putting pressure on the government to obtain either a special status for Scotland or a deal which organised the right of remaining within the internal market. The Scottish Members of the Westminster Parliament have used the threat of Scottish independence to push for a second referendum on the possibility for the UK to remain within the EU. Such a situation was not unforeseen; Scotland already voted in a referendum on its independence in 2014 and decided to stay within the UK, for the very reason that it was a Member State of the Union, with 55.3 % of the votes. The 2016 Referendum could therefore be interpreted as an indirect referendum on Scottish independence. Scotland felt betrayed by the second deal as Boris Johnson preferred getting the UK – and therefore Scotland – out the EU customs union. Nicola Sturgeon has explicitly called for independence to prevent Scotland being "ripped from her European family" against its will on the 2nd of November 2019.[44] Brexit has a direct effect on the acceleration of the Scottish independence will.

The situation in Northern Ireland was the direct result of the decision of the UK government to use article 50 TEU just after the 2016 vote in favour of the Leave. The relationships between Northern Ireland, the rest of the UK and the Republic of Ireland have been pacified by the Good

---

[43] In Scotland 62 % of the votes have been in favour of the Remain and 55.8 % in Northern Ireland, see https://www.electoralcommission.org.uk/who-we-are-and-what-we-do/elections-and-referendums/past-elections-and-referendums/eu-referendum/results-and-turnout-eu-referendum.

[44] "Scotland will be 'ripped from Europe' without independence, says Nicola Sturgeon", *Euronews*, 3.11.2019.

Friday Agreement, ratified in 1998 under the silent supervision of the EU which invested a lot in peaceful processes at the Irish border[45]. In case of Brexit, the Republic of Ireland will be staying in the EU and the 27 Member States decided to protect the Irish interests in the chess game of Brexit. The question of the Irish Border was therefore one of the three preliminary questions which were to be resolved before any Brexit deal. The Europeans steadily supported the necessity for the Irish border to be opened and to allow free movement of goods and workers without any controls. It is worth noticing that free movement has been considerably intensified since 1998. At the same time, the EU 27 obliged the UK to organize its own border for controls to defend the security and integrity of the EU internal market. As a third country, the UK products should be controlled at the EU external border, playing the role of a natural filter to avoid any dangerous products and to respect EU security standards.[46] The British government was not able to give any efficient answer to these requests which explains the negotiation of the backstop, finally accepted by Theresa May. If no solution was organised by the UK in the course of the negotiation of the agreement on the future relationships with the EU, the UK would still be part of the EU customs union to avoid any control at the Irish border on the island. This decision has never been democratically accepted by the UK. The blockage of the Northern Irish devolved institutions resulted in a debate on Northern Ireland centred on the will of the Democratic Unionist Party (DUP) at Westminster. The Irish border was never considered as a democratic object in the Brexit negotiation on the part of the UK. The EU acted just in the opposite way, pushing to obtain clear guarantees for Northern Ireland and Eire.

Boris Johnson decided to get rid of the backstop in September 2019 for the negotiation of the second deal of the EU. He "discovered" the political sensitivity of the Irish border in the late September 2019[47] and advocated for "no controls" at the Irish Border. As the UK is not part

---

[45] Hayward, K., Wiener, A., "The Influence of the European Union towards conflict transformation on the island of Ireland", in Diez, T., Albert, M., Steller, S. (eds.), *The EU and Border Conflicts: the Power of Integration and Association*, Cambridge, Cambridge University Press, 2008, pp. 33–63.

[46] See regulation EU n° 2019/1020 of the European Parliament and of the Council of 20.6.2019, on market surveillance and compliance of products, OJEU, 25.6.2019 L 169, p. 1.

[47] O'Carroll, L., Mason, R., Rankin, J., "Boris Johnson and Leo Varadkar say they see pathway to Brexit deal", *The Guardian*, 10.10.2019.

of the EU customs union, to recover its sovereignty according to the British government, it has been accepted by the EU and the UK that Northern Ireland would remain within the normative influence of the EU and would be integrated in a British Customs union. Controls of goods, VAT controls and control of persons would be organized in the Irish Sea or in the UK maritime harbours. This was acceptable for the Northern Irish wishing to avoid any sort of terrestrial border controls. But it was interpreted as a betrayal by the DUP because such an organization was creating a border between Northern Ireland and the UK. In this perspective, the second deal can be interpreted as a blunt concession of the Prime Minister in the direction of a political disconnection between Northern Ireland and the rest of the UK.

The question of the reunification of Ireland has been at stake since the difficult negotiation of the first deal because of the incapacity of the British government to give credible answers to the question of the securing of the Irish Border as an opened European border. The Prime Minister of the Republic of Ireland had explicitly evoked such a possibility as a possible political solution in case of serious crisis.[48] Northern Ireland is also considering this option which was politically unforeseeable before the 2016 Referendum. The reality is a regain of tensions in Northern Ireland making the return to violent riots possible.[49] If reunification is achieved on the island of Ireland, the United Kingdom will lose one of its constituent nations because of a consultative referendum interpreted by British governments as urging a definitive Brexit.

New Legislative Elections on Brexit

In a last (?) attempt to find a way out of the legislative blockage and to avoid that MPs decide to vote too many amendments to the second deal during the debates on the implementation act in October 2019, Boris Johnson proposed new general elections and the dissolution of the House of Commons. The MPs have obtained his promise not to propose the ratification of the second deal before the elections. Boris Johnson

---

[48] Humphries, C., "Irish PM says hard Brexit would raise issue of Irish unification", *Reuters*, 27.7.2019.

[49] Ourdan, R., "'L'idée d'une réunification se répand': en Irlande du Nord, les troubles du Brexit", *Le Monde*, 1.11.2019.

was also obliged to ask for a new delay to solve the Brexit.[50] The EU 27 has accepted a new (and ultimate) delay for Brexit until the end of January 2020. A strong majority of the House of Commons voted for the organization of new elections on the 12th of December 2019.

This strategy has already been used in 2017 by Theresa May. She wanted to concentrate the debates during the elections on the consequences of Brexit, to reinforce her conservative majority at the House of Commons. She lost the game. She obtained a small majority and had to form an alliance with the DUP. The elections have showed a profound division of the British society. Westminster was not able to be the heart of a peaceful democracy. Divisions might have killed any Brexit deal but even more British unity. Even if autumn 2019 was different from spring 2017 and Brexit finally did happen on 31st January 2020, it is not the end of the story of the Brexit. For the UK and the EU have to join again the table of negotiation to determine, in details, the legal conditions of their future relationships.

---

[50] Contrary to what he has promised, he has used a very uncommon (unlawful?) means. He sent a first letter asking for a delay without his signature and a second one signed by him saying that a new delay is not the best idea. See a comment and the two letters here: "Brexit: les deux lettres adressées par Boris Johnson aux Européens", *Le Monde*, 19.10.2019.

Part 2

The Social Consequences of Brexit

The Right to Family Reunification after Brexit: the Impossible Status Quo

AUDE BOUVERESSE

The impact of Brexit on fundamental rights are, like the rest, difficult to assess. It is nevertheless interesting to focus, in particular, on the right to family reunification as it is particularly representative of the concrete issues related to Brexit and the difficulties to face it, even though a consensus on the maintenance of acquired rights had emerged from the beginning of the negotiations.

The respect of the fundamental right of family reunification often comes directly in conflict with a State wishing to exercise a restrictive migratory policy. In this regard, European rights appear to be strong allies to counter it. European Union (EU) law promotes indeed family reunification, as a part of the European mobility as well as inherent in its objectives. Furthermore, it has acquired a constitutional status, since it is enshrined in the EU fundamental rights charter in Article 7.[1] Thenceforth, it is not surprising that it was also one of the main reasons put forward in support of Brexit, its supporters thinking to regain full control of their migration policy by leaving the EU.

However, the very existence of a State makes sense only if it contributes to the well-being of the society it intends to govern. The United Kingdom, although it decided to leave the EU, could not neglect the importance of safeguarding the rights of British citizens living or having lived in other Member States and citizens of the EU living or having lived in the UK and their family. On this point, at least, an agreement between the negotiators was found. The attached agreement, which was

---

[1] See Choudhry, S., "Article 7 – Right to Respect for Private and Family Life (Family Life Aspects)", in Peers, S., Hervey, T., Kenner, J., Ward, A. (eds.), *The EU Charter of Fundamental Rights: A Commentary*, Oxford, Hart Publishing, 2014, pp. 183–221.

adopted on 8 December 2017, states that "it is of paramount importance to give as much certainty as possible to UK's Citizens 'living in the EU and EU Citizen living in the UK about their future rights". The reality could be different. The draft agreement of 14 November 2018 considered that it was only "necessary" to provide for reciprocal protection. Albeit the rejection of the Withdrawal Act of 2018, the revised Withdrawal Agreement published on 17th October 2019 (thereafter the "Withdrawal Agreement") reaffirms the will to maintain a *status quo* for British and EU citizens.[2]

So far, and in view of the main texts available, a consensus emerged from negotiators (the British government and the EU) who affirmed, since the very beginning, the maintenance of existing rights, referring in particular to the freeze on rights acquired, especially fundamental rights.

However, first, it might be noted that the prevailing and persistent uncertainty already represents a violation of fundamental rights. Even more fundamentally and without raising an unsustainable suspense, the *status quo* is actually impossible to defend. Indeed, the scope of family reunification appears to be impaired, especially the legal and normative guarantees attached to the protection of the rights cannot be regarded as equivalent. They are even asymmetrical depending on whether they cover the EU nationals in the UK or the UK citizens in the EU. In addition, the guaranties of the protection cannot be seen as equivalent in the sense of a *status quo* despite what has been hammered by both sides, the EU and Great Britain, since the very beginning of the negotiations.

The purpose of this article is not to be exhaustive on the issue but to identify the main risks and challenges for family life after Brexit. In this perspective, it seems important to focus on the current interest of family reunification, as guaranteed by EU law, in order to be able to assess the modification of this right in the context of Brexit.

---

[2] The EU Withdrawal Agreement bill re-affirms in that respect "Recognising that it is necessary to provide reciprocal protection for Union citizens and for United Kingdom nationals, as well as their respective family members, where they have exercised free movement rights before a date set in this Agreement, and to ensure that their rights under this Agreement are enforceable and based on the principle of non-discrimination; recognising also that rights deriving from periods of social security insurance should be protected".

The Interest of Family Reunification as Guaranteed by European Union Law

Falling into the scope of EU law appears to be a major interest for the family member concerned in order to exercise the right to family reunification in accordance with its content, its warranty and its scope. Nevertheless, it is important to note also that, if this interest is undeniable since the citizen falls within the scope of the treaties and can rely on his European citizenship, it is more limited in the context of secondary law.

The European Court of Justice (ECJ) initially refers to family reunification as a part of the economic freedom of movement. In short, the right to family reunification was mainly a corollary of the exercise of free movement. Thus, as early as in 1986, the Court recognized the right to family reunion, not as a subjective right essential to the individual, but as an attribute necessary for the free movement of persons. Given the importance of free movement in EU law, the association of the right to family life with this fundamental economic freedom has been an opportunity to strengthen both its content and its guarantees.

The reasoning of the EU legislator[3] and the ECJ is crystal clear and pragmatic when it ruled "if Union citizens were not allowed to lead a normal family life in the host Member State, the exercise of the freedoms, guaranteed by the Treaty, would be seriously obstructed".[4] If one wants an effective and operational free movement of the salaried or independent workers, the latter must meet any obstacle. Depriving him of his family may hinder his mobility. Thus, any State regulation that would hinder family reunification has to be considered as an obstacle to the free movement of workers and shall be eliminated or justified under the control of the Court.

This idea of the effectiveness of free movement of economic agents actually made it possible to give an effective content to the reunification right. Far from being limited to a non-removal right, it implies the recognition of an arsenal of rights for the benefit of family members, regardless of their nationality, without which it would be emptied of its content. Thus, the family can claim a derived right of entry on

---

[3] See Regulation 15 [1961] *JO* of 26.8.1961.
[4] Case C-127/08 Metock [2008], para. 62; see also Case C-60/00 *Carpenter* [2002] para 38; Case C-459/99 *MRAX* [2002] para 53.

presentation of a passport and, if a visa could be required in certain circumstances for third country nationals, they can obtain it accordingly simplified administrative formalities. The family can also claim a right of residence and a right of access to a salaried activity, a right of social benefits after three months' residence, the schooling of their children, etc. It is important to note that an effective family reunification right under EU law is not limited to a right to non-removal, which is often best available to individuals on the basis of Article 8 of the European Convention of Human Rights (ECHR).

A new step has been taken with the enshrinement of European citizenship in the Maastricht Treaty in 1992. Directive 2004/38[5] of the European Parliament and of the Council on the right of citizens of the Union and their family members to move and reside freely within the territory of the Member States emphasises in recital 5: "The right of all Union citizens to move and reside freely within the territory of the Member States should, if it is to be exercised under objective conditions of freedom and dignity, be also granted to their family members, irrespective of nationality".

However, the Directive 2004/38 does not confer any autonomous right on family members of a Union citizen who are third-country nationals. Thus, any rights that may be conferred on those nationals by the directive are derived from the rights which the Union citizen concerned enjoys, as a result of having exercised his freedom of movement.

But, even outside the scope of the Directive, the Court has reproduced the argument of effectiveness and applied it to the concept of European citizenship based on article 21 of the Treaty. In this respect, the Court has developed the personal scope of application of Union law in such a manner that a EU citizen who has never moved to another Member State can claim the benefit of his rights as an EU citizen for himself, but also for its family even if the latter are third-country nationals, when it is necessary in order to ensure that the Union citizen can exercise his freedom of movement effectively. In the *Zambrano*[6] judgment, indeed,

---

[5] European Parliament and of the Council, Directive 2004/38/EC on the right of citizens of the Union and their family members to move and reside freely within the territory of the Member States (L158), 29.4.2004, *Official Journal of the European Union*, 30.4.2004, p. 77.

[6] Case C-34/09 *Ruiz Zambrano* [2011], see also: Case C-165/14, *Rendón Marín* [2016]; Case C-133/15 *Chavez-Vilchez and Others* [2017].

the ECJ ruled that Member States are precluded from refusing a third country national upon whom his minor children, who are EU citizens, are dependent, a right of residence in the Member State of residence and nationality of those children, and from refusing to grant a work permit to that third country national, in so far as such decisions deprive those children of the genuine enjoyment of the substance of the rights attached to the status of EU citizens. These rights, in the light of case law, cover both the right of residence and the right to family reunification. However, the EU citizenship status of a citizen who has never exercised his/her right of free movement did not include the protection of this right to family life under EU law since it did not involve "the denial of the genuine enjoyment of the substance of the rights conferred by virtue of his status as a citizen of the Union".[7]

Among other things, the *Zambrano* judgment marks a substantial change in the Court's reasoning taking into account the respect of family life as a part of the fundamental status of EU citizens.[8]

In that respect, the Court has acknowledged, in certain cases, that third-country nationals, family members of a Union citizen, who were not eligible, on the basis of Directive 2004/38, for a derived right of residence in the Member State of which that citizen is a national, could, nevertheless, be accorded such a right on the basis of article 21 Treaty on the Functioning of the European Union (TFEU).[9] In the *Lounes*[10] judgment, the Court ruled that the rights which nationals of Member States enjoy under Article 21 TFEU include the right to lead a normal family life, together with their family members, in a host member state even if it is the Member State of which that citizen is a national since he has exercised previously his right of freedom of movement by settling in a Member State other than that of which he is a national. By consequence, even though Directive 2004/38 does not cover such a situation, the

---

[7] Case C-434/09 *McCarthy* [2011]; Case C-256/11 *Dereci* [2011].
[8] Case C-184/99 *Grzelczyk* [2001].
[9] In *Singh* case law (Case C-370/90 *Singh* [1992]), the Court already recognized such right for a national of Member state to claim his right to family reunification in the member state of which he is a national since he previously exercised his of freedom of movement but the status was different since M. Singh was a worker in the meaning of EC Law.
[10] Case C-165/16 *Lounes* [2017].

Court considers that the EU citizens must be entitled to the right to family reunification as protected by the Treaties under article 21 TFEU.

The Court retains the same reasoning in the *Cowan* judgment.[11] "It follows that the refusal by the authorities of a Member State to recognise, for the sole purpose of granting a derived right of residence to a third-country national, the marriage of that national to a Union citizen of the same sex, concluded, during the period of their genuine residence in another Member State, in accordance with the law of that State, may interfere with the exercise of the right conferred on that citizen by article 21(1) TFEU to move and reside freely in the territory of the Member States. Indeed, the effect of such a refusal is that such a Union citizen may be denied the possibility of returning to the Member State of which he is a national together with his spouse."[12]

Thereby, it results from this that the rights, which nationals of Member States enjoy under article 21, include the right to lead a normal family life, together with their family members, both in the host Member State and in the Member State of which they are nationals when they return to that Member State.

Finally, the Court stressed a complete and particularly wide protection of the right to family reunion by combining the case law developments developed on the basis of article 21 TFUE and those developed on the basis of Directive 2004/38. In that perspective, it ruled that "the conditions for granting that derived right of residence must not be stricter than those provided for by Directive 2004/38 for the grant of a derived right of residence to a third-country national who is a family member of a Union citizen who has exercised his right of freedom of movement by settling in a Member State other than that of which he is a national."[13] Even though Directive 2004/38 does not cover a situation such as that mentioned in the preceding paragraph of this judgment, it must be applied, by analogy, to that situation in order to ensure the effectiveness of European citizenship taking into account that the rights which nationals of Member States enjoy under Article 21 TFEU include the right to lead a normal family life, together with their family members.

---

[11] Case C-673/16 *Coman* [2018].
[12] Case C-673/16 *Coman* [2018] para 40.
[13] Case C-165/16 *Lounes* [2017] para 61.

Thus, as is apparent from the case-law referred, any national measure that is liable to obstruct the exercise of freedom of movement of persons or deprived of the genuine enjoyment of the substance of the rights conferred by virtue of the status of citizen of the Union may be justified only where such a measure is consistent with the fundamental rights guaranteed by the Charter, including article 7 enshrined the right to family reunification.

However, in the present state of negotiations, and in the best hypothesis of a deal, the *status quo* is based solely on the secondary legislation which raises the issue of a possible alteration of the right of family reunification post Brexit.

The Alteration of Family Reunification in the Context of Brexit

It is mentioned from the recitals of the Withdrawal Agreement that the primary objective is to ensure reciprocal protection for European and British citizens so as to allow them an effective exercise of the rights which they derive from the right to the Union and which derive from their previous life choices.[14]

A first reading of the Withdrawal Agreement suggests a *status quo*. Thus, it is understood that they must be able to claim the same rights, including the fundamental right to equal treatment and therefore also to the same social benefits as nationals and under the same conditions as previously as long as they remain in the host State. In addition, the right of residence is confirmed for family members who already reside legally in the territory in question and the possibility, whatever their nationality, to join the EU or UK citizens provided that their family ties are established before the end of the transition period.

---

[14] Recognising that it is necessary to provide reciprocal protection for Union citizens and for United Kingdom nationals, as well as their respective family members, where they have exercised free movement rights before a date set in this Agreement, and to ensure that their rights under this Agreement are enforceable and based on the principle of non-discrimination; recognising also that rights deriving from periods of social security insurance should be protected, p. 3.

However, a more in-depth reading of the text reveals that this protection is more restrictive for those affected by Brexit than the one they currently have.

The Impossible Status Quo for the Benefit of the British Citizen on European Soil

In any event, it should be recalled that any British citizen, who has not activated his European citizenship on the date of exit, will no longer be able to benefit from the freedoms of movement and the rights which accompany them. As a third-country national of the Union, his access to European territory will be limited and logically less favourable to that of a European citizen. The Directive 2003/86[15] on the right to family reunification confers no subjective right to family reunification and the Court preserves, in this field, a particularly important margin of appreciation for States which may impose much more restrictive conditions of integration on the applicant. Thereby, it can only benefit the spouse and minor children who hold British citizenship and their entry may be subject to conditions of integration, a check of their criminal record and a visa as any foreigner.

In addition, even the British citizens, who would have exercised their right to free movement in accordance with Union law before the end of the transition period, such as covered by the Withdrawal Agreement, would not be able to claim the maintenance of these rights, if they leave the Member State in which they exercised their right of residence.[16] After the transition period, if the British citizen leaves the so-called Host Member State to another, he would not be able to benefit from right to reunification under EU law, as his situation is no longer covered by the Agreement.

There is no maintenance of existing rights here. His/her status will necessarily become that of a third-country national. Thus, if a British national, who works in France, wants to respond to a job offer in Germany, his Congolese husband who still benefits from family reunification to stay and respond to jobs in France will lose this protection in Germany.

---

[15] European Commission, Directive 2003/86/EC on the right to family reunification (L251), 22.9.2003, *Official Journal of the European Union*, 3.10.2003, pp. 12–18.

[16] Article 9 c) ii and Article 10 1 a).

Fundamental Rights Potentially Limited to the Scope of Directive 2004/38

Even in the situation covered by the Withdrawal Agreement, a British or European citizen, who has exercised his right to reside in a Member State in accordance with Union law before the end of the transitional period and who subsequently continues to reside there, it seems difficult to consider that his/her right to family reunification will be exercised with the same guarantees as before Brexit.

Part 2 of the Agreement, dealing with "Citizens' Rights", has so far considered the definition of "family" and their rights mainly in the light and by reference to Directive 2004/38. According to the Directive 2004/38, family members enjoy the same rights identified by the Court in its case law, namely: entry, stay and social benefits. The Directive even offers specific and individual protection to family members, since it is intended, under certain temporal and economic conditions, to maintain their rights, in particular those of residence, in the event of the death of the Union citizen, of divorce, annulment of marriage or termination of registered partnership.

However, although the Directive 2004/38 largely overlaps with the rights identified, its scope is, on the other hand, more limited and does not cover all the hypotheses that the Court may have submitted to the scope of the treaties authorizing citizens to rely on article 21 TFEU.

First of all, concerning the direct beneficiaries,[17] the directive only applies to "Union citizens who move to or reside in a Member State other than that of which they are a national". Thus, the citizen who has never left the territory of the host Member State (*Zambrano* hypothesis) are outside the scope of Directive 2004/38. In addition, a person who returns to his country of origin, such as the *Singh*, *Lounes* or *Coman* hypothesis, cannot rely on the directive to obtain a derived right of residence for his family. The Court has held on a number of occasions, that "it follows from a literal, contextual and teleological interpretation of Directive 2004/38 that the directive governs only the conditions determining whether a Union citizen can enter and reside in Member States other than that of which he is a national and does not confer a derived right of residence on third-country nationals who are family members of a Union citizen in the

---

[17] Article 3)1° Directive 2004/38.

Member State of which that citizen is a national".[18] So, other situations like *Ibrahim*[19] and *Chen*[20] also rest outside the scope of the directive.

As articles 9 and 10 of the Withdrawal Agreement aim primarily at the situation covered by the directive and do not refer in a general way to article 21 TFEU, the right to family reunification, as guaranteed by EU law, could therefore be restricted. Put in other words, according to the agreement, EU and UK citizens who have exercised their rights are targeting a smaller category of citizens since those who derive rights directly from their sole status as citizens on the basis of article 21 TFEU may no longer be entitled to the right to family reunification as guaranteed by Union law.

However, some corrections were made during the negotiations, the *Zambrano hypothesis*, which was not covered in the Attached Agreement of December 2017, now seems to be integrated since article 9 (a) (ii) stated that: "persons other than those defined in Article 3(2) of Directive 2004/38/EC whose presence is required by Union citizens or United Kingdom nationals in order not to deprive those Union citizens or United Kingdom nationals of a right of residence granted by this Part". This hope seems confirmed by the drafting of article 13 of the Withdrawal Agreement which notes in paragraph 3 that "family members who are neither Union citizens nor United Kingdom nationals shall have the right to reside in the host State under article 21 TFEU and as set out in article 6(2), article 7(2), article 12(2) or (3), article 13(2), article 14, article 16(2), article 17(3) or (4) or article 18 of Directive 2004/38/EC, subject to the limitations and conditions set out in those provisions".

Despite these precisions, some doubts remain concerning the situation of a British or EU citizen who, in the past, stayed in a host Member State and returns to his country of origin as well as for the *Chen* and *Ibrahim* hypothesis.

Admittedly, the agreement mentions that the concepts stemming from EU law concerning citizens' rights are interpreted in relation to the case-law of the Court,[21] but in the absence of an express mention, the

---

[18] *Coman* para 20; 2014, Case C-456/12 *O. and B* [2014], para. 37; Case C-133/15 *Chavez-Vilchez and Others* 2017], para.53; *Lounes* para 33.

[19] Case C-480/08 *Teixeira*; C-310/08, Ibrahim [2010].

[20] Case C-200/02, *Zhu Chen*, 2004.

[21] Article 4(4) and (5).

guarantee of retaining a right of residence remains precarious especially after the end of the transition period. But in which extent the case law of the Court will be taking into account after it?

Second, concerning the members of the family, the Withdrawal Agreement indicates that it is the only one constituted before the end of the period of transition. For all others, national law will apply. One step forward, however, is that the agreement reintroduces the obligation not only to promote reunification with the partner and other family members but above all to carry out a detailed examination of the situation justifying the refusal.[22]

Finally, without being exhaustive, there is a real practical difficulty for European citizens residing on British territory to prove their status and the period of residence. Even if the EU has attached particular importance to the existence of smooth and simple administrative procedures for the citizens covered by the agreement to exercise their rights.[23]

An attempt could be made to qualify this possible move away from rapprochement by pointing out that the British citizen on European soil, who would be travelling in another State, could still claim the family reunification directive. However, it does not offer as much protection as that granted to European nationals. Similarly, it could be objected that the right is insured under article 8 of the ECHR. But this legal basis does not provide the same guarantees.

The Weakening of the Guarantees Surrounding the Right to Family Reunification

The rights to which the citizens concerned by Brexit can still claim and their future presuppose to be protected as long as they can be included in a higher standard of law. In other words, normative safeguards must be set up, but individuals shall also be able to defend these rights before an autonomous judicial body. The Withdrawal Agreement provides this double guarantee but does not remove any ambiguity as regards both

---

[22] Article 10(4) and (5).
[23] Article 18.

the prevalence of standards in each of the legal systems and the bodies competent to ensure them.

Normative Guarantees

The problem focuses on the normative value attached to the Withdrawal Agreement and the UK's concession to transform the status of EU citizens into a national law statute. It is a source of many uncertainties. According to article 4(1):

> "The provisions of this Agreement and the provisions of Union law made applicable by this Agreement shall produce in respect of and in the United Kingdom the same legal effects as those which they produce within the Union and its Member States" and Article 4(2): "The United Kingdom shall ensure compliance with paragraph 1, including as regards the required powers of its judicial and administrative authorities to dis-apply inconsistent or incompatible domestic provisions, through domestic primary legislation".

Especially, some difficulties are involved by the British dualism, which prevents the immediacy of rights. Indeed, to the extent that the UK intends to adopt legislation to ensure that the rights of citizens referred to in the agreement will prevail over contrary national laws, it is part of the dualism which presupposes receipt of the agreement in national law in order for it to have its effects. There may already be at this stage a gap in the transposition of the agreement into national law and within British law between the law transposing the agreement and the law set up in the EU Withdrawal Agreement.

In any case, it must be understood that the transcription of these rights and their normative value becomes a question of domestic law. The constitutional or legislative value of the debatable text and the possibility for the British Parliament to limit the content and scope of its rights remains open. Indeed, even if the repeal can only be express, if politically it is hardly conceivable, it is nevertheless legally possible.

These few clarifications call for two remarks. On the one hand, the principle of reciprocity of rights governing negotiations concerning citizens' rights cannot be affirmed since the guarantees granted to them cannot be regarded as equivalent. British citizens enjoy constitutional protection enshrined in the Treaties. On the other hand, the risks of a weakened normative guarantee make even more imperative the existence of judicial guarantees regarding the review and implementation of the agreement.

Jurisdictional Guarantees

In a State governed by the rule of law, it is generally accepted that the protection of fundamental rights cannot be regarded as assured in the absence of jurisdictional guarantees.

In this context, the protection of fundamental rights, within the framework of the Treaties, can be considered as safe if no European or national provision which violates these rights can be opposed to citizens. Above all, the ECJ can effectively sanction any infringement. Thus, it can annul a contrary European act[24] and pronounce with pecuniary sanctions in support of the failure of a Member State.[25] In addition, the individual may engage the responsibility of the author of a violation of fundamental rights and be compensated accordingly.[26] The European Communities Act of 1972 made it possible to integrate this protection by allowing British Courts to defeat parliamentary sovereignty if it proved to be deviant. This will be repealed.

Remember that the law of the ECHR gives no equivalent guarantee. While the adoption of the Human Rights Act – HRA-98 – now requires the UK Courts to take into account the requirements of the ECHR, they do not have the power to cancel the provisions violating the fundamental rights that will remain until that the Government or the Parliament modifies them. This system is so unsatisfactory that the Court may have considered "that it would be premature to say that such a procedure offers an effective remedy to individuals who complain about domestic law".

However, respect for fundamental rights as imposed by the European Court of Human Rights was already felt as a subjection of the Common Law to the standards contained in the ECHR and the decisions of the European Courts. The Brexiters relayed these positions ardently. Therefore, it is not surprising in this context that one of the cornerstones of the negotiation of the exit agreement remains for the UK to limit the jurisdiction of the Court.

The compromise obtained, to use the words of the Strasbourg judges, gives the feeling that "it would be premature to affirm that such a

---

[24] Article 263 TFEU.
[25] Article 258-260 TFEU.
[26] Article 340 al. 2 TFEU in the case of infringement ascribable to an EU institution; see also in the case of infringement ascribable to a Member state: Case 6 and 9/90 *Francovich*, 1991.

procedure offers an effective remedy to individuals who complain about domestic legislation."[27]

These reasons suggest that any withdrawal of the competence of the ECJ to ensure the protection of fundamental rights will inevitably be analysed as a lessening of the protection of these rights in Europe, and particularly of the British citizen.

On the effective date of Brexit, British judges regain jurisdiction. This competence remains nevertheless framed. Indeed, even after effective exit, the agreement specifies that British judges in the context of the application and interpretation of the rights of the citizens concerned take "due consideration" of relevant decisions of the Court and especially that during the 8 years following that date, it will be possible to question the ECJ for a preliminary ruling on interpretation in this field.[28]

Three remarks nevertheless. Firstly, jurisdictional guarantees seem more important for British citizens on European soil than for European citizens remaining on British territory. UK citizens will continue to be able to avail themselves of Union law before the ECJ and in accordance with its protective case-law, which conforms in principle to its positions. But it is certain that European citizens in the United Kingdom do not benefit from the same guarantees, if only in terms of continuity, since supervision is left to an independent body, that the respect of their rights will be entrusted to national judges, who will be required only to "take into consideration" the jurisprudence that the Court developed before the date of exit.

Secondly, while some people welcome the fact that the Court's case law will be duly taken into consideration, this obligation seems very weak in such a sensitive area. There is in fact no legal obligation on the British Courts to develop an opinion contrary to the ECJ and more generally to European law, since it states that it nevertheless "duly considered" its case-law. In fact, even though the Attached Agreement makes it clear that the Court is the ultimate arbiter of interpretations of EU law in relation to citizens' rights and even assumes that UK Courts take into account its case-law until effective date of exit, this consideration remains limited. Any evolution of the jurisprudence of the Court after this date will no longer be enforceable against the UK Courts. There is a serious

---

[27] ECHR Case 13378/05, 2008, ECHR 357 *Burden v. the United Kingdom*.
[28] Article 158, para 3 of the Withdrawal Agreement.

risk of discrimination and infringement of the rights of Union citizens who remain in British territory.

Finally, all situations have not yet been considered and may not be. Especially the question of the jurisdiction of the ECJ, maintained, even after the exit, for the disputes which are pending before the actual exit.

In conclusion, it seems impossible to advance any *status quo* concerning such fundamental issues as the protection of fundamental rights. The right to family reunification directly affects the lives of citizens involved in a European network. In that perspective, it must be reminded that Brexit cannot be summarized as a deal or a no deal that would be just harmful to politicians and economic operators.

Brexit and Its Impact on the Integration of Migrants in the UK

Seiko Oyama

Although long-term net migration continues to add to the United Kingdom (UK) population, according to the Office for National Statistics, different trends have been observed since 2016. After the Brexit referendum, the number of European Union (EU) citizens coming to the UK for work has decreased while the number of those leaving the UK has increased. Since 2016, EU net migration has fallen, although EU citizens still arrive for long-term settlement. Non-EU net migration has continued to increase since 2013. In 2019, approximately 642,000 people moved to the UK, while 402,000 left.

Although Brexit might cause a change in the pattern of movements for EU and non-EU citizens, it will hardly stop the inflow of new arrivals for settlement. The integration of migrants is a challenge for a host country because national economic and social policies need to not only provide for their needs but also ensure that have access to public services and the labour market. Without effective integration policies and measures, migrants are more likely to be exposed to the risk of social exclusion or poverty. Being a Member State of the EU, the UK has benefited from the policy framework and support tools for integration provided across the EU. Since the Justice and Home Affairs Council adopted the Common Basic Principles for Immigrant Integration Policy in the EU in 2004,[1] the European Commission has provided the framework and many tools such as handbooks, networks and National Contact Points for the EU integration policies.

---

[1] Council of the EU, 2618th Meeting of the Justice and Home Affairs, Press Release, 14615/04 (Presse 321), 19.11.2004.

As stated in Article 79(4) of the Treaty of the Functioning of the European Union (TFEU), the Member States are primarily responsible for effective integration, and these measures and policy frameworks are provided to support, stimulate and coordinate their actions and policies to integrate migrants. The integration indicators, adopted in 2010, were in four areas – employment, education, social inclusion and active citizenship – and they have been used to monitor the progress and results of integration policies.[2] The European Commission set out a European Agenda for the integration of third-country nationals in 2011 and emphasized that priorities should fully take into account different policy areas and the involvement of a wide range of actors at various levels.[3] In addition to a legislative framework to ensure equal treatment and grant proper rights, integration as an evolving process requires monitoring, assessment of the progress, innovative approaches for support and action and constant financial support. The European Commission has played an important role in establishing partnerships among relevant stakeholders at all levels of governance, in coordinating and monitoring policy developments, and in providing the EU financial support.

Despite the migration challenges caused by a steep increase of new arrivals in the EU, the European Agenda on Migration in 2015 emphasized the need for effective integration policies for third-country nationals.[4] The Action Plan in 2016 insisted on the importance of the use of the EU's common policy framework, which strengthens national integration policies, especially EU tools such as policy coordination and funding.[5] Although the UK has effectively used such beneficial EU tools for a variety of integration measures in priority policy areas, it has had to renounce them for migrant integration post Brexit.

This article will argue that migrant integration in the UK has been supported and assessed by soft-governance through the EU tools of comprehensive policy coordination and multi-annual financial support.

---

[2] The indicators were adopted in the Zaragoza Declaration in April 2010 by EU Ministers. For a pilot study of these indicators, see *Indicators of Immigrant Integration – A Pilot Study*, Eurostat Methodologies and Working Papers, 2011.

[3] European Commission, European Agenda for the Integration of Third-Country Nationals, COM (2011) 455 final.

[4] European Commission, A European Agenda on Migration, COM (2015) 240 final.

[5] European Commission, Action Plan on the integration of third country nationals, COM (2016) 377 final.

Without a national strategy on the integration of migrants, which has devolved to each of the constituent nations and local authorities, the UK will face a number of barriers to develop a strategic, coordinated, and multi-dimensional policy framework for successful migrant integration at the national level after leaving the EU.

Policy Coordination

EU Networks of Multi-Level Stakeholders

Effective integration of migrants has to be realized at national, regional and local levels by involving various types of stakeholders. The EU has contributed to establishing networks and coordinating dialogues between the different actors and stakeholders in the field of immigrant integration.

In 2002, National Contact Points on Integration were established as an intergovernmental network for the exchange of information among representatives from the ministries responsible for migrant integration. The Handbooks on Integration for policy-makers and practitioners were largely based on the information and practices provided by the National Contact Points on Integration.[6] With the initiative of the European Commission published in its Action Plan of 2016, the Network of the National Contact Points on Integration turned into the European Integration Network (EIN) with a stronger coordination role and mutual learning mandate. The EIN gathers representatives from the ministries responsible for national integration strategies and encourages them to exchange knowledge and good practices for mutual learning. The representatives also consult with the European Commission on developments and policy agenda in the field of integration; therefore, the EU policy agenda could reflect not only some good practices but also the necessity of financial support or tools for specific migrant integration measures of the Member States.

Since 2008, the Directorate General (DG) for Migration and Home Affairs has coordinated an EU network of migration and asylum experts

---

[6] European Commission, *Handbook on Integration for Policy-Makers and Practitioners*, Third edition, DG Justice, Freedom and Security, 2010.

called European Migration Network (EMN) to provide comparative policy-relevant information.[7] EMN National Contact Points coordinate a national network of various stakeholders specialized in migration and asylum to exchange information and knowledge on emerging issues. Based on this information and the statistics collected by the EMN National Contact Points, the EMN provides publications and further information such as country factsheets, bulletins, glossaries, and reports. In addition, it establishes Ad-Hoc Queries (AHQ), which allow Member States (and Norway) to obtain information on a specific topic on asylum- and migration-related issues from other countries in a relatively short time through the online platform on the EMN site. For example, the UK inquired about Member States' views and data on the labour market outcomes of the successful interventions for former asylum seekers and resettled refugees in March 2019; before the end of April 2019, it received responses from 22 countries including the UK itself and Norway.

The inquiries refer to the results from the 2014 EU Labour Force Survey which suggested that refugees in the UK have relatively poor labour market outcomes in comparison with those from other European nations, and the available support to overcome these barriers is limited in the UK. It continues as follows:

> This AHQ is designed to identify the impact providing employment support has on refugee employment rates, both granted asylum seekers and resettled refugees. We are keen to seek Member States' views and data on the labour market outcomes and demographics of refugees as well as seeking evidence of previous successful interventions. This would enable us to develop our understanding as to why refugees in the UK suffer worse labour market outcomes, as well as the scale of potential improvements that could be made, compared to other Member States.[8]

This enquiry reveals that the UK has benefited from the AHQ portal in terms of collecting data and good practices from other countries to analyse the negative factors that cause poor labour market outcomes among refugees in the national context. Post Brexit, the UK will no longer be a member of the EU networks of multi-level stakeholders such

---

[7] Council Decision of 14 May 2008 establishing a European Migration Network (2008/381/EC).

[8] EMN, ad hoc query on 2019.36 Refugee Employment Support, Requested by EMN NCP United Kingdom on 15.3.2019, https://ec.europa.eu/home-affairs/sites/homeaffairs/files/201936_refugee_employment_support.pdf (5.4.2020).

as EIN and EMN, developed across the Member States. The new British Cohesion and Integration Network (COIN) was launched in 2019 to bring together organizations and individuals including policy makers and practitioners from all cohesion and integration sectors. However, it would serve mainly as a national network across the UK. Non-membership of the EU networks will thus prevent stakeholders from having access to effective facilities, opportunities to exchange information and peer learning activities.

Governance by Monitoring

Integration is a constant process and its progress has to be assessed according to the set targets. The assessment of the progress requires the evaluation of various policy fields and actions. Integration measures and policies for migrants have been studied based on the degree of mainstreaming priorities across general policy areas such as education, employment, and social cohesion in European countries.[9] An editorial team of the European Website of Integration assesses whether the long-term integration measures are available in the 27 EU Member States and the UK, in policy areas such as language, employment and vocational training, education, health, housing and anti-discrimination.[10]

Common European "indicators" for migrant integration have been used to monitor results of integration policies through comparative data collection and peer learning activities. Migrant integration has been increasingly assessed in relation to European targets in the areas of employment, education and social inclusion because it is considered an important issue to achieve the targets set by the Europe 2020 Strategy for Growth and Jobs. Migrant integration outcomes in the Member States have been analysed and monitored within the Country Reports and Analysis in the framework of the Education and Training Monitor and

---

[9] For these studies, see Collett, E., Petrovic, M., *The Future of Immigrant Integration in Europe Mainstreaming Approaches for Inclusion*, Brussels, Migration Policy Institute, 2014. Scholten, P.W.A., Van Breugel, I., *Mainstreaming Integration Governance New Trends in Migrant Integration Policies in Europe*, Chippenham, Palgrave Macmillan, 2018.

[10] European Website on Integration, "What measures are in place to ensure the long-term integration of migrants and refuges in Europe?", 31.3.2020, https://ec.europa.eu/migrant-integration/feature/what-measures-are-in-place-to-ensure-the-long-term-integration-of-migrants-and-refugees-in-europe (5.4.2020).

the European Semester, with a focus on education and integrating youth into the labour market.[11]

Early school leaving from education and training,[12] one of the benchmarks set for a strategic framework for European cooperation in Education and Training over the last 20 years, has been a headline target for Europe 2020. Early school leavers (ESLs) face a higher risk of being unemployed or becoming inactive. The employment rate for young people aged 20–34 who completed the highest level of education less than three years ago is 51.2 % for those who completed the International Standard Classification of Education (ISCED) 0–2, compared to 76.8 % for those who completed ISCED 3–4.[13] In 2018, the EU average revealed that early school leaving rates amongst the foreign-born population (20.2 %) are more than twice as high as those for the native-born population (9.5 %). Migrant integration measures such as inclusive education systems and vocational training for better inclusion into the labour market have been therefore monitored and analysed as solutions to close the gap between foreign-born and native-born ESLs.

ESL rates in the UK have been monitored and reduced from 15.7 % in 2009 to 10.7 % in 2018, although it is a little above the benchmark (10 %) for Education and Training 2020 and Europe 2020. The Education and Training Monitor analyses the countries in which there is no significant improvement towards the ESL headline target in the last few years, despite their relatively low ESL rates. For example, the UK was considered to be in stagnation between 2010 and 2011 according to the Education and Training Monitor 2012. In addition, within the framework of European Semester, the Council of the EU, in its recommendation of 9 July 2013 related to the UK National Reform Programme 2013, referred to the youth unemployment rate which, at 20.7 %, was much higher than the overall unemployment rate which remained relatively low at 7.8 %. The Council recommended improvements to the quality of apprenticeship

---

[11] European Commission, COM(2016)377 final, *op. cit.*

[12] Early leavers from education and training (early school leavers) are defined as persons aged 18 to 24 fulfilling the two conditions: (1) the highest level of education or training attained in ISCED 0, 1, 2 or 3c short, (2) no education or training has been received in the four weeks preceding the survey. The early school leaving rate consists of the total population of the same age group, see: Education and Training Monitor 2012, SWD (2012) 373 final, 20.11.2012, p. 14.

[13] European Commission, Education and Training Monitor 2019.

programmes and the reform of complex qualifications systems to tackle the high unemployment rate (37.2 %) of poorly skilled 15–25 year olds.[14] In order to reduce the ESL rate, secondary schools managed to keep students in education longer in European countries, and the UK was not an exception. The compulsory participation age in education and training is 16 years in Scotland, Wales, and Northern Ireland, but in England this was raised to 17 years in 2013 and to 18 since 2015. Existing apprenticeship frameworks were replaced by new employer-designed apprenticeship standards with vocational qualifications that "support labour mobility into Europe".[15] The Department for Education considers that participating in education or training for longer contributes to an increase of young people in the more highly skilled, productive, and internationally competitive workforce.[16]

"Soft-governance", which comprises regular monitoring, country reports, comparative data, and country specific recommendations within the framework of the European Semester and the Education and Training Monitor, has succeeded in promoting structural reforms in the fields of education and employment of the youth and reducing ESL rates in the UK for the last 10 years. However, post Brexit, the UK will be out of such monitoring and evaluation frameworks and lose soft pressure on achieving the targets related to social inclusion of vulnerable youth through education and training.

ESL rates show distinct characteristics in the case of the UK because its rate of foreign-born (8.9 %) is lower than that of native-born (11.0 %). Specifically, the rate of EU-born (12.5 %) is much higher than that of those born outside the EU (6.0 %).[17] The relatively high rate of ESLs among the EU-born has not been changed, although it dropped about four points from 16.1 % in 2012. The underachievement of EU-born students, especially those from new Member States after

---

[14] Council Recommendation of 9.7.2013 on the National Reform Programme 2013 of the United Kingdom and delivering a Council opinion on the Convergence Programme of the United Kingdom, 2012/13 or 2017/18, 2013/C 217/23.

[15] Department for Business Innovation & Skills, "Getting the job done: The government's reform plan for vocational qualifications", 2014, p. 19.

[16] CEDEFOP, "Leaving education early: putting vocational education and training in centre stage, United Kingdom", 2017, pp. 16–19.

[17] Education and Training Monitor 2019.

2004, could be one of the factors for the higher rate of ESLs,[18] because language competence is crucial for access to higher education and the labour market. The Ethnic Minority Achievement Grant was abolished in 2012 and it is up to each school or academy to decide whether they will provide specific support for the students for whom English is an additional language.

Not all will be lost due to Brexit, for there are also some national measures. For example, in the UK "Integrated Communities Action Plan" of 2019,[19] a monitoring of integration is promised in a forthcoming technical paper with 20 indicators proposed by the Ministry of Housing, Communities & Local Government (MHCLG) on measuring outcomes for integrated communities in England.[20] The issue concerning the lack of data on the integration of immigrants within the UK has been raised by the All Party Parliamentary Group (APPG) on Social Integration.[21] Particularly, there are major gaps between data at local authority and neighbourhood levels and the availability of data on integration outcomes by certain socio-demographic characteristics.[22] The MHCLG has identified 20 indicators of integration – in the language, education, and employment fields – with which they monitored the integration of immigrants at national and regional levels in a technical note published in 2019. However, it will likely take a few years to fill the gaps in collected data and monitor the outcomes.

---

[18] Strand, S., Malmberg, L., Hall, J. analyse that, among "White Other" students, "there is roughly a 20 point gap in Best 8 score for Polish, Turkish, and Portuguese speakers, a 50 point gap for Lithuanian, Romanian and Latvian speakers and a 120 point gap for Slovak speakers" compared to the average Best 8 score for English speakers, see Strand S., Malmberg, L., Hall, J, *English as an Additional Language (EAL) and Educational Achievement in England: An Analysis of the National Pupil Database*, Oxford, University of Oxford, 2015, p. 72.

[19] HM Government, Integrated Communities Action Plan, February 2019.

[20] Ministry of Housing, Communities & Local Government (MHCLG), "Measuring outcomes for Integrated Communities", 2019, https://assets.publishing.service.gov.uk/government/uploads/system/uploads/attachment_data/file/819701/Integrated_Communities_Measurement_Technical_Note.pdf (8.4.2020).

[21] APPG, Interim Report into Integration of Immigrants, 2018.

[22] MHCLG, *op. cit.*, p. 6.

EU Funding for Migrant Integration

Asylum, Migration and Integration Fund (AMIF) and European Social Fund (ESF)

The EU has provided financial support for the integration of third-country nationals. The European Integration Fund financed projects in Member States between 2007 and 2013 worth 825 million euros via the so-called SOLID programme. The Asylum, Migration and Integration Fund (AMIF) succeeded the SOLID programme (including the European Integration Fund) and a total of 3.137 billion euros was then allotted for the 2014–2020 period. The principal objectives of the AMIF include supporting legal migration to EU Member States in line with labour market needs and promoting the effective integration of third-country nationals.

The UK has benefited from these measures by approximately 260 million euros in the 2014–2020 period.[23] A minimum of 20 % is required to be allocated to integration priorities under the AMIF National Programmes. Despite this allocation quota for different objectives, "the UK's priority was to continue to encourage voluntary return as the preferred option" in the period between 2014 and 2017.[24] The AMIF provided integration assistance to 4714 individuals for the first four years, compared to the 69,764 individuals who have been supported in 3.5 years under Asylum objectives and to the 26,000 returnees who were co-financed annually by the AMIF.[25] Facing high levels of inward migration in the 2014–2017 period, the UK prioritized the reception and short-term integration of asylum applicants and unaccompanied children with co-financed projects including training in asylum-related topics and the development of the reception conditions.

The European Social Fund (ESF) and the European Regional Development Fund (ERDF) are the major financial instruments of

---

[23] European Commission, Summary of the allocation received per Member State under the AMIF and the ISF border, visa and police, posted on the site of DG Migration and Home Affairs on 26.3.2020.

[24] AMIF UK Responsible Authority, Asylum Migration and Integration Fund United Kingdom Interim Evaluation report, December 2017, p. 9.

[25] *Ibid.*, p. 5–9.

the European Structural and Investment Funds (ESIF) that invest in promoting social inclusion, education and training opportunities, as well as access to labour markets. ESF allocates approximately 10 billion euros a year to the Member States to co-fund job prospects programmes and projects by investing in human capital such as workers and youth to combat poverty and discrimination. For the 2014–2020 period, 199 billion euros have been allocated to the ERDF for measures supporting investments in infrastructure for employment, social inclusion, education, housing, health, etc., in order to correct disparities between regions. The UK has benefited by around 11.8 billion euros from the ESF and ERDF during the 2014–2020 period.[26] ESF-funded programmes have provided vocational training and invested in education and lifelong learning across the UK. ESF funding is tailored to local needs by focusing on the labour market activation of disadvantaged groups such as migrants and refugees, long-term unemployed young people and people with disabilities to combat social exclusion.

Since there is no single national operational programme for migrant inclusion, the local dimension of the ESF is crucial in the UK.[27] For example, in Greater Manchester, which comprises 10 local authorities, eight ESF programmes are being operated with a budget of 186 million euros for the 2014–2020 period. The Working Well programme had already supported over 16,500 people, before it began being funded by the ESF since 2019 with a budget of 38 million euros. It was introduced as a good practice of city-led interventions with ESF support.[28] ESF funding scaled up the size of the Working Well programme, supporting 45 % more people than it did before.[29] In 2018, it was believed that "with central government budget cuts and austerity still the norm, the ability to secure ESF funding has and continues to add significant value

---

[26] See the website of European Social Fund, "The ESF in the United Kingdom", https://ec.europa.eu/esf/main.jsp?catId=381 (9.4.2020).

[27] Ahad, A., Schmidt, T., *Mainstreamed or overlooked? Migrant inclusion and social cohesion in the European Social Fund*, Brussels, European Programme for Integration and Migration (EPIM), 2019, p. 35.

[28] Euro-cities, "Boosting employment and social inclusion in EU cities Lessons learned from cities experiences with the European Social Fund in 2014–2017", Technical report, 2018, p. 40.

[29] *Ibid.*

to the lives of people supported by the Working Well programme".[30] It has been analysed in Greater Manchester that Brexit would impact the labour market in which EU nationals have been the major workforce in distribution, hotels, banking and finance, manufacturing, etc. After losing ESIF funding in the post-Brexit era, the UK government is required to allocate national funds to replace the ESIF by providing flexibility to local authorities and beneficiaries for its use during a multi-year funding period.

As we have discussed, the UK has allocated a large part of the AMIF for the reception and return of asylum seekers between 2014 and 2017. The AMIF was used for short-term integration of asylum applicants, while the ESF was allocated for longer-term integration measures in the UK. For the funding period 2021–2027, the AMIF shall be allocated on early integration measures such as assessment of skills and qualifications, establishing reception accommodation, civic orientation courses, and professional guidance, and so on, while the ESF+ will be focused on the provision of longer-term integration by improving access to employment and public services, fostering active inclusion with equal opportunities and active participation, improving accessibility of healthcare systems and long-term care services, etc.[31] The EU structural funds enable the Member States to tackle migrant integration issues using a comprehensive approach by utilizing all different sorts of EU financial instruments, promoting social cohesion and inclusion, economic growth, employment and education. The beneficiaries of such EU funds have been regularly monitored and assessed on their progress and the outcomes of the policies and investments by the Member States. The UK will lose such an international strategic framework with holistic and comprehensive approaches to tackle migrant integration issues post Brexit.

The EU structural funds have focused on "less-developed" areas across the UK; the highest per capita aid levels are in Wales (690 pounds per head), Northern Ireland (300 pounds per head), North East England

---

[30] Greater Manchester Combined Authority, "Brexit and Greater Manchester", 2019, p. 14, https://greatermanchester-ca.gov.uk/media/1624/gmca___brexit_v2__.pdf (10.4.2020).

[31] Wolffhardt, A., *Making the most of EU funds to support a comprehensive approach to migrant integration*, Policy Option Brief, RESOMA, 2020.

and South West England (both 250 pounds per head).[32] In dealing with the pressure on social policy budgets, the UK "government will be therefore obliged to decide if it should maintain the distinctive support for the most disadvantaged" post Brexit.[33] Furthermore, Polverari and Bachtler observed expanded economic development activity triggered by a considerable leverage of other funding sources, including public investment, especially private funds, entailed by the EU programmes.[34] Thus, without EU structural funds, the UK may face barriers to maintaining public and private investment for multi-annual programmes. With greater autonomy to target domestic priorities after Brexit, the UK regional and local economic development policy will hardly prioritize an interconnection between economic and social cohesion, which has been emphasized by the EU structural funds, but would rather focus on economic objectives like productivity, innovation and entrepreneurship.[35]

Financial Instruments to Support a Heterogeneous Group of Migrants

Although the current ESF supports social inclusion of vulnerable participants with foreign and minority backgrounds through national and local-level operational programmes, it is difficult to assess the proportion of the fund that is spent on migrant integration. Migrants are a very heterogeneous group in terms of nationality, legal status, length of stay, ethnicity, language proficiency, etc. and certain migrant populations such as Roma are more visible to policy makers than others.

High mobility and the unsuccessful integration of Gypsy, Roma, and Travellers within the EU have been matters of great concern for Member States. The European Commission set out the EU Framework for National Roma Integration Strategies to be achieved by 2020. In

---

[32] Bachtler, J., Begg, I., "Cohesion policy after Brexit: the economic, social and institutional challenges", *Journal of Social Policy*, vol. 46/4, 2017, p. 750.
[33] *Ibid.*, p. 753.
[34] Polverari, L., Bachtler, J., with Davies, S., Kah, S., Mendez, C., Michie, R., Vironen, H., *Balance of Competences Cohesion Review: Literature Review on EU Cohesion Policy*, Final Report to the Department for Business, Innovation and Skills, The University of Strathclyde, 2014, p. 8.
[35] Stewart, K., Cooper, K., Shutes, I., "What does Brexit mean for social policy in the UK?", *Social Policies and Distributional Outcomes in a Changing Britain (SPDO) research paper 3*, February 2019, p. 70.

response, the Commission's Communication – the Local Engagement for Roma Inclusion (LERI) project – was launched in 21 localities across 11 EU Member States. From 2013 to 2016, the LERI project was conducted in Medway, a south-eastern region in England with a population of 264,000.[36] In this region, between 2001 and 2011, the number of those who identified as "White Other" increased, with the largest such groups reported as European Mixed (1703) and Polish (1327).[37] There are no official figures for the population of Roma, but it is reported that approximately 3000 to 4000 Roma, largely from Czech Republic and Slovakia, live in Medway – one of the largest groups of Roma in England.[38]

Medway has benefited from several sources of EU funding for the development of local and regional government networks and stakeholders to reduce inequalities and improve social cohesion. Within the framework of the Interreg programme, which provides funding for a series of cross-border and interregional cooperation across Europe, Medway participated in the Achieving the Integration of Migrant Communities and Ethnic Residents (AIMER) project[39] between 2009 and 2012, as well as the Action to Generate Inclusion for Residents of Migrant Background (AGIR) project[40] between 2013 and 2015. Medway also participates in the European Territorial Cooperation Programme (URBACT) and benefits from EU funding to develop exchange and learning networks with other European cities and find the solutions to urban challenges such as sustainable housing for social mix and gender equality in the employment sector.[41] With the recent increase in Roma and EU migrants and an attempt to mainstream the integration policies of Roma with EU funding, LERI local interventions were developed in Medway. Through interactive consultations with local Roma and EU migrants as well as local

---

[36] Medway Council, Medway 2011 Census Report, 2013.
[37] Ibid.
[38] Smith, D., *Local engagement for Roma inclusion, Locality study Medway (United Kingdom)*, Vienna, European Union Agency for Fundamental Rights, 2016.
[39] See the outline of AIMER project, http://archive.interreg4a-2mers.eu/admin/page_ext_attachments/2009_11_06_Presentation_6_Nov_Cambridge.pdf (25.5.2019).
[40] See the outline of AIGIR project, http://www.sfdeurope.com/resources/Agir-leaflet.pdf (25.5.2019).
[41] See the interactive map of URBACT programme, https://urbact.eu/interactive-map (25.5.2019).

officials and professionals, LERI interventions took place with regard to the following issues: inclusion through language, family based learning, extra academic support for high school pupils, integration through dialogue and community engagement events.[42] The LERI project emphasised the importance of education, especially the development of language skills for adults because inadequate language skills pose barriers to engaging with the public sector on issues related to housing, employment, wages, and security. The LERI project sought to "act as a template of best practice for organisations looking to develop local interventions".[43] LERI participants succeeded in establishing the Medway Czech Slovak Society and encouraging local stakeholders to continue running some of the interventions that LERI initiated. Importantly, LERI has achieved its objective by bringing together various stakeholders and Roma community members and increasing Roma involvement in educational projects, with Roma residents showing improvements in their language skills and confidence while simultaneously acquiring important life skills through the interventions.[44]

Brexit will prevent UK stakeholders from benefiting from the various EU financial instruments and related networks to promote local and regional development. Although the Integrated Communities Action Plan proposed in 2019 mentions the steps to be taken to continue addressing the challenges that Gypsy, Roma and Traveller communities can encounter during integration, specific ethnicities will hardly be targeted objectives through other integration programmes.[45] Because of significant funding cuts by the government, local communities are dependent on the work of voluntary and community organisations such as Medway Plus.[46] The local authority does not favour a distinct integration policy for migrant populations because "UK born residents also experience low skills, unemployment, poor job prospects and poverty".[47] The number of

---

[42] Smith, D., *op. cit.*, 2016.
[43] *Ibid.*, p. 18.
[44] *Ibid.*
[45] HM Government, *op. cit.*, 2019.
[46] Medway Plus is a charitable incorporation organization and empower and strengthen residents' participation in local community and coordinate the management of community facilities and resources through the projects, https://medwayplus.wordpress.com/about-us/ (25.5.2019).
[47] Smith, D., *op. cit.*, 2016.

votes in favour of leaving the EU was 88,997, almost double that of those in favour of remaining (49,889) in Medway.[48] It is doubtful whether a post-Brexit UK policy would recreate multi-annual programmemes as in cohesion policies, co-funded by the EU structural funds, and "there is a risk of reverting to an ad hoc, politics-driven approach to creating short-term instruments and funds."[49] The Brexit referendum and budget cuts might result in local authorities in areas such as Medway facing greater difficulty in promoting projects that aim for better social cohesion between diverse residents, including those from Roma communities.

Conclusion

The UK had made progress on migrant integration through networking among multi-level stakeholders, monitoring and assessment of the outcomes according to the benchmarks set at the EU level and EU financial instruments that cover different policy areas to pursue a comprehensive approach on migrant integration. However, Brexit will prevent national and local stakeholders in the UK from profiting from this EU strategic framework on migrant integration in the future.

Without a UK-wide strategic policy framework on migrant integration, the responsibility for migration policy remains with the Home Office, while the MHCLG takes the lead on community cohesion in England and other departments take the lead on initiatives in their own policy areas. In the Integrated Communities Action Plan (2019), some cross-departmental action was proposed, but most of the actions remain under a single leading department. Each of the devolved administrations has developed its own distinctive approach to integration policy, and there is "a lack of clarity on where responsibility lies in Whitehall, or between national and local government; differing definitions of integration used and some lack of consistency."[50] A Controlling Migration Fund of 26 million pounds was announced[51] to fund successful projects, but

---

[48] See the Medway County site, https://www.medway.gov.uk/info/200168/elections_and_voting/376/election_results/3 (25.5.2019).

[49] Bachtler, Begg, op. cit., p. 758.

[50] Broadhead J., *Policy Primer Integration*, The Migration Observatory at the University of Oxford, 3.2020, p. 5, https://migrationobservatory.ox.ac.uk/wp-content/uploads/2020/03/Policy-Primer-Integration.pdf (11.4.2020).

[51] HM Government, op. cit., 2019, p. 7.

funding can only be granted to a local authority, not other stakeholders. Post Brexit, the UK government is required to develop a comprehensive and proactive strategy for migrant integration[52] with clarified integration policy goals by making good use of its own experience of being a former Member State of the EU strategic policy framework.

---

[52] APPG, *op. cit.*, 2018.

Effects of Brexit on UK Nationals Living in France*

Noriko Suzuki

Nationals of the Member States of the European Union (EU) fear an increase in migrants coming from other EU Member States (EU migrants) or non-European refugees. Others complain about the EU because the State loses powers over the EU's decisions, especially in the EU's policy of controlling borders. This dissatisfaction appears everywhere in Europe with anti-EU movements or anti-EU votes that are often picked up by left-wing or right-wing extremists or "populism" movements. This phenomenon has recently happened in the United Kingdom (UK). The British people, well known as Eurosceptic among EU countries for a long time, according to the Eurobarometer polls, decided to exit the EU by referendum in June 2016.

The 2016 referendum was not the first referendum in the UK that asked its citizens whether or not to remain in the European Community (EC). In 1975, the British people chose to stay in the EC. However, during the recent referendum in 2016, a majority of the British voted for the exit of the EU in order to regain their sovereignty from the EU, especially so as to control migration flows. Moreover, supporters of Brexit wanted to take back control by saving the money that the UK feeds into the EU budget and to use it instead for internal policies such as the National Health Services (NHS). This Brexiter opinion shows that there is a perceived link between internal EU migration and the degradation

---

* Acknowledgment: This paper was supported by JSPS KAKENHI Grant Number JP15K03871, and Waseda University Grants for Special Research Projects Number 2019BARG005927.

of the NHS, because EU migrants are blamed for taking health benefits thanks to their status of European citizenship.[1]

From the EU's point of view, it is the first time in the history of European integration that a Member State secedes from the EU. However, since the Member States have been working ever more closely together after the Maastricht Treaty in 1992, Brexit will bring about enormous institutional and legislative changes both for the UK and for the EU. From a citizen's point of view, Brexit will result in the loss of the benefits of European citizenship as one the major consequences of the process of withdrawal from the EU. There are two main types of citizens who are at the centre of this topic. First, Brexit will affect an estimated 2.5 million EU citizens who have migrated to the UK. These people will eventually lose the rights they have enjoyed thus far as European citizens. If the UK is no longer an EU Member State, people from other EU countries will not be able to benefit from their status as EU citizens. Second, there are about 1.3 million UK nationals living in other EU countries and they have been enjoying EU citizen privileges.[2] These UK nationals are very much afraid of the consequences of Brexit, because if they lose their status as EU citizens, they can no longer live nor work in other EU countries freely. Instead they must obtain proper permissions as non-EU citizens in order to travel to, stay and work in an EU Member State. Moreover, UK nationals who were living abroad could not vote in the 2016 referendum due to their long stay abroad. These nationals are concerned about not only losing their political rights as EU citizens but also limiting their political rights as British citizens after Brexit.

In this situation, what does it mean for British citizens living abroad after Brexit? In response to this question, this paper will analyse the results of a field research in France from March 2017 to March 2019 in which UK nationals living in two areas of France were interviewed. It will first deal with European citizenship and the rights of UK nationals living in other EU countries after Brexit. It will then investigate UK nationals' reactions to Brexit, their exercise of political rights and their consideration of citizenship. In conclusion, the paper will determine that a significant number of UK nationals who live in France try maintain

---

[1] "#BrexitOrNot: paroles d'électeurs britanniques à l'heure du choix pour ou contre l'Europe", *Le Monde*, 21.6.2016 (1.11.2018).

[2] Nardelli, A., Traynor, I., Haddou, L., "Revealed: thousands of Britons on benefits across EU", *The Guardian*, 19.1.2015, (1.11.2018).

their rights in their resident community in various ways including by acquiring the nationality of their host country.

European Citizens and Brexit

The Rights Granted to European Citizens

In 1992, the Treaty of the EU introduced citizenship of the Union and has recognized the nationals of the Member States as European citizens. European citizenship shall be an addition to the national citizenship rather than a replacement of it (TEU Art. 9, TFEU Art. 20). This grants European citizens the following rights: freedom of movement and residence in the other Member States (TFEU Art. 21), voting rights and eligibility for local elections and the European election in the State of which they are not nationals (TFEU Art. 22), diplomatic protection by the other Member States in any third State where their State is not represented diplomatically (TFEU Art. 23), the petition to the European Parliament (TFEU Art. 24) and the request to the Ombudsman appointed by the European Parliament (TFEU Art. 30) in any of the Treaty languages.

Thus, this treaty allows European citizens to move, live and work in the EU as well as to have the ability to be elected as municipal councillors without having access to nationality in their country of residence. When European citizens are in the territory of a third country in which the country of nationality is not represented, they have the right to enjoy the protection of the diplomatic and consular authorities of any EU Member State on the same conditions as the nationals of that State. So, the citizenship of the Union creates a European area without borders. Yet, these rights are applied only to those who move to Member States other than their own because European citizenship does not replace the nationality of each Member State by "the principle of subsidiarity" and the notion of the European citizen completes it (TFEU Art. 20-1-2). Thus, these rights are reserved for mobile Europeans.

In addition, the "Citizenship Directive"[3] has recognized the freedom to move and reside in the EU for all economically active and inactive

---

[3] European Parliament and Council, Directive 2004/38/EC on the right of citizens of the Union and their family members to move and reside freely within the territory of

European citizens.[4] This freedom is admitted to their family regardless of whether there are Europeans or non-Europeans. Apart from these political rights of European citizenship, European citizens also have social rights that start with the rights of immigrant workers and can be described as "the principles of non-discrimination" by nationality in the conditions of work, payment, etc. (TEU Art. 45), medical and pension benefits (TEU Art. 46). The EU has established these rights for workers in the EU Member State other than that of their nationality. Benefits are allowed not only for these workers but also for their families.

The European Health Insurance Card (EHIC) is issued freely to people from the EU Member States. This card allows for European citizens to access medical services during temporary stays in other Member States. These citizens are insured or covered by the social security system of the 27 EU Member States (plus Iceland, Liechtenstein, Norway or Switzerland) under the same conditions and at the same cost (free in some countries) as people insured in each country.[5] Thus, EU citizens are guaranteed civil rights such as freedom of movement, residence and employment, but also social rights in the countries where they moved within the EU. Moreover, their family members are similarly protected even without having the nationality of an EU Member State. This European citizenship is therefore a new and very different from the traditional nationality-based idea.

The Characteristics of European Citizenship

First, European citizenship is based on the concept of a multiple citizenship. To begin with, different from nationality, citizenship is a relational contract and a legal link between individuals and the State. In this contract, the individuals have rights and obligations conferred by the State, whereas nationality is based on a filiation and community. The concept of multiple citizenship has been developed by Derek Heater.[6] He explains that the assumption of citizenship as a singular, bilateral relationship between individuals and the State is deeply rooted in our

---

the Member States (L 158/77), 29.4.2004, *Official Journal*, 30.4.2004.

[4] They have sufficient resources and comprehensive security for the disease if they reside there for more than a month.

[5] European Commission about European Health Care Insurance. See: https://ec.europa.eu/social/main.jsp?catId=563&langId=en (2.5.2019).

[6] Heater, D., *What is Citizenship?*, Cambridge, Polity, 1999, pp. 115–116.

understanding of this concept, but that it can no longer be understood today without the additional idea of multiple citizenship. This citizenship is formed by parallel citizenship and citizenship in layers. The citizenship of the European Union is indeed categorized in layers, since the individuals are citizens of their Member State and then also of the EU. Levels of citizenships are functioning between the State and the EU as in a quasi-feudal system, at the level of supra-national Europe. In this point of view, we can say that the EU citizenship is a multiple citizenship as it adds to national citizenship "but does not replace it" (Art. 20 of TFEU). Therefore, European citizenship differs from national citizenship and constitutes a legal link between the citizens of the Member State and the EU.

Second, European citizenship can be characterized as a citizenship of residence. The principle of a Nation-State has supposed the existence of a dichotomy that opposes the nationals and the foreigners. The former has the rights recognized by the State, such as rights of residence, voting and eligibility, as well as the social protection, whereas the latter does not have these rights. There are exceptions to this rule. Thus, citizens' rights can be extended to foreigners who have resided for a long time in some European States.[7] For example, some Nordic countries have changed the rule that only nationals have the right to vote. Sweden is the first country to grant foreign residents the right to vote in municipal elections in 1976 and this new rule was also adopted in Norway and Denmark.[8] In these countries, foreign residents have local voting rights that are part of the rights for nationals without having access to nationality. These foreigners that reside for a long-time in other countries are therefore considered resident citizens – *denizens* as called by Tomas Hammar – and possess substantial rights and privileges by their residence. These long-time foreign residents do then not need to apply for the nationality of the State where they reside, especially if they have to lose their original nationality through naturalization. In this situation, citizenship is associated not only with nationality but also with residence. Thus, this citizenship of residence is a new concept which can be applied to European citizenship

---

[7] Soysal, Y., *Limits of Citizenship*, Chicago, The University Chicago Press, 1994.
[8] Back, H., Hammar, T., Malmstrom, C., Soininen, M., "La participation électorale des immigrés en Suède", in Le Cour Grandmaison, O., Wihtol de Wenden, C. (eds.), *Les étrangers dans la cité. Expériences européennes*, Paris, La Découverte, 1993, pp. 121–131.

because the latter is recognized by the nationals of Member States and granted to people in the Member States where they reside even if they do not acquire the nationality of that country.

Third, European citizenship allows to be extended, under certain circumstances, to Third Country Nationals (TCNs). As mentioned above, the "Citizenship Directive" has recognized the freedom to mobility and residence in the EU for all economically active and inactive European citizens and for their family members, regardless of whether the latter are Europeans or non-Europeans. European social rights are also based on the principles of non-discrimination by nationality and can be granted to family members of EU citizens. The EHIC is therefore issued to people from non-EU countries who are legally residing in the EU and are covered by a Member State social security scheme[9]. This extension of European citizenship is allowed by "modernized coordination" to legal residents of TCN in the EU and in a cross-border situation. EU citizen family members and survivors are also covered if they are in the EU[10]. Thus, people benefitting from European citizenship have a tendency to dissociate from nationals of EU Member States and to be based on residence in the EU. In principle, the extension of the status of European citizenship to non-EU nationals could also be applied to political rights. Thus, EU non-nationals could have the local voting right in the country of their residence because of European citizenship, without having the nationality of that State. However, EU Member States show resistance to this logic. In France, for example, non-EU citizens do not have the rights of local or national votes even if they reside for long-term stays. The French right to vote is strongly linked to nationals and only extended in 1994 to European citizens by the Directive 94/80 on local elections, without extending it to non-Europeans. For this reason, one can say that within the EU, there exists still some national power of discretion for the decision on political rights. In comparison to the rights of free movement and social security that all Member States extend to family members of European citizens and legal residents regardless of their nationality, the right to vote is still limited to nationals of European Member States.

---

[9] However, nationals from non-EU countries cannot use their EHIC for medical treatment in Denmark, Iceland, Liechtenstein, Norway and Switzerland.

[10] European Parliament and Council, Regulation (EU) No. 1231/2010, 24.11.2010, *Official Journal of the European Union*, 29.12.2010. It does not apply to Denmark or the United Kingdom.

In sum, we can see that European citizenship is an enlarged concept with regard to national citizenship. According to T. H. Marshall[11], citizenship is composed of civil, political, and social elements and these three elements are gradually obtained by the nationals. However, the analysis of the European citizenship shows that some of the rights of European citizenship exceed the national citizens' rights and are extended to non-Europeans, so that European citizenship is different from Marshall's interpretation of national citizenship.

Effects of Brexit on European Citizens: Who Is at Risk?

European citizenship has expanded the beneficiaries of rights, but withdrawing from the UK will lead to a loss of citizenship. Three type of people are affected by Brexit and most at risk of a loss or "downgrading" of citizenship rights following Brexit: UK nationals currently residing in another EU Member State (group 1); EU nationals currently residing in the UK (group 2) and UK nationals living in the UK (group 3).[12]

Group 1 faces, along with European citizenship, losing the right to remain in their country of residence. Those who have European citizen family members can rely on the "Citizenship Directive", but those who do not, may have to seek a TCN long-term residence permit. On the contrary, people in group 2 who have "been amply considered in political and legal debates"[13] will find themselves with an uncertain status following Brexit. If these people in group 2 wish to remain in the UK in the long term, they may be forced to naturalize, due to absent adequate safeguards in the Withdrawal Agreement. But if their country of origin does not allow dual nationality, this would entail giving up their initial nationality, together with their European citizenship[14]. Finally, group 3 is in opposition to the majority who voted to leave the EU: this group is composed of voters who want to remain in the EU.[15]

---

[11] Marshall, T. H., Bottomore, T., *Citizenship and Social Class*, Tokyo, Horitsu Bunkasha, 1992 (in Japanese).
[12] European Citizen Action Service, "Brexit and Loss of EU Citizenship: Cases, Options, Perceptions", Brussels, Citizen Brexit Observatory, 2017.
[13] ECAS, *ibid.*, p. 5.
[14] ECAS, *ibid.*, pp. 5–6.
[15] ECAS, *ibid.*, p. 6.

Within group 1, there are two categories among UK nationals living in another Member State of the EU: group 1 A voted in the referendum and group 1 B could not vote in the referendum because of a long absence from the UK, even if this person wanted to cast their vote. Some UK nationals living abroad were unable to vote in the 2016 referendum because they were under the age of 18. These young people will nonetheless lose the opportunity to exercise their European citizenship rights. However, most group 1 B people who did not vote had their voting rights lost due to living abroad for long periods of time. According to the UK government, people moving or living abroad can register as an overseas voter for up to 15 years after leaving the UK, as long as they are British or eligible Irish citizens and registered to vote in the UK within the previous 15 years.[16] If not registered to vote in the UK within the previous 15 years, these people lose their voting rights, including those for the Brexit referendum: 700,000 British were estimated to be in this group during the referendum of 2016[17] among over 5.6 million British citizens living abroad.[18] Thus, 12.5 % of UK nationals living abroad could not vote in this referendum although it is decisive for their future as they will lose their citizenship status following Brexit, not only losing their political rights to vote at local elections as European citizens, but also limiting their national political rights as British citizens. Thus, they will lose political rights to all elections in the UK even if they are UK nationals, as well as in the country of residence which does not allow any voting rights to foreigners.

It therefore appears that UK nationals living abroad are the most at risk among the three groups, because they are deprived of their voting rights. (See Table 1).

This is also the case for UK nationals in France. French electoral laws allow European citizens to have voting rights for only local and European elections because of European citizenship, but not for national elections. Moreover, they do not allow non-European migrants any political rights in France, because of the principal of national sovereignty. If the UK does find an agreement with the EU,

---

[16] https://www.gov.uk/voting-when-abroad (30.4.2019).

[17] "I was one of the 700,000 British people denied a vote in the first EU referendum – that's why we need another Brexit vote", *The Independent*, 8.8.2018 (30.4.2019).

[18] The British Irish Chamber of Commerce, "British abroad voting in Brexit" (30.4.2019).

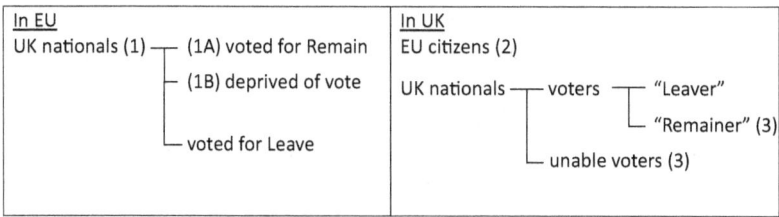

Table 1 of groups at risk as a result of Brexit

UK nationals living in France could no longer be European citizens, thus they would be treated as migrants of TCN. Therefore, we focus on UK nationals living in France as the group most at risk among the three groups above and evaluate their situation and rights in France after the referendum of 2016.

UK Nationals Living in France

A Picture of UK Nationals Living in France

There are 4.4 million foreigners living in France, 1.49 million of whom are from EU countries.[19] Thus, a third of foreigners living in France are European citizens. Among those Europeans, there are 152,000 British residents, as well as Spaniards, the fourth most abundant group after the Portuguese and Italians.

In terms of migration flows, British citizens who come to France have been increasing since the 2000s. Despite the total number of entrants dropping after 11 September 2001, the British alone made up more than 12.9 % of the share of entrants in 2002 and more than 33.8 % in 2003. Thus, in the period between 2001 and 2003, while other Europeans in France were decreasing in abundance, British people entering France doubled. Since 2004, more than half of the people that have moved to France were born in the UK, Portugal or Spain.[20] Like the Germans and Dutch, British people residing in France for more than a

---

[19] INSEE, Répartition des étrangers par nationalité en 2015.
[20] INSEE, "Les immigrés récemment arrivés en France", INSEE première, No.1524, 2014.

year are primarily in the country for pleasure and not for work. In 2012, more than 70 % of Portuguese and Spanish Europeans entering France claimed to hold a job, while only 45 % of British people say they were in employment.[21] More than half of the British immigrants coming to France have immigrated there for pleasure. Since visitors include those who are economically inactive, the British people moving to France are generally retired and pensioners.[22] Indeed, the average age of British immigrants in France is statistically higher than those immigrating from other countries. For example, the average age of immigrants from Europe to France lies between the age of 19 and 40, while one in four of the British immigrants is over the age of 56.[23]

Compared to the other Europeans, the residential place of the British is quite unique. Most immigrants live in or near large cities because they come to work. For example, the Portuguese, who are the most populated among European nationalities, massively came to France between 1960 and 1975. They worked in construction sectors and car industries, so they concentrated in Île-de-France (Paris and this region) and Rhone-Alpes (Lyon and this region).[24] However, British people living in rural areas are scattered. The region that welcomes the most British immigrants is Nouvelle-Aquitaine[25] (26 %), before Occitanie[26] (17 %) and Île-de-France (13 %).[27] Thus, the British prefer the southern region of France to the Paris region, where also many Portuguese live. The following map illustrates the geographical situation of the French regions.

---

[21] *Ibid.*

[22] Régnard, C., *Immigration et présence étrangère en France 2003*, Rapport annuel de la Direction de la population et des migrations, Paris, La Documentation française, 2005.

[23] INSEE, *op. cit.*, 2014.

[24] De Portugal Branco, J., "Évolution des caractéristiques et des conditions de vie au Portugal", Polycopie, 1998, pp. 91–129; Suzuki, N., *EU Citizenship to Shimin Ishiki no Dotai*, Tokyo, Keio University Press, 2007 (in Japanese).

[25] Nouvelle-Aquitaine is a new administrative regions, which was merged of three old regions (Aquitaine, Limousin and Poitou-Charentes), by the French law concerning the territorial reform, la loi n° 2015-29 du 16 janvier 2015 relative à la délimitation des régions, aux élections régionales et départementales et modifiant le calendrier électoral.

[26] Occitanie was also created of the old regions of south, Languedoc-Roussillon and Midi-Pyrénées, by the territorial reform of 2015.

[27] INSEE, "Flash, Nouvelle-Aquitaine", No. 28, 2017.

Map of French Regions[28]

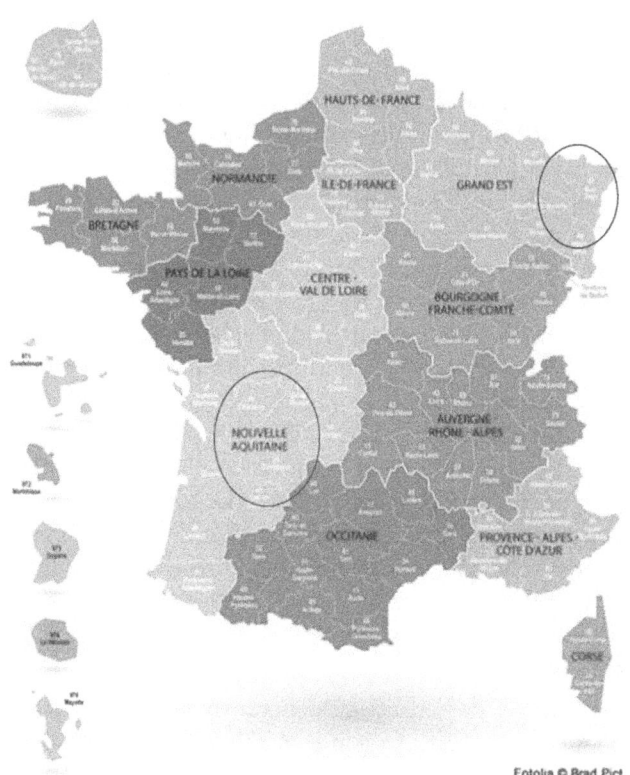

Fotolia © Brad Pict

UK Nationals in the Nouvelle-Aquitaine

The region Nouvelle-Aquitaine, situated in the south-west of France, has a historical link with the UK. The town Bergerac in the department of Dordogne has indeed been under British rule for about 300 years from the middle of the 12th century, via the centenary war, until 1450.[29] However, despite these historical and resulting cultural ties, the massive

---

[28] Source: Fotolia Brad Pict.
[29] Labroue, E., *Bergerac sous les Anglais*, Cressé, Éditions des régionalismes, 2004/2010.

settlement of the British and their economic activities has only occurred recently.

According to a study conducted by the French regional statistics Office INSEE in 2017[30], only 840 British lived in this region in 1968 (two British per ten thousand inhabitants on the region), but they settled intensively from 1999 onwards and they numbered 39,000 residents in 2014. This means that 50 times more British resided there than in 1968. The migration of British residents to this region has increased sharply in the last 20 years and now they constitute the second foreign nationality after Portuguese and a quarter of the British living in France. Exceptionally in Poitou-Charente, the former region of Nouvelle-Aquitaine, the British were already the most numerous to live, about twice as many as the Portuguese in 2009. The number of British immigrants was about 13,000 compared to the total foreign population of 41,300, especially in the departments of Charente where 5000 British residents lived.[31] Therefore, the region of Nouvelle-Aquitaine is the place where most British people are living in France and people call them "Dordogneshire".[32] Regarding the settlement of British people living in Nouvelle-Aquitaine, they are quite scattered. They are more numerous in the municipalities of the departments of Charente and Dordogne. Also, the British population is high along these departmental borders. And, most British residents own their homes.[33]

In terms of age, the British residents in Nouvelle-Aquitaine are on average 52 years old, half of them over the age of 58, and most often 65 years old. When compared to the total population of the region, the British are mostly retired. This region attracts an increasingly aging population that settles for retirement. This is contrary to the British in Hauts-de-France[34] who are economically active migrants.[35] This feature

---

[30] INSEE, *op. cit.*, 2017.
[31] INSEE, "Près de 13 000 Britanniques ont choisi de vivre en Poitou-Charentes", No. 3, 11.12.2009 (25.5.2019).
[32] "Brexit: suspense en Dordogneshire", *Le Point.fr*, 21.6.2016 (25.5.2019).
[33] INSEE, *op. cit.*, 2017.
[34] Hauts-de-France was also merged of the old regions of north, Nord-Pas-de-Calais and Picardie, by the territorial reform. This region is the closest region to the UK in France.
[35] INSEE, *op. cit.*, 2017.

of British immigrants who are elderly and retired is unique in Nouvelle-Aquitaine. Thus, our research will focus on this region, especially the departments of Charente and Dordogne.

Our Field Survey

Survey Method

We conducted a field research in Dordogne and Charente in August 2017 and March 2019. There is a commune of Dordogne, Eymet, where British residents represent about 10 % of the population. In order to be able to conduct a comparative approach, we also surveyed in the city of Strasbourg, in the eastern part of France, in March 2017. The city of Strasbourg is called "the Capital of Europe" because the Council of Europe and the European Parliament are in this city.

We used semi-structured interviews totalling 10 UK nationals. Among them were four people living at a municipality of Dordogne (Eymet) and two municipalities of Charente (Cognac and Nercillac), who were interviewed twice, one year after the referendum and just before the scheduled date of the EU withdrawal. This was done in order to know if they changed their opinions or attitudes. The other UK nationals work or used to work for European institutions in Strasbourg.

In comparison to these two groups of UK nationals, the first group came to France in order to live freely and independently of their State, because they have the rights of living and working as European citizen. The second group came to France in order to work in European institutions as representatives of their Member State, so they are dependent on their State and nationality.

We asked them three questions: First: Did they vote in the referendum about the exit of the UK in 2016?; second: What is their reaction to Brexit?; and third: What effect and what concern did this result have? We will analyse their answers to clarify the Brexit effect on the UK nationals and their perception of citizenship.

Exercise of Voting Rights

Among the people we interviewed, only three British voted at the referendum. The other British residents did not vote, although they wanted to. These people could not vote because of the long duration of their residence abroad in France. In 2015, the EU Referendum Act was enacted in the UK which stated that UK nationals residing abroad for more than 15 years would lose the right to vote. One of these persons we interviewed who was working for a European institution had voted for the legislative elections in 2002, but he could not vote at the referendum because he had been residing in France for 28 years. He was very disappointed that he could not vote in the referendum but he wanted to vote for remain.[36]

On average, the people we interviewed had been abroad for 26 years, thus their right to vote was taken away due to the EU Referendum Act. Therefore, despite wanting to vote in the 2016 referendum, they were deprived of this right. Only one interviewee was able to vote, notwithstanding his residing abroad for 24 years, because he had an office in the UK and paid taxes for this building until 2004. As it was 12 years before the referendum, he could vote in 2016, although next time he will lose this right.[37]

For the international civil servant, there is a specific reason concerning their status and the deprivation of voting rights. One retired man could not vote in the referendum of 2016 because he stayed in France for over 30 years. During this time, he received a salary and now receives a pension from the European institution and had not paid income tax in the UK. If he had paid income tax in the UK, he would have been able to vote. "No taxation without representation" – he did not agree with the fact that the British government does not give the British living abroad the right to vote.[38] On the other hand, one of the British interviewees living in France for more than 15 years as a winegrower and who could also not vote for the referendum, found that this deprivation of voting rights for people not living for a long time or paying taxes in the UK was rather normal.[39] And, finally, a British woman whose husband is French and who has a son studying in Scotland told us that her son has dual citizenship and wanted to vote for the referendum in Scotland, but that

---

[36] Interview on 2.3.2017 at Strasbourg.
[37] Interview on 30.3.2017 at Strasbourg.
[38] Interview on 31.3.2017 at Strasbourg.
[39] Interview on 31.8.2017 at Eymet.

he could not because he missed the voting age by some months. He was disappointed.[40]

Dissatisfaction with the Result of Brexit

Our interviewees generally deplored the results of the referendum. They not only complained that it was impossible or difficult to vote for them, even though this referendum is very important for UK nationals living in the EU. But they also wanted to retain their European citizenship which guarantees them their European rights in their country of residence. They took advantage of European rights as European citizens – a majority of the people questioned exercised their right to vote in the local elections in France and some of them were even elected as local councillors in France.

The rights of European citizens to benefit from medical services were also of great concern to them, especially the elderly. A retiree said he could receive these services almost free in France like the French, while it was expensive in the UK. The result of the referendum was therefore a problem directly related to the daily life of the UK nationals in France.[41] A retired British couple was extremely worried about the economic impact on their life since the result of Brexit. They said that the 20 % decline in the pound sterling (from 1.30 euro to 1.08 euro) had a significant impact on their daily lives, especially for them living on their pension.[42]

Brexit was a very important issue for all our interviewees' lives and none of them were happy about it. The British councillor in France said that he was "disappointed, demoralized, defeated, and confused", when he heard the result. He was very upset that he did not have dual citizenship and could not run for mayor without taking the French nationality. That is why, before the referendum, he had already intended to apply for French nationality because he just wished to continue his integration in France and to obtain the right to vote in elections other than local, but now he felt "obliged" to do so. By avoiding the loss of his current rights, he thought of asking for the

---

[40] Interview on 30.3.2017 at Strasbourg.
[41] Interview on 31.3.2017 at Strasbourg.
[42] Interview on 30.8.2017 at Charente.

nationality of the State of residence. But still, he hesitated because the process is very long.[43]

Applying for French Nationality

Since the Brexit result, British nationals are increasingly asking for citizenship of their State of residence. Most of our interviewees thought to apply for French nationality. Most of the respondents thought they would apply for French nationality, although half of them working in the European institutions are closely linked to the UK. One woman thought it was "necessary" because she felt European more than British now. Before the referendum, she had not thought of French nationality, because she had married a Frenchman and could live in France and vote in local and European elections through European citizenship. But after this result, she deemed it necessary, because she would lose her political rights even if she continued to live and work in France.[44]

Some of our interviewees had already applied for naturalization after the result of Brexit. One person said that he had applied for naturalization because of Brexit. And he answered that the reason for thinking about naturalization was to have "stability" in order to be able to stay in France without worry.[45] He believed this, although he was able to vote in the referendum as a European citizen, because his period of residence in France was only 14 years. So, after about a year and half of administrative procedures, he and his partner have been naturalized French. They got a French passport and their French birth certificates. They were feeling more secure in their live in France, especially when Brexit happened.[46]

A British councillor in France began the process of naturalization in November 2017. This was his third request, because his last two requests were not completed due to the collection of documents being insufficient and complicated. This was why he gave up originally, but this time the file was accepted. Now, he was waiting for the result. He decided to apply for French nationality because he had lived in France for 28 years. His wife was French and he could live and work without problems because

---

[43] Interview on 30.3.2017 at Strasbourg.
[44] Interview on 30.3.2017 at Strasbourg.
[45] Interview on 30.8.2017 at Charente.
[46] Interview on 8.3.2019 at Charente.

he was a European citizen. He had therefore not seriously considered naturalizing French before Brexit but now he wished that he could vote in the UK referendum, and also when there were national elections in France. And he wanted to continue to be able to participate in local life: until now, European citizenship had allowed him to vote in local elections, but, after Brexit, he did not know if he could remain a local councillor. At our meeting, he insisted, that he should keep the right to remain a local councillor and that he would support the polling station in national and European elections, even if he did not have the right to vote. He felt frustrated by this situation.[47] Where does this frustration come from?

Consideration of Nationality and Citizenship

We learned from Brexit that British nationality no longer granted British residents living abroad the political rights of the State of their nationality. This is because UK nationals living abroad for over fifteen years could not participate in the referendum in the UK or in the State of their residence. Also, they would lose their European citizenship because the UK is no longer a Member State of the EU. So, UK nationals will lose their rights to freely travel, live and work in the EU despite their integration into the community of their host country. To compensate for the gap between their nationality and their citizenship, some of them have applied for naturalization.

In theory, it is not necessary to naturalize, but rather to have a residential permit. For the moment, it is not necessary because the UK nationals have the European residence card, but some have already asked for the national security card if Brexit happens.[48] The French government has for its part prepared the rules for Brexit: according to the Ministry of the Interior[49], UK nationals present in France before 31 December 2020 will have to apply for the new title provided in the Withdrawal Agreement between the UK and the EU. With the agreement, UK nationals will be

---

[47] Interview on 7.3.2019 at Eymet.
[48] Interview on 7.3.2019 at Eymet.
[49] Interieur.gouv.fr, "Le ministère de l'intérieur se prépare au Brexit", https://www.interieur.gouv.fr/Actualites/Le-ministere-de-l-Interieur-se-prepare-au-Brexit/Sejour (4.5.2019).

treated under the same criteria as EU nationals for the recognition of the right of residence.[50] Without the agreement, UK nationals residing regularly for more than 5 years in France before the date of withdrawal would only have access to a resident card.[51] But, in the case of their residence in France for less than 5 years, they may apply for a residence permit of EU law depending on their situation of economically activity or inactivity in France. Thus, it will be much easier for British residents with the UK adopting the Withdrawal Agreement because the British residents will then be treated as EU citizens like now.

Following the Withdrawal Agreement signed on 24 January 2020, there is also a possibility for UK nationals it to continue their professional activity in France. With the agreement, UK nationals who started their professional activity in France before 31 December 2020 will not need a work permit. However, even with the agreement being accepted, UK nationals arriving in France after the date of withdrawal now must obtain a work permit.[52] Still, compared to these two conditions regarding the working permit, the agreement brings more advantage and freedom for many British residents. Without the agreement, they would have needed to apply for a residence card to exercise their right to work. This means the same status as TCNs.

With these considerations, we assume that the British living and working in France are not pleased with Brexit but are relieved that the Withdrawal Agreement has been signed, because they will not have to give up their status as European citizens and become TCNs. To avoid the loss of their acquisition rights, some of them have however already requested a residence card to ensure legal residence in France, while others apply for naturalization for greater stability.

---

[50] By these criteria, British nationals must prove one of their following situations: to have a professional activity, to have sufficient resources for themselves and their family, as well as health insurance, to study or take vocational training, to have a health insurance, or to be a family member of a British or European Union citizen living in France before 1.1.2021 and having a right of residence.

[51] This resident card issued in France will allow to live in France and to circulate in the other states of the Schengen area for periods not exceeding three months.

[52] Interieur.gouv.fr, *op. cit.*

Conclusion

The 2016 referendum which determined that the UK should exit the EU was very important for all UK nationals, but especially for those who live outside of the UK. This is because the result of Brexit is directly related to their lives and their political and social rights. Despite the importance of this referendum, most of the UK nationals living abroad could not vote because they have lived outside of their country for more than fifteen years. This long absence from the UK deprived them of their voting rights. And, once the UK exits the EU, they will lose the rights that European citizens had exercised previous to the Brexit decision. It is for this reason that they are dissatisfied with the result of Brexit. Because of this dissatisfaction, more than half of our interviewees have decided to apply for French nationality in order to have the stability of living in France. The withdrawal agreement which keeps certain of the European citizens' rights for certain British residents abroad does not change this general trend. One interviewee even clearly stated that she felt more European now than she felt British.

As regarding citizenship, one has to emphasize, however, that it is different from nationality; the first means the rights of the citizens, while the second means the membership of the State. In the case of the British observed in our field study, even if they have British nationality, with Brexit, they feel deprived of their rights, at the level of their State of nationality and at European level. Therefore, the British people living in the EU are seeking to maintain European citizenship in order to retain their citizenship rights, and if they cannot, they apply for the nationality of their country of residence. The tendency to apply for French nationality may also be attributed to the fact that the UK and France recognize multiple nationalities. In countries of residence that do not allow dual citizenship, different responses may be considered.

European citizenship has introduced a new concept that is dissociated from nationality and supports the idea of citizenship of residence. However, Brexit makes us reconsider the relationship between citizenship and nationality. Because UK nationals living abroad for over fifteen years lose some of their British citizens' rights and European citizenship, they ask for nationality of residence in order to obtain citizenship. Their citizenship does not dissociate nationality. Thus, the exit of the EU turns UK nationals living in the EU towards their "new" nationality: nationality of residence.

PART 3

THE ECONOMIC AND LEGAL CONSEQUENCES OF BREXIT

The "Real" Costs of Brexit

Emmanuel Brunet-Jailly

On 23 June 2016, Britain decided to leave the European Union (EU) in a referendum vote. Since then, the results have remained controversial for several reasons. First of all, the referendum revealed deep regional cleavages in opinions with regards to EU membership, as evidenced by the defeat of Brexit ideas in Scotland and Northern Ireland. Those were confirmed by the results of the last parliamentary elections in December 2019. Secondly, since the referendum, there is emerging evidence that several misleading claims were made by the Brexit campaign. As a result, many have asked for a second referendum or an election; a new election was held on 12 December 2019 and brought a large majority to the conservatives. Key misrepresentations of a number of important determining issues, including the cost of being in the EU and the cost of leaving the EU, remained under-explored. These form the core elements of this paper, which focuses on the costs of leaving the EU with a specific focus on the implementation of border infrastructures, staff, and necessary reforms across government offices necessary to implement UK custom borders.

Costs, obviously are varied and thus assessing costs is complex. Also, as discussed in this chapter polarized opinions on the overall Brexit costs led to toxic debates; There is however consensus among experts which guides our assessment; for instance at the end of 2019, it is important to acknowledge that all international financial institutions were predicting that Brexit will have (variable) but negative impacts on the British economy.[1] The estimates were "an output loss of between 5 and 8 percent in the World Trade Organization (WTO) scenario compared

---

[1] Arregui, N., Chen, J., "United Kingdom", Washington, International Monetary Fund, Country Report 18/317, 25.10.2018.

with non-Brexit scenarios."[2] Adding as well, "in a more benign Free Trade Agreement scenario, output falls by between 2.5 and 4 per cent relative to continued EU membership in the long run."[3] Such assessments have been confirmed by more specialised studies on Brexit and energy,[4] Brexit and tariff costs to the UK and EU trade regimes,[5] as well as Brexit and foreign investments[6]. "Economists for Brexit" disagree but "uncertainty" is agreed upon as the ineluctable negative factor impacting the British economy post Brexit by most economists.[7]

Indeed, economists around the world suggested two possible outcomes; both grim: First, the Free Trade Agreement outcome would lead to a shrinking of the UK Gross Domestic Product (GDP) by 3 % by 2020, then 1 % by 2025 and 2030. Second, the WTO "most favoured nation" type agreement would have pricier consequences with a reduction of the size of the UK economy by 5.5 % by 2020, then 4 % by 2025 and 3.5 % by 2030.[8] Also, WTO forecasts of trade relations becoming more difficult across the channel would lead to many less goods being exported, a reduction of minus 11 % to minus 7 % in exports from Britain and the rest of European Member States. Germany, the Netherlands, France and Ireland would be the countries most affected because these are the UK top four client-countries. In short, while 51.4 % of all UK export are going to the EU, those exports would be reduced year after year because of the likeliness of tariffs and quotas walls, or simply because of uncertainty. Clearly, the impact for EU Member States would also be

---

[2] *Ibid.*, p. 24.
[3] *Ibid.*
[4] Pollitt, M., "The economic consequences of Brexit: Energy", *Oxford Review of Economic Policy*, vol. 33/S1, 2017, pp. 134–143.
[5] Protts, J., *Potential Post-Brexit tariff costs for EU-UK trade*, London, Civitas, 2016.
[6] Dhingra, S., Ottaviano, G., Sampson, T., Van Reenen, J., "The Impact of Brexit on Foreign Investment in the UK", London, Center for Economic Performance, Paper Brexit 03, 2016.
[7] Minford, P., Gupta, S, Le, V. P. M., Mahambare, V., Xu, Y., *Should Britian Leave the EU? An Economic Analysis of a Troubled Relationship*, Cheltenham, Edward Elgar Pub, 2016. See also a critique of Minford, P. views in: Dhingra, S., Ottaviano, G., Sampson, T., Van Reenen, J., "Economists for Brexit: a Critique", London, Center for Economic Performance, Paper Brexit 03, 2016.
[8] Nabarro, B., Schulz, C., *UK Economic Outlook in Four Brexit Scenarios*, London, Institute for Fiscal Studies, 2019.

severe with exports to the UK being reduced by 5 to 15 % for Northern Ireland, with a pan EU average impact of about 6.6 %. In sum, it is not clear how much exiting the EU would cost the UK economy, but scenarios are generally not favourable to Brexit.[9]

This chapter starts with a critical review and discussion of the various Brexit arguments and a detailed analysis of the various costs considered during and after the referendum campaign: Was being a member of the EU expensive? Will the EU be able to survive a British exit, and should UK custom borders be decisional factors, in particular, because of the situation of Northern Ireland. In turn, the arguments presented in this paper are, first, that Brexit should not have been justified by costs of EU membership because it was the cheapest of all EU memberships; second, that Britain had extensive control over its migration borders and third that although it had limited control over its custom borders, those benefited the UK in the form of important economies of scales. Post Brexit, Britain will need to settle a separation bill, legal costs associated to separation and will also need a new custom policy, which is estimated in this paper at about 65 billion euros, including expanded infrastructures and staff, as well as internal reform across over 100 departments and agencies of the Crown, as well as new fiscal and staff costs to 180,000 small and medium enterprises. Also, immigration policies are likely to suffer from not being part of the EU intelligence and border enforcement cooperative institutions.

Section one of this chapter focuses on the pre-referendum arguments and section two looks at the post referendum discussion while answering three questions: First: What were the debates about costs and estimates before and after the Brexit referendum? Because being an EU member was argued to be expensive, fights over costs and estimates are debated in this chapter to try to answer the second question: What are the real costs to the EU and EU Member States? Can the EU afford to lose the UK as a Member State and can the UK afford to leave the EU? And, third: What are the Brexit implications for control over customs and immigration policies and ultimately their costs?

---

[9] Black, A., *"Hard Brexit", International Trade and WTO Scenario*, London, Federal Trust for education and research, 2017.

Pre-Referendum Cost Arguments

Building a strong European Union was Winston Churchill's idea, who stated, in 1946, that "we must build a kind of United States of Europe."[10] But full British membership was vetoed by French president Charles de Gaulle in 1963 when he opposed the UK joining the European Economic Community (EEC). A conservative Prime Minister, Harold Macmillan, launched the application process again in the early 1960s before the end of his Prime Ministership. However, De Gaulle's veto was renewed in 1967. It was only under Edward Heath's Prime Ministership, in 1973, that the UK joined the EEC. And, the UK position in the EEC was solidified in Britain thanks to the 1975 referendum whereby 67 % of the "yes" won the day. It was further hardened thanks to Margaret Thatcher's negotiation of a rebate[11] regarding a contention over the British financial contributions to the EEC's annual budget, and, many threats to suppress payments. Again, in 1993, Prime Minister John Major had to threaten resignation to see his country sign the Treaty of Maastricht. This treaty was foundational for the creation of the EU. However, it is notable that neither the 1975 referendum, nor the generally engaged position of British Prime Ministers such as John Major or Tony Blair, ever defeated a deep seated hard-core "Eurosceptic" group of Members of Parliament (MPs) found both among Labour and Tory back benchers.

In June 2016, once again Euro-sceptics, primarily found in the Conservative Party (Boris Johnson) and Nigel Farrage (a Member of the European Parliament (MEP) and leader of the United Kingdom Independence Party (UKIP)[12] argued that the EU was too oppressive and expensive a membership, while Tory Prime Minister David Cameron and the Labour party leader, both "unconvincing" pro-Europe leaders, defended the stay side of the campaign. Notably interesting is that, at the time of the campaign, nearly 51 % of the British electorate was convinced that the UK exit from the EU would have no significant effect of their lives or businesses, while 4 % thought it would be beneficial or

---

[10] Churchill made a direct reference to the "United States of Europe" on 19.9.1946 at the University of Zurich, Switzerland.

[11] Barker, A., "Margaret Thatcher's prised 'rebate' dragged into Brexit bill talks", *Financial Times*, 18.7.2017.

[12] United Kingdom Independence Party (UKIP), *Manifesto for Brexit and Beyond*, Bodmin, Printbridge.

strongly beneficial; only 35 % assumed that it would have a detrimental or strongly detrimental impact. The overarching theme of the campaigns was that Brexit was about sovereignty: European integration was a threat to British economic and political sovereignty, because important decisions were "not made in the UK anymore" (according to Michael Gove, then Minister of justice).[13] In Europe, the idea of a transnational state was not a good idea, as suggested by Boris Johnson: "Napoleon, Hitler, various people tried this out, and it ends tragically."[14] The remain side, however, may not have been convincing because, for instance, the EU President Donald Tusk suggested that the Union was the best protection against wars only; while David Cameron suggested that, although the EU was not necessarily an ever-closer Union, it was also "to secure prosperity."[15] On the economic front, issues of cost loomed high and where harshly debated: Ian Duncan Smith (former Minister of labour) and Boris Johnson (then former Mayor of London) both argued that membership had very high costs: Duncan Smith suggested payments of 350 million pounds weekly could go the UK health deficits and Johnson that control over Value Added Tax (VAT) would benefit UK business. Echoing Cameron, defenders of the Union suggested that exiting would be an economic disaster. For instance, Finance Minister Osborne submitted that GDP growth would drop by 3.4 to 9.5 % annually and that global loss of about 47 billion euros in trade should be expected. Although controversial, these figures have been corroborated now by a number of international organizations including the International Monetary Fund (IMF), the Bank of England and others.[16]

Above and beyond economic and trade issues, the main debate was about the cost of membership: The core issue presented by the Brexit side was that the UK paid more into the EU budget than it received, which is uncontested. Indeed, the UK, like most other larger EU national economies, paid more into the EU than it received. But the pro-Brexit

---

[13] Gove, M., "EU referendum: Michael Gove explains why Britain should leave the EU", *The Telegraph*, 20.2. 2016.
[14] Ross, T., "Boris Johnson: The EU wants a superstate, just like Hitler did", *The Telegraph*, 15.5.2016.
[15] David Cameron's EU speech – full text, *The Guardian*, 23.1.2013.
[16] Cappariello, R., "Brexit: estimating tariff costs for EU countries in a new trade regime with the UK", *Questioni di Economia e Finanza, Banca D'Italia Eurosystema*, vol. 381, 2017.

campaign argued that in 2015, the UK was paying 18 billion pounds into the EU annual budget. This did not include two important caveats: First, the UK paid 18 billion minus a 5 billion annual rebate negotiated by Margaret Thatcher in 1973; second, Britain received funds from the EU policies as well. In reality, Britain paid 18 billion minus five billion and minus the funds (about 5 billion again) coming from EU policies implemented in the UK. These two numbers are important. The first one is a 5 billion rebate. The second one is the amount spent by the EU in the UK. Both are controversial: For instance, when checking with the UK ministry of finance (Exchequer) the real figures are substantially different: in 2018 the UK had to pay 17.4 billion pounds into the EU budget but also received a 4.2 billion pounds rebate, which is automatic so the UK only paid 13.2 billion pounds. Also, the amount received back by the UK from the EU in 2018 was 4.3 billion pounds for both agriculture and for regional policies. And, it is notable that direct funds transferred to private entities such as businesses are not accounted for by the Exchequer because these do not transit through the UK Treasury, which make estimates more complicated; the European Commission notes an average of 6.63 billion euros being transferred to the UK annually between 2000 and 2018. In all, it was not 350 million per week as argued during the referendum campaign that was paid into the EU budget (or 18.2 billion pounds).[17]

Also, the Exchequer notes that such a budget allowed the UK to trade with all EU Member States; a relationship that accounts for a little over 50 % of all UK exports world-wide and for a trade figure in excess of 656 billion yearly. In sum, the UK paid into the EU about 9 billion pounds to facilitate trade in excess of 338 billion pounds annually. And, during the referendum campaign; the European Commission President, Jean-Claude Junker, attempted to redress those arguments but was not very successful. Some of his arguments suggested that Brexit would affect 100 billion in trade, including 36 Financial Times Stock Exchange (FTSE) businesses out of the top 100, and would also affect 3 million jobs in the British Isles. The latest parliamentary report published in 2019 confirmed this contribution to the EU of 8.9 billion pounds down from 17.4 billion VAT, Gross National Income (GNI) and custom receipts minus a rebate

---

[17] "The UK's EU membership fee", *The UK's Independent Fact Checking Charity*, 8.7.2019.

of 4.2 billion pounds, and the EU transfers to the UK for 4.3 billion pounds.[18]

These acrimonious debates expanded then into looking at alternative models of relations with the EU such as the Swiss or Norwegian relationships. Indeed, Norway is not a fully-fledged member of the EU. It is part of the European Economic Area (EEA)[19] and as such does not have full membership, which implies that the Norwegian-EU relationship is dictated by a large number of internal decisions of the Union. Also, Norway contributes about 1 billion euros per year to EEA Member States and the EU budget (391 million euros to the EEA, 447 million to the EU and 6 million to the Schengen cooperation).[20] Switzerland's option is also not so linear because it is a member of the European Free Trade Association (EFTA) but is not a member of the EEA, which means trading with EU Member States is less expansive and also bound to less protections, but it also includes Schengen. The Comprehensive Economic and Trade Agreement (CETA) signed with Canada was also a quickly dismissed option because of the lack of knowledge and understanding of the consequences of this Canada/EU free trade agreement on government procurements and agriculture products. Clearly, the last option may be the WTO – the worse option for the UK because such an option implies duties and quotas on both sides of the Channel and would cost the UK about as much as membership or about 2–5 % on all 335 billion per year trade done with the EU, or about 6.5 to 15 billion per year, which

---

[18] Keep, M., "The UK's contribution to the EU budget", London, House of Commons Library, Briefing Paper CBP 7886, 4.11.2019. The full report on this policy brief is at: https://researchbriefings.parliament.uk/ResearchBriefing/Summary/CBP-7886#fullreport (4.11.2019).

[19] The membership of the European Economic Area and the European Free Trade Association (EFTA) as Norwegians have would lead the UK to: retain access to the single market, contribute to the EU budget, Subject to EU standards and regulation, and acceptance of the EFTA court. A membership of the European Free Trade Association as Swiss do, would lead the UK to negotiate bilateral agreements governing the UK access to the single market on a sector to sector basis and to follow EU regulation in the sectors covered but would otherwise negotiate free trade agreements. A last model could be to have a relationship similar to Turkey; it is a custom union with the EU that is limited to trade in industrial and agricultural products. This is a custom union that would not apply to services. It would mean that the UK would have to comply with a significant portion of the EU trade policy.

[20] "Financial Contribution", Mission of Norway to the European Union, 1.3.2017, https://www.norway.no/en/missions/eu/areas-of-cooperation/financial-contribution/ (21.12.2019).

is 75 % to 150 % of the cost of EU membership in 2018; Thus trading globally has a cost, and being in the EU also has specific costs. In sum, neither options are much better than full membership in the EU with 'rebate'. But, what remains important then is understanding the nature of all other post-Brexit costs in details.

Pre-Referendum Arguments over Immigration and Costs

A second politically very important issue was about control over immigration. During the pre-referendum campaign, the UKIP party of Nigel Farage used immigration as a core issue to very successfully scare people about the risk of migrant waves moving into the UK. Posters suggesting a "Breaking Point" or "Out of Control or On the Move" suggested that the UK immigration and border policies were out of control and that the key culprit was a welcoming EU. UKIP posters stated "We must break free of the EU and take back control of our borders".[21] Clearly, poll and referendum results point to the effectiveness of this campaign. Unfortunately, there are no facts to back up anyone's fear that this fabricated idea of invasion was remotely close to reality.

In fact, Eurostat's data[22] on asylum and new asylum application for January to March 2015 indicates that the UK were only the seventh largest recipient of asylum applications in the EU then, with 7395 registered applicants. Hungary placed second, behind Germany with 32,810 applications (Germany tops the list with 73,135). They are followed by Italy, France, Sweden and Austria. Looking at the 2014 data is interesting for a comparative perspective on those numbers. The total amount of applications then was 630,000 for the year: with Germany processing 200,000 applications, Sweden 90,000, Italy 80,000, France 70,000, Hungary 40,000 and the UK 35,000. Similarly, looking at the 2013 data from Eurostat, the numbers place the UK fifth in the EU: Germany was topping the list with 76,165 applications, France received 61,715,

---

[21] Stewart, H., Mason, R., "Nigel Farage's anti-migrant poster reported to police", *The Guardian*, 16.6.2016.

[22] Eurostat, "Asylum Statistics: Asylum applications (non-EU) in the EU-27 Member States, 2008–2019", Statistics Explained, 2019. See also Eurostat, "Migration and migrant population statistics", Statistics Explained, 2019, https://ec.europa.eu/eurostat/statistics-explained/pdfscache/1275.pdf (4.7.2019).

Sweden 45,005, Italy 23,565 ad the UK 22,355, followed thereafter by Belgium, Austria, Switzerland, Holland and Greece. To put all figures in perspectives with a comparison outside the UK and the EU, in 2014, Canada accepted 285,000 new immigrants and processed many more applications. In relations to their relative size, Canada welcomed about 1 % of its total population as new migrants while the United Kingdom welcomed 0.05 %.

Because of the implication that there was potential for invasion (as suggested by Farage[23]), knowing where migrants to the UK come from is also very interesting: according to the UK Office for National Statistics, migrants of Chinese and Indian origin are the first two groups. They are followed by eight groups that are either Anglophone or from the EU.[24] Interestingly, as well, there are broadly speaking two very distinct groups of immigrants that are known to strengthen the UK economy. In 2014, these are, first, people applying successfully to work in the UK, i.e. 228,000, out of which a majority came from the EU and, second, the 177,000 people applying to study in the UK, where Universities are on the top of the world's list and extremely attractive because less expensive than in the United States.

Also important is the question: Are these migrants a burden on the UK economy? On the one hand, 1.25 million non-nationals settled in the UK since 2004 and 270,000 of those are EU nationals, hence growing the numbers of non-UK born residents / non-nationals to about 8 million by 2015. On the other hand, only 500,000 of those non-UK born 8 million are a burden on social and health benefits in the UK. Indeed, of the 5 million recipients, 90 % are UK citizens: the *Daily Telegraph* suggested that EU nationals cost 4 billion, while non-EU nationals cost 118 billion and UK born nationals cost 591 billion pounds in 2011.[25] Also, it is notable that 37,000 professors in the UK are from outside the UK as well as 70 % of all UK University registered graduate students.[26]

---

[23] Stewart, H., Mason, R., "Nigel Farage's anti migrant poster reported to police", *The Guardian*, 16.6.2016. Unison's Dave Prentis said poster showing a queue of migrants and refugees incites racial hatred.

[24] "Migration Statistics Quarterly Report May 2019", Office for National Statistics, 24.5.2019.

[25] "Immigration: the real cost – the fiscal effect of immigration 1995–2011", *The Telegraph*, 6.11.2014.

[26] "International Migration and the Education Sector: what does the current evidence show", Office for National Statistics, 8.5.2019.

In sum, immigration provides both costs and benefits to the UK economy. These are difficult to assess, however, with four different agencies having four different ways of measuring the positive or negative effects. The UK department of the Home Office actually underscores a net benefit to the UK economy of 2.5 billion pounds annually: it balances costs of migration in the amount of 28.8 billion being offset by nest fiscal contributions of 31.2 billion pounds annually. Two other institutes' research findings suggest marginally different results: the Institute for Public Policy Research[27] and the Migration Watch UK conclude that depending on years, between 2000 and 2004, net benefits vary between plus 1.9 billion to minus 5 billion pounds. In other words, what is important to our discussion is that those studies agree that the positive or negative impacts of migration are less than 1 % of the growth domestic product. But immigration costs had a determining impact on the referendum results as detailed below.

Referendum Results

The referendum results and subsequent election in the fall 2019, however, confirmed the electorate's will to exit the EU; the December 2019 elections confirmed the referendum results as well as the divide between Britain, Scotland and Northern Ireland, and the urban-rural voters split, and polarization between educated and less educated voters.

At the 2016 referendum 33,577,345 voted: 17,410,742 or 51.89 % in favour of Brexit (leave camp) while 16,141,241 or 48.11 % voted against (remain camps) and the rest cast invalid or blank votes. These numbers however, do not picture the results across the UK with equal accuracy because, in Northern Ireland and Scotland, about two third of the votes were against Brexit, with 62 % pro-remain and 38 % pro-leave in Scotland and 55.8 % pro-remain and 44.2 % pro-leave in Northern Ireland. In fact, Brexit also set the stage for a breakdown of common UK politics, when taking into account Britain's (53.4 %) and Wales' (52.5 %) majority in favour of leaving.

---

[27] Griffith, P., Morris, M., *An Immigration Strategy for the UK. Six Proposals to Manage Migration for Economic Success*, IPPR, 2017. See also Migration Watch for a contrary view: https://www.migrationwatchuk.org/briefing-papers/category/2 (4.11. 2019).

When looking inside the demographics of the polls, it is also striking that urban, educated and young voted to remain (57 % with a university degree, 64 % with higher education (4 or 5 years), 81 % in the education sector, 67 % Asian, 73 % Black, 70 % Muslim), while rural, less educated and older voted to leave (60 % White, unemployed, 66 % retired). For instance, 73 % of voters under the age of 24 voted to stay while 60 %, aged 65 or older voted to leave. Similarly, most of Britain's urban regions voted to stay with London being overwhelmingly in favour of the remain side, with just over 2/3 of the votes being remain.[28]

Confirming those trends, the election of December 2019 gave Prime Minister, Boris Johnson a firm and rare majority of 365 seats out of the 650 seats in the House of Parliament. Yet, notably in Scotland, the Scottish National Party won 13 additional seats or 48 out of the 59 available seats, whereas in Northern Ireland, the Democratic Unionist Party lost two seats (from 10 to 8). In sum, immigration and immigration costs had a determining impact on votes for Brexit.

Brexit and Ongoing Negotiation over Cost Issues with the European Commission and EU Member States

In February 2017, Theresa May had gone to Italy to present the British Brexit plan. Her proposal stood on twelve points:

> to provide a process, to control UK laws, to strengthen the relationships between Northern Ireland, Scotland, Wales and Britain, and the European Union. To maintain the common travel area with Ireland, to control migration; to protect the rights of British nationals in the EU and of EU nationals in Britain; to align workers' rights; to trade freely with the EU and to expand trade agreements with other; to support science and innovation; yo keep cooperation on terrorism with the EU and to guaranty a peaceful and orderly Brexit.[29]

She suggested focusing parliamentary efforts on legalising EU regulations and to exit EU dispute resolution systems to rely on private ones. She acknowledged having to settle the separation (also called

---

[28] "EU Referendum in full", *BBC NEWS*, https://www.bbc.com/news/politics/eu_referendum/results (13.7.2019).

[29] Dominiczak, P., Wilkinson, M., "The 12-point Brexit plan explained: Theresa May warn EU she will walk away from a 'bad deal' for Britain", *The Telegraph*, 17.1.2017.

"divorce") bill first but also pointed to what was encouraging outcomes when she suggested that the best systems of two worlds would emerge, with, for instance, the EU custom union being phased out for selective custom unions in the areas where they serve best (automobile and pharmaceuticals). Indeed, the costs she envisioned included having to settle for all the divorce bill and shared programmes in the amount of about 20 to 40 billion euros and savings from the EU contribution of about 8 billion euros yearly.

At the time, both the legal and separation bills were underestimated because Theresa May hoped to separate in under 24 months of a phased process which would result for the UK in either a good deal or no deal. This would allow the UK to lower corporate tax rates to 17 %, resulting in market share expansion and loss of regulatory constraints and a new economic model of freer trade with much less regulations and taxation. Indeed, a no deal Brexit, then was assumed to lead to a lowering of business taxes on EU markets. In her speech, a number of uncertainties were identified by the media: there was, for example, no mention of collaborations on foreign and security matter or terrorism and crime. For the rest, the UK would make all the EU "*acquis communautaire*" UK law, but would then take the time to review them one by one. The UK would leave the Single market by nationalizing it, and, in case of disputes, a free trade agreement dispute resolution system would provide arbitration, not EU law. Also, the UK would agree to a series of custom agreements but would leave the custom union, hence focusing its efforts on those few UK industries that were particularly Europeanised such as Pharmaceuticals and Automobile. This is a model both Norway and Sweden relied upon when negotiating with the EU. Also, the budget payments were assumed to stop because they would no longer be part of the EU and in particular the Single market.

Pro-Brexit commentators noted that this was likely going to result in a deficit in the EU budget of 9 billion euros per year, that the EU may still require some forms of payments similar to Norway's. Also, there would be a significant impact on the EU budget because the UK was one of the largest economies in the EU and because it was a net contributor to the EU budget. This led to a controversy about the size of this net annual contribution to the EU budget, and the public rediscovery that the UK was the only of 28 Member States to benefit from a rebate of about 5 billion euros per annual budget. Indeed, that rebate had been negotiated by Margaret Thatcher when Prime Minister. Also, the exact contribution of the EU to the UK was somewhat controversial because it would impact the so called "divorce" settlement, both in terms of financial obligations and legal costs, because each item of negotiation also led to a new financial obligation; as early as in 2017, it was clear though that the "divorce" settlement included payment obligations that had already been agreed upon as far ahead of time as 2028.[30] The House of Commons summarised the settlement components in three chapters of expenditures: one is the UK contribution to the EU annual budget until 2020 amounting to 10.9 billion pounds; two are liabilities running for 2021–2028 amounting to 19.6 billion pounds, and third are other liabilities (2.3 billion pounds), all adding up to a total amount of 32.8 billion pounds.[31] In estimates of August 2019, the *Financial Times* of London was reporting Boris Johnson's threat that, in the case of a "no deal" Brexit, the UK would refuse to pay 39-billion-euros separation bill.[32]

When looking at the impact of the Brexit on the EU, a counter intuitive finding was that a small number of EU Member States would actually benefit financially from the Brexit because their share of the EU cost would come down: the annual contribution to the EU budget of Bulgaria, Greece, Latvia and the Netherlands are thus expected to drop between 4.3 % and 9 % (Netherlands and Latvia).[33] Indeed, when the UK contribution is brought down to "0", the EU budget will be impacted: the biggest impact is on Germany and France, which will have to pay respectively 9 % and 4 % more per year into the EU budget (or 2.56 and 1.5 billion euros each). On the contrary, the UK gains are forecasted to stand at about 7 billion euros per year but this scenario may be a *mirage* because if WTO tariffs[34] come into force, a worst case scenario, tariffs would bring current average tariffs with the EU of 2.8 % for instance on agricultural product to much higher tariffs, for instance

---

[30] Keep, M., "Brexit: the financial settlement", London, House of Commons Library, Briefing Paper Number 8039, 22.10.2019.
[31] *Ibid.*
[32] Payne, S., Peel, M., Blitz, J., "UK will refuse to pay 39bn divorce bill in no-deal Brexit", *Financial Times*, 26.8.2019.
[33] Nuñez Ferrer, J., Rinaldi, D., "The Impact of Brexit on the EU Budget: A Non-Catastrophic Event", Brussels, Centre for European Policy Studies, Policy Brief, No. 347, 7.9.2016, p. 4.
[34] Morris, C., "Brexit: What is the 'no deal' WTO option?", *BBC News*, 29.7.2019.

35 % for dairy products, 24 % for jams, jellies and marmalades, 9.6 % for onions, 8 % for peas, and manufacturing would also increase to 10 % for cars.

Other options such as having access to the EU market through a European Economic Area (EEA) status, similar to Norway, would have a cost estimated at about 8 billion euros per year, suggesting that savings of 7 billion may not be possible at all: indeed, UK the independent fact checking *Full Fact* showed that the per capita cost of Norwegian membership was 140 euros per year while UK's was 220 euros per capita.[35] Assuming a similar partnership would cost the UK 140 euros per capita, totals at about 9 billion per year, a cost similar to EU membership including both the "rebate" and EU Commission policies expenditures in the UK.

In sum, a WTO status or a customised custom union similar to Norway, or EEA membership, or even a specific tailored agreement, all have costs ranging from several billion more than EU membership without "rebate". In the end, it seems that the mathematics of real gains are very limited.

Those figures also impact the particularly important political case of Northern Ireland, which, as of November 2019 has been set to be a continuous full-stop – and not back-stop in the Irish Sea – means a full integration of Northern Ireland in the EU market for the next four to eight years with changes only possible with a vote from the Stormont Assembly.[36] This Boris Johnson compromise is very important decision because although the primary markets of the British economy are the EU Member States, the dependency for Northern Ireland is much higher, with over 65 % of all sales going to the EU through the Republic of Ireland. This dependency is at its highest in the case of Northern Irish agri-food products (farming and agri-food industries) because exports to the EU account for 62.3 % or about 3.599 billion euros per year in a context where Northern Ireland's agri-food products receive EU regional

---

[35] McKinney, C. J., "Norway's EU payments", *The UK's Independent Fact Checking Charity*, 4.8.2019.

[36] The "Stormont assembly" is the legislative body of Northern Ireland – it is the Parliament Building of the Northern Ireland Assembly, which is located on the Stormont estate area of Belfast. The seat of the executive is located in the Stormont Castle. Details are available at: "Brexit: MPs pass withdrawal agreement bill by 124 majority", *The Guardian*, 20.12.2019.

development subsidies as high as 87 pence to a pound earned by a farmer. Also, it is notable that for the period of 2014–2020, Northern Ireland was a recipient of EU funds in areas such as agriculture (2.229 billion euros per year), rural development (227 million euros), fisheries (24 million euros), Peace programmes (229 million euros), Interreg programmes (240 million euros) and European Social and Regional Development fund programmes (491 million euros). In all, post Brexit, agriculture and Peace programmes in Northern Ireland could have been losing access to about 3.5 billion euros in funding. This is now alleviated. In sum, Boris Johnson's proposal to keep Northern Ireland inside the EU for at least four years post Brexit is possibly, politically, and from a cost perspective, a good political and economic solution for Northern Ireland, the Republic of Ireland, the UK and the EU.[37]

Post Brexit Costs: New Custom Borders and Border Infrastructures

In 2019, the British civil service was the smallest it has ever been since 1945. It has shrunk, losing staff in many areas, yet because of Brexit it may have to grow again because Britain's membership to the EU includes important economies of scales in the area of customs, in particular, in maritime trade. Staying inside the EU customs union may have been a better option, because all in all the UK deals about 55 million custom declarations yearly, but post Brexit it will have to deal with 200 million more, i.e. 255 million per year. Those new post Brexit declarations will include 200 million having to be filed by businesses that never had to file one before, i.e. since the entry of the Britain in the EEC in 1973. A Parliamentary report indicates that the economies of scales resulting for EU custom dealers being in the Netherlands or Denmark will not be available and reveals a need for 3000 up to 5000 new staff in custom. Also, a new relationship with the EU means new custom relationships as well; which suggests applying rules of origins that are much more onerous for the 180,000 small and medium size businesses trading with customers

---

[37] "Northern Ireland Protocol: Unfettered access to the UKIM", HM Treasury, 2019, https://www.politico.eu/wp-content/uploads/2019/12/LSRFUR-slides.pdf (21.12.2019); Osborne, H., "Can Boris Johnson's Brexit deal avoid a border in the Irish Sea?", *The Guardian*, 6.12.2019.

and clients in the EU. The lack of port and harbour infrastructures is also underscored and estimated at the cost of about 39 billion euros.[38]

Also, many government department and agencies will have to adapt to the new custom environment and new systems of rules and processes. Prior to Brexit, rules were EU rules and thus implemented trade borders away from the boundary lines such as enforcing rules and regulations, inspections and issuing licences, but also registering businesses across the EU on behalf of UK traders. Post Brexit it is estimated that in all thirteen government departments and agencies would have to adapt to a work load five time larger than prior Brexit. In all, this concerns about 100 local authorities, agencies across the public sector from revenue and custom to horticultural marketing inspectorate, from border force to over 100 port health authorities across the UK that will have to adapt to a new regulatory environment and a much larger clientele.[39]

In 2015, the UK was equipped to deal with 6 million custom declarations in the UK while 49 million were dealt with on the continent through brokers and agents, freight operators and transportation agencies. Post Brexit, Information Technology (IT) custom declaration (also called maximum facilitation or "mac fac") may help but there are about 180,000 businesses that are affected and a lot of those are small and medium sized traders, who will need to modernise in order to face the reform. Interestingly, the House of Lord also published a report on the impact of customs onto small and medium size businesses: it estimated that "if custom declarations were introduced between UK and the EU, there would be between 17 billion and 20 billion pounds of administrative cost per year."[40] Although 20 billion pounds is a large number, what is most worrisome for small and medium sized businesses is that Jürgen Maier, UK chief executive for Siemens suggested it would cost much

---

[38] "Brexit: the customs challenge – 20th Report of Session 2017–19", London, European Union Committee, House of Lords, 2018; "Contingency preparations for exiting the EU with no deal", Cabinet Office, Civil Contingencies Secretariat, 12.3.2019; Byrne, S., Rice, J., "Non-Tariff Barriers and Good Trade: A Brexit Impact Analysis", Banc Ceannais na hEireann/Central Bank of Ireland Research Technical Paper, 2018/7, 2018; Hadfield, A., *Kent and Medway: Delivering a Brexit Border Policing, security, Freight and Customs*, Center of European Studies CEFEUS Canterbury Center for Policy research and Canterbury Christ Church University, 2018.

[39] Owen, J., Shepheard, M., Stojanovic, A., *Implementing Brexit: Customs*, London, Institute for Government, 2017.

[40] "Brexit: the customs challenge – 20th Report of Session 2017–2019", *op. cit.*, p. 20.

more because "it does not include the cost of delays."[41] For instance, the Animal Plant Health Agency (ALPHA) works at 20 points of entry in the UK thanks to 2300 staff. It issues 12,000 exportation certificates and inspections per year. ALPHA deals with EU and non-EU food, feed and drink, i.e. 70 % of all UK imports and 61 % of all UK exports to the EU. Post Brexit ALPHA will have to deal with this new situation in house.

In 2019, the UK Institute for Government wrote that "Custom is undoubtedly… the biggest challenge facing government"[42] because there is a capacity increase need with new border posts, roads, truck parks, warehouses and service stations that are needed. Dover would need to expand as well but has a geographical, geological situation: it has no space because the harbour lies between the city and a cliff. Modernising its current ports is estimated to cost between 19 and 26 million pounds or about 31 billion euros. The situation has been acknowledged by two major seaports partners of Dover. Dunkirk is implementing a 250 million euros modernisation plan including a harbour expansion, greater custom capacity, border inspection, greater consignment capacity from 1000 to 5000 square meters, and a new 4000 square meters logistics warehouse. Calais is also investing 862.5 million euros in harbour enlargementing.

In sum, new custom borders are necessary and will progressively become reality in the post-Brexit era. Costs, however, are high: with infrastructures estimates set at 31 billion euros and costs to small and medium size businesses set at a minimum of 25 billion euros. In all, the new custom borders of the Britain will cost about 50 billion euros.

Conclusion

In 2020, a lot of uncertainties remain: after the Art. 50 declaration, the UK entered a period of negotiation and implementation of a difficult Brexit deal with two or more years of settlement, a separation process and scheduling, including reciprocal financial schedules. Post referendum, for Theresa May, and today post-election, for Boris Johnson, the positive outcomes for the UK are likely to be in the best case a deregulation and lower taxes for UK businesses.

---

[41] Blitz, J., "Is UK custom chief right that 'max fac' will cost 20 billion pound per year?", *Financial Times*, 25.5.2018.
[42] Owen, J., Shepheard, M., Stojanovic, A., *op. cit.*, p. 5.

However, when cross examining data on the costs of Brexit for the UK and the EU, it becomes clearer that many referendum (and electoral campaign) claims regarding the costs of EU membership were erroneous and that true costs were extremely close to the praised EU-Norwegian association: indeed, no other options could be more competitive than the UK position when benefiting from both an EU annual "rebate" and EU policies.

Uncertainty, however, according to most respected international estimates now will likely undermine the UK economy for the next 10 years. And, in the meantime, the overall and cumulated costs of exiting the EU, including the settlement bill, as well as new necessary custom infrastructures and policies are very likely to be higher than 100 billion euros; also, and most importantly, projected annual savings on EU membership will not happen because trading internationally has a cost, whether it is being part of a free trade agreement or being outside a free trade agreement: there are financial and regulatory costs born onto government agencies and businesses. Indeed, the evidence presented in this chapter points to the fact that the worst option would be a Brexit without a free trade deal of some kind. Economic uncertainties and custom borders will make economic costs very real for the foreseeable future in the UK.

From Opting Out to Brexit in the Area of Freedom, Security and Justice

CATHERINE HAGUENAU-MOIZARD

Since the referendum on Brexit, Theresa May has had to change her mind on many topics. Though she had campaigned in favour of remaining in the European Union (EU), she must fulfil her mission as a Prime Minister and negotiate the conditions of Brexit.

On the Area of Freedom, Security and Justice (AFSJ) though, she has been much more consistent as on other topics. The AFSJ covers immigration, asylum, control of borders, judicial cooperation in civil and criminal matters, police cooperation, customs cooperation, harmonisation of criminal law. During the referendum campaign, she explained that her "judgment, as Home Secretary, is that remaining a member of the European Union means we will be more secure from crime and terrorism".[1] A few months later, she proposed a "bold new strategic agreement that provides a comprehensive framework for future security, law enforcement and criminal justice cooperation".[2] Basically, she wanted the rules to stay the same because it would be in the best interest of both parties.

It was not really surprising, since the UK has obtained a special status towards the AFSJ in the Lisbon Treaty of 2007. The British were already partly out of the EU in that respect. Brexit will only make things more complicated but not really different in the long run. The AFSJ provides a very good example of the bad faith of the Brexiters and the inability of the Remainers to explain the situation properly. Indeed, the UK is partly

---

[1] May, T., "Home Secretary's speech on the UK, EU and our place in the world", London, 25.4.2016.
[2] May, T., "PM's Florence speech: a new era of cooperation and partnership between the UK and the EU", Florence, 22.9.2017.

out of the AFSJ and partly in. The future options remain unclear but most of the present rules will probably be kept, one way or another.

Partly Out and Partly In

The UK government has managed to negotiate a very special status within the AFSJ. The other governments have long thought that if they refused anything asked by the British, the UK would leave. It has eventually left but in the meantime, beforehand, they have been able to get almost everything they wanted. The UK is already partly out and stays partly in.

Partly Out

The UK has never been part of the Schengen area but takes part to some Schengen measures. It has negotiated a general right of opt out under the Lisbon Treaty.

Schengen

The UK has always been reluctant towards the Europeanisation of border controls. It has never joined the Schengen area. When the Schengen agreements were adopted, in 1985 and 1990, Margaret Thatcher was Prime Minister. She did not want the UK to join and explained it in her usual harsh manner in a speech to the College of Europe in 1988 known as "the Bruges speech": "it is a matter of plain common sense that we cannot totally abolish frontier controls if we are also to protect our citizens from crime and stop the movement of drugs, of terrorists and of illegal immigrants".[3]

Over the years, the UK has always remained outside the Schengen area. But they were keen to have access to the database created by the Schengen States, the Schengen Information System (SIS) and to benefit from the measures of police cooperation. Through the SIS, the authorities have access to information on missing persons or objects all over the Schengen area. The British authorities have access to this information,

---

[3] May, T., "Speech to the College of Europe", Bruges, 20.9.1988.

but they cannot issue nor access Schengen-wide alerts for refusing entry or stay into the Schengen area because they are not part of this area.

The UK managed to get access to the SIS following the treaty of Amsterdam in 1997. Art. 4 of the protocol to the Amsterdam Treaty integrating the Schengen *acquis* into the framework of the EU provided that the UK (and Ireland) could at any time ask to participate in the Schengen *acquis* or to depart from it. In May 1999, the EU Council adopted two decisions on the integration of the Schengen *acquis* and the British government immediately asked to take part in some of it, the SIS and the police and judicial cooperation in criminal matters and the fight against drugs trafficking. Its request was accepted by the EU Council in May 2000.[4] Other decisions have been adopted since then under protocol 18 to the Lisbon Treaty, which repeats the same provisions as the protocol to the Amsterdam Treaty. The UK has recently been allowed to participate in the Large-Scale IT Systems in the Area of Freedom, Security and Justice (LISA) agency within the AFSJ.[5]

The overall impression we may get from those decisions is that the UK was able to pick and choose from the Schengen *acquis*. This is true most of the time but the British did not always get what they wanted. In 2008, the EU Council rejected the request of the UK to take part in the exchange of data on visas (VIS). The UK brought an action for annulment against that decision. The European Court of Justice (ECJ) dismissed the action because VIS concerned the common visa policy, although it also related to police cooperation. The UK did not take part in the common visa policy.[6]

The General Opt out under the Lisbon Treaty

Apart from the control of borders and the visa policy, the UK took part in decisions taken in what is now called the AFSJ. This has changed under the Lisbon Treaty. During the negotiations of the treaty, the Labour Prime Minister Gordon Brown drew "red lines", that is to say

---

[4] EU, "Council Decision concerning the request of the United Kingdom of Great Britain and Northern Ireland to take part in some of the provisions of the Schengen acquis (L131/43)", 29.5.2000, *Official Journal*, 1.6.2000.

[5] EU, "Council Decision on guidelines for the employment policies of the Member States (L267/328)", 5.9.2018, *Official Journal*, 25.10.2018.

[6] EU, "European Court of Justice (ECJ), Grand Chamber, UK v. Council, (C-482/08)", ECLI:EU:C:2010:631, 26.10.2010.

subject matters which were not open to negotiation from the British point of view. Among others, he told the other Member States in a letter of June 2017 that "we will not agree to give up our ability to control our common law and judicial and police system".[7] As a result, the UK got the possibility to exercise a general opt out of the acts adopted in the AFSJ before the Lisbon Treaty entered into force, that is to say before 1st December 2009. The UK thus got the right to unbind itself from previously binding legal acts. The UK government was mainly reluctant towards one of the main changes brought about by the Lisbon Treaty in the AFSJ: the overall jurisdiction of the ECJ.

This right of opt out was secured through Protocol 36 of the Lisbon Treaty on transitional provisions. Under Art. 10 § 4 of the protocol, the British government was allowed to notify to the EU Council that it no longer accepted the acts adopted before 1st December 2009 in the AFSJ. It could send this notification until 1st June 2014 (six months before the end of the transition period). After the notification, all the acts would cease to apply to the UK. The British government did not wait that long. A debate was organised in both Houses of Parliament in July 2013 and Theresa May, as Home Secretary, sent the notification on 24 July 2013: 185 acts were covered by the opt out.

But the government managed to re-opt in some of them.

Partly In

Basically, the UK was allowed to cherry-pick in the AFSJ. Concerning the acts adopted until 1st December 2009, Art. 10 § 5 of Protocol 36 gave a right of re-opt in to the UK. After the general opt out, the British government could notify at any time its wish to participate in acts which have ceased to apply. The re-opt in would apply if the EU Council, deciding unanimously, accepted it.

The government published a list of acts it wanted to re-opt in because the advantages were superior to the costs. Most of them dealt with police and justice cooperation in criminal matters, such as the framework decision on the European arrest warrant or the decisions on Europol and

---

[7] Quoted by Blair, A, Monnet, J., "Britain and the Negotiation of the Lisbon Treaty", in Laursen, F. (ed.), *The Making of the EU's Lisbon Treaty*, Brussels, P.I.E. Peter Lang, 2012, pp. 97–121.

Eurojust. Negotiations took place between the British government and the governments of the other Member States. In the end, the EU Council adopted a decision, in November 2014, which listed 35 acts which would still bind the UK.[8]

As far as the acts adopted since December 2009 are concerned, Protocol 21 to the Lisbon Treaty applied. The UK had a right to opt in. It may decide if it was interested or not by a proposal. It must notify its intention to be bound within three months after a proposal has been sent to the EU Council. The other Member States must accept the opt in unanimously. If it was accepted, the UK could take part in the adoption of the act. The UK may also notify its intention after the act has been adopted. If the UK does not opt in an amendment to an act, the EU Council, by a qualified majority of the other Member States, may try and convince the UK to opt in or to bear the financial consequences of not opting in, if any.

An example of such a situation has arisen when the "asylum package" was amended in 2013. The British government has decided to opt in the Dublin III and Eurodac regulations adopted in 2013 but not in the new directives on asylum. The government explained that the rights given to asylum seekers by those new directives would cost too much.

As a result of the right to re-opt in and the right to opt in, one must carefully look into each measure to check whether the UK is bound or not by EU regulations. It means that without Brexit, the UK could very much do what it wanted in the AFSJ. It might not be that comfortable in the future.

The Future Options

Everyone agrees that cooperation in criminal matters should not stop after Brexit. The UK uses a lot the various instruments of cooperation.[9]

---

[8] EU, "Council Decision determining certain consequential and transitional arrangements concerning the cessation of the participation of the United Kingdom of Great Britain and Northern Ireland in certain acts of the Union in the field of police cooperation and judicial cooperation in criminal matters adopted before the entry into force of the Treaty of Lisbon (L343/11)", 27.11.2014, *Official Journal*, 28.11.2014.

[9] Hanratty, R., "The effect of Brexit on the fight against crime", *Archbold Review*, 4.5.2018, pp. 4–9.

Around 1000 persons are arrested by the UK every year under a European arrest warrant, and 200 are extradited to the UK. The databases such as the SIS or the European Criminal Records Information System (ECRIS) are also used a lot. Brexit means that this might no longer be possible and this endangers the fight against crime on both sides of the Channel. After the referendum, some politicians defended a Norwegian solution. But Norway might not be a proper model. The UK is not Norway. The only solution might be to negotiate a future partnership.

The Norwegian Model

Norway is a third country and it has concluded a number of treaties with the EU. It has joined the Schengen area in 1996 and participates in Frontex.[10] It is also bound by bilateral agreements on judicial or police cooperation. In 2001, it has signed an operational agreement concerning Europol, which means the Norwegian authorities take part in the exchange of information organized by Europol.[11] Norway is also part of Eurojust under an agreement concluded in 2005.[12] More recently, Norway has signed an agreement on the European arrest warrant, which has not entered into force yet.[13] The negotiations lasted for thirteen years, between 2001 and 2014. The agreement extends the European arrest warrant to Norway, with two differences. The national authorities may refuse to extradite their own nationals and to extradite someone accused of a political offence.

---

[10] Under an arrangement ratified by the Council in 2007: EU, "Council Decision on the conclusion, on behalf of the Community, of an Arrangement between the European Community and the Republic of Iceland and the Kingdom of Norway on the modalities of the participation by those States in the European Agency for the Management of Operational Cooperation at the External Borders of the Member States of the European Union (L188/15)", 15.2.2007, *Official Journal*, 20.7.2007.

[11] Europol, "Agreement between the Kingdom of Norway and the European Police Office".

[12] Eurojust, "Agreement between the Kingdom of Norway and Eurojust", Oslo, 2005.

[13] EU, "Council Decision on the conclusion of the Agreement between the European Union and the Republic of Iceland and the Kingdom of Norway on the surrender procedure between the Member States of the European Union and Iceland and Norway (L343/1)", 27.11.2014, *Official Journal*, 28.11.2014. The text of the agreement was published in 2006, L292/1, *Official Journal*, 21.10.2006.

The Norwegian model of police and justice cooperation was defended by the UK National Crime Agency because it makes things simpler and quicker. The problem is that, contrary to Norway, the UK is not member of the Schengen area. Third countries such as Norway and Iceland which have close links with the EU in police and justice cooperation were able to enter agreements because they had joined the Schengen area. They had to accept the rules on border controls in order to get access to other measures. It is highly unlikely that the EU will accept to extend those facilities to a third country outside Schengen.

From the UK's point of view, the Norwegian model has other drawbacks. Although Norway participates in the exchange of information within Europol and Eurojust, it has a limited power of decision. The legal framework (the decisions on Europol and Eurojust) were adopted by the EU Member States only. Norway is not represented in the management board, which decides on the policy of the agencies. It is represented in the management board of Frontex but has limited voting rights, according to Art. 1 § 2 of the 2007 arrangement. The jurisdiction of ECJ is another cause for concern. The agreements with Norway do not give any direct power to the ECJ over Norway. The Frontex arrangement provides though that Norway must "recognize the jurisdiction of the ECJ over the Agency" (Art. 6 of the arrangement). The agreement about the extension of the European arrest warrant sets "the objective of arriving at as uniform an application and interpretation as possible of the provisions of this Agreement" and provides that the Norwegian authorities "shall keep under constant review the development of the case law of the Court of Justice of the European Communities" (Art. 37). Such a rule would never be accepted by the British government. Theresa May has repeated that the UK "should take back control of our laws".[14] The paper on enforcement and dispute resolution published in August 2017 insisted that the UK would no longer be subject to the ECJ and that it would not reduce the rights of anyone in the UK.[15]

All these reasons explain why, in a report published in 2016, the House of Lords' EU Committee concluded wisely that the Norwegian model was not adapted to the UK.[16]

---

[14] Quoted by *The Guardian*, 23.8.2017 (6.10.2019).

[15] HM Government, "Enforcement and dispute resolution: A future partnership paper", London, 23.8.2017.

[16] "Brexit: Future UK-EU security and police cooperation – 7th Report Session 2016–2017", London, European Union Committee, House of Lords, 2016.

A Future Partnership?

Something new should be invented to continue cooperation after Brexit. The British government has published a paper on "a future partnership" in security, law enforcement and criminal justice in September 2017.[17] It emphasized the leading contribution of the UK to the development of EU law in this field and stresses that an ongoing cooperation is necessary for the security of British and EU citizens.

The Withdrawal Agreement does not say much about the AFSJ. The present law will apply until the end of the transition period, on 31 December 2020 but the UK will no longer have the right to opt in new measures adopted between Brexit day (31 January 2020) and the end of the transition period.

In the political declaration made in November 2018, the EU and UK agreed that they "should establish a broad, comprehensive and balanced security partnership". The UK should continue working with Europol and Eurojust, should be able to exchange data in order to fight against crime and have an arrangement on the swift extradition of suspects or criminals.[18] The declaration also refers to the ECJ. The UK agrees to respect "the integrity of the Union's legal order such as with regard to the alignment of rules and the mechanisms for disputes and enforcement including the role of the Court of Justice of the European Union". It is vague enough but does not close the door to some kind of taking into account of the ECJ's case law.

The intention to continue cooperation in criminal matters is clear. The process will probably be long and hard. Before agreements are found, the EU Member States and UK will have to fall back to the existing multilateral treaties such as agreed in the Council of Europe, for example the 1957 Convention on extradition or the 1959 Convention on mutual assistance in criminal matters. Those instruments are not as efficient as EU law. As an example, the Convention on extradition does not provide for any time limit for the extradition, contrary to the framework decision on the European arrest warrant. The Convention on mutual assistance does not have as broad a scope as the European Investigation Order created in 2014.

---

[17] "Security, law enforcement and criminal justice – a future partnership paper", London, HM Government, 18.9.2017.

[18] "Brexit: leaked political declaration in full", *The Guardian*, 22.11.2018.

Conclusion

As far as the AFSJ is concerned, "Brexit does not mean Brexit."[19] The UK was already out of the EU as far as a number of AFSJ measures were concerned. Brexit simply makes things more complicated than they already were. The Withdrawal Agreement has repeatedly been rejected by the House of Commons until it was finally adopted on 24 January 2020. Since then, the UK has been trying to keep its special status regarding the AFSJ but no one knows what will happen at the end of the transition period.

---

[19] Tekin, F., "The Area of Freedom, Security and Justice: Brexit does not mean Brexit", Berlin, Jacques Delors Institut, Policy Paper 205, 13.9.2017.

PART 4

THE (GEO-)POLITICAL CONSEQUENCES OF BREXIT

The Consequences of Brexit for the Island of Ireland 'Deal or No Deal'

RUTH TAILLON

In the 23 June 2016 referendum, the United Kingdom (UK) decided by an overall majority of 52 % to 48 % to leave the EU. In Northern Ireland, however, the vote was 56 % to remain as opposed to 44 % supporting leave. Since then, the "special circumstances" of Northern Ireland and the land border between Ireland and Northern Ireland have become central issues in the withdrawal negotiations; despite hardly featuring in the pre-referendum deliberations. Since the 2016 referendum campaign and increasingly since the publication of the draft Withdrawal Agreement negotiated between then Prime Minister Theresa May's government and the EU, the "backstop" arrangement – in which Northern Ireland and perhaps all of the UK "will maintain full alignment with rules of the Internal Market and Customs union which are relevant to the avoidance of a border, north-south cooperation and the all-island economy," – has come to be recognised as the most significant obstacle to achieving a deal that will facilitate an "orderly withdrawal."[1]

Irrespective of the ongoing Westminster melodrama, there has been some consistency of approach from both Prime Minister May and her successor, Boris Johnson. The common thread is the mantra "nothing is agreed until everything is agreed" and that agreement could only be achieved on arrangements for the Irish border along with other border arrangements; i.e. access to the single market and customs union. As the clock ticked down, the outcome of the dramatic machinations within

---

[1] Until September 2019, at the insistence of the UK Government the backstop as set out in the Withdrawal Agreement applied to the entire UK. On 17 October 2019, the President of the European Commission and Boris Johnson decided that the backstop would apply to Northern Ireland only, as originally proposed by the EU.

the British Parliament prompted Prime Minister Johnson to insist that he preferred a deal with the EU over leaving with no deal. He was also adamant that the so-called Irish backstop must be removed from the Withdrawal Agreement. However, irrespective of the Prime Minister's protestations, there has been little evidence of serious efforts to put forward credible alternatives to the backstop. Johnson's strategy has for a long time been a "No Deal" exit by 31 October 2019; after which it was presumed the way would be open for unencumbered negotiations on a "comprehensive free trade agreement".

The flaw in this strategy was that the Irish Government and the EU Council have repeatedly warned that in such a scenario, trade negotiations could start again only on the basis of new proposals from London that are "compatible with the Withdrawal Agreement". Thus, in September 2019, EU chief negotiator Michel Barnier ruled out abolishing the backstop and said that alternative arrangements for the border could only be considered after the Withdrawal Agreement was ratified.[2]

Nevertheless, with no alternative proposals coming from the UK side, the prospect of the UK's withdrawal without a deal – with all its predicted negative consequences and more – was beginning to appear inevitable. These consequences would be particularly damaging in Ireland, as the Centre for Cross Border Studies (CCBS) has argued in November 2019:

> Failure to reach agreement on the UK's orderly withdrawal from the EU will have the most adverse negative impacts on socio-economic relations within and between these islands, on the operability of the 1998 Belfast/Good Friday Agreement in all its parts, and on the nature of the UK's borders. No deal will lead to physical border infrastructure, with serious consequences for the social and economic stability of the island of Ireland.
>
> The Protocol on Ireland/Northern Ireland contained in the draft Withdrawal Agreement comes closest to providing a legally binding framework that can "maintain the necessary conditions for continued North-South cooperation" and "avoid a hard border" on the island of Ireland. No other existing proposal or agreement achieves this.[3]

---

[2] Barnier, M., quoted in *Irish Times*, 3.9.2019.
[3] Centre for Cross Border Studies, "Statement on draft Agreement on the withdrawal of the United Kingdom from the European Union", 20.11.2018, https://bit.ly/2lW2Uuj.

The 1998 Belfast/Good Friday Agreement

In November 2016, the Irish Taoiseach (Prime Minister) Enda Kenny and British Prime Minister Theresa May agreed that as co-guarantors of the 1998 Agreement, both governments remained fully committed to the Belfast/Good Friday Agreement (GFA) and that there would be "no return to the borders of the past"; that the retention of an open border is critical; the benefits of the Common Travel Area would be preserved; and "Northern Ireland and the peace process is front and centre of our priorities."[4]

These commitments were in alignment with the European Council guidelines, which committed the Union to continuing to support peace, stability and reconciliation on the island of Ireland (paragraph 14):

> Nothing in the [Withdrawal] Agreement should undermine the objectives and commitments set out in the Good Friday Agreement in all its parts and its related implementing agreements; the unique circumstances and challenges on the island of Ireland will require flexible and imaginative solutions. Negotiations should in particular aim to avoid the creation of a hard border on the island of Ireland, while respecting the integrity of the Union legal order. Full account should be taken of the fact that Irish citizens residing in Northern Ireland will continue to enjoy rights as EU citizens. Existing bilateral agreements and arrangements between Ireland and the United Kingdom, such as the Common Travel Area, which are in conformity with EU law, should be recognised. The Agreement should also address issues arising from Ireland's unique geographic situation, including transit of goods (to and from Ireland via the United Kingdom).[5]

Since the referendum in 2016, many voices have raised concerns about the dangers posed by Brexit to the Belfast/Good Friday Agreement. The agreement has two parts. The Multi-Party Agreement is a multilateral agreement between the UK and Irish governments and political parties in Northern Ireland. The British-Irish Agreement is a bilateral international agreement ratified by the Irish and UK governments.

---

[4] Speech by Kenny, E. T. D. at the First Meeting of the All-Island Civic Dialogue on Brexit, 2.11.2016.

[5] Council of the EU, "Directives for the negotiation of an agreement with the United Kingdom of Great Britain and Northern Ireland setting out the arrangements for its withdrawal from the European Union", Brussels, 22.5.2017.

In May 1998, referenda were held on both sides of the border. The question put to Northern Ireland voters was whether they supported the Multi-Party Agreement. Of a turn-out of 81 % of the eligible electorate, the vote was 71 % in favour. The Democratic Unionist Party (DUP) was the only major political group in Northern Ireland to oppose the agreement. Voters in the south were asked if they would allow the state to sign the agreement and amend the Constitution of Ireland to be consistent with the agreement; specifically, it provided for the removal of the "territorial claim" contained in Art. 2 and 3 – thus accepting Northern Ireland as part of the UK sovereign territory until such time as majorities in both jurisdictions voted for Irish unification. It is the provisions of the new Art. 2 that protects the EU citizenship rights of Irish citizens in Northern Ireland post-Brexit:

> It is the entitlement and birth-right of every person born in the island of Ireland, which includes its islands and seas, to be part of the Irish nation. That is also the entitlement of all persons otherwise qualified in accordance with law to be citizens of Ireland. Furthermore, the Irish nation cherishes its special affinity with people of Irish ancestry living abroad who share its cultural identity and heritage.[6]

While the southern turn-out was lower (56 %), the "Yes" vote was 94 %. It is worth reminding ourselves here that the GFA is an internationally-recognised, legally-binding treaty between Ireland and the UK.[7] Together with common EU membership of its co-guarantors (Ireland and UK), it has provided the spirit and the common legal basis for rights, safeguards and equality of opportunity, the all-island economy and institutions of North-South and East-West cooperation.

Brexit represents a fundamental challenge to the 1998 Agreement, to its practical application on the island of Ireland and to the totality of the relationships set out in the agreement, including to cross-border cooperation in all of its forms. The future of the UK-Ireland border, the totality of relations that cross it and frame how we live with one another within and between these islands will be determined by the

---

[6] Agreement reached in the multi-party negotiations, Annex B: "Irish Government Draft Legislation to Amend the Constitution".

[7] A detailed legal analysis is provided by Austen Morgan, a barrister involved in the negotiation and implementation of the Agreement at in Austen, M., *The Belfast Agreement a Practical Legal Analysis*, Belfast, Belfast Press, 2000.

future relationship between the UK and the EU that will be shaped in coming years.

The Protocol on Ireland/Northern Ireland in the Withdrawal Agreement represents the best deal on offer for Northern Ireland that safeguards against a "hard" border on the island and protects North-South cooperation. As it presently stands, however, the protocol does not protect the totality of existing socio-economic relations within and between these islands, notably the East-West dimension of the 1998 Belfast/Good Friday Agreement.[8]

Prior to the 2016 referendum, the Centre for Cross Border Studies warned that "… a decision to leave the EU would require revisions to the Belfast Agreement and associated legislation. While some of these changes appear relatively minor, others have the potential to raise serious political difficulties."[9] The 1998 Agreement maintains a version of sovereignty and border management informed by a tradition of EU that regards national borders as sites of integration and cooperation. A principal element of the agreement is rights and their protections, which are either directly or indirectly underpinned by EU law. Having to disassociate parts of the agreement from EU law as a result of Brexit will have consequences for such rights and their protections and may result in differential treatment of Irish, British and other EU citizens, as well as among different categories of EU citizens – with direct consequences for social cohesion.

The agreement between the UK and Irish Governments presupposed continued membership in the EU by both parties: "Wishing to develop still further the unique relationship between their peoples and the close cooperation between their countries as friendly neighbours and as partners in the European Union".[10] This declaration can be interpreted as recognition by the two governments of the opportunity the 1998 Agreement represented to fully capitalise on their countries' common membership of the EU. The commitment of the signatories to the agreement reached in the multi-party negotiations to, among other principles, "exclusively democratic and peaceful means of resolving

---

[8] *Ibid.*
[9] "EU Referendum Briefing Papers, Briefing Paper 2 – The UK Referendum on Membership of the EU: Potential Constitutional Consequences", Armagh, Centre for Cross Border Studies and Cooperation Ireland, 2016, pp. 6–7.
[10] British-Irish Council, Agreement between the Government of the United Kingdom of Great Britain and Northern Ireland and the Government of Ireland, 1998.

differences on political issues", would transform the physical nature of the border between Northern Ireland and Ireland. The security infrastructure that was no longer necessary in the absence of an armed conflict has been gradually removed and in doing so has transformed daily life in border communities.

In triggering Art. 50 of the Treaty on European Union (TEU) on 29 March 2017, Theresa May's government set in motion the procedures towards the UK's exit from the EU. At that time, it was expected by most observers that the UK and the EU would have ratified a Withdrawal Agreement and that the date of the UK's exit from the EU would be 29 March 2019. Particularly in 2016, there was much unfounded optimism among Conservative Members of Parliament (MPs) about how easy negotiations would be. David Davis, for instance, commented: "We're not really interested in a transition deal, but we'll consider one to be kind to the EU"; and Michael Gove claimed: "The day after we vote to leave, we hold all the cards and we can choose the path we want." Similarly, John Redwood opined: "Getting out of the EU can be quick and easy – the UK holds most of the cards". Even by 2017, there appeared to be little comprehension of the complexities involved. Liam Fox, International Trade Minister, claimed that: "The free trade agreement that we will have to do with the European Union should be one of the easiest in human history."[11]

Sequencing the Negotiations

At the outset, the EU Council guidelines set out the sequencing of Brexit negotiations, based on a phased approach requiring "sufficient progress" on conditions for withdrawal before going on to discuss the future EU/UK partnership. These conditions covered the protection of EU citizens in the UK, the financial settlement, and the fate of the GFA concerning Northern Ireland.[12]

The UK, on the other hand, wanted the Withdrawal and Future Relationship agreements negotiated alongside each other because in their view, the UK would be disadvantaged by an early agreement regarding its

---

[11] "11 Brexit promises the government quietly dropped", *The Guardian*, 28.3.2018.
[12] Barnier, M., "Speech in front of the Committees of Foreign Affairs and the Committees of European Affairs of the Italian Parliament", Rome, 21.9.2017.

financial obligations and the future status of the Northern Irish border. Secretary of State for Brexit, David Davis, predicted it would be "the row of the summer". He asserted that it was "wholly illogical" to address the issue of the border in Ireland "unless you know what our general borders policy is, what the customs agreement is, what our trade agreement is". The UK would argue that "nothing was agreed until everything was agreed."[13]

Within just weeks, however, the UK had, as the *Financial Times* put it, "capitulated" and accepted sequencing, i.e., negotiating the Withdrawal Agreement first. It was not the row, but the "row-back" of the summer. The newspaper suggested that the reversal reflected the lack of preparation and clarity on the UK side. Britain needed, the *Financial Times* argued, to raise its game and stop underestimating its opponents. "The current ploy is to hide under the "nothing is agreed until everything is agreed" phrase of the EU, but without realising (or acknowledging) that that mantra is for the divorce deal not the trade deal."[14]

Although the UK quickly conceded on sequencing, its position throughout the negotiations has been that the Withdrawal Agreement and Agreement on Future Relations between the UK and EU could not and should not be disconnected. In particular, they argued that the future status of the border between Ireland and Northern Ireland could only be resolved in the context of negotiations on future trade relationships. This position was reiterated by Theresa May in October 2017, when she said that: "The point of the implementation period is to put in place the practical changes necessary to move to the future partnership, and for that you need to know what the future partnership is going to be."[15]

The Joint Report

In December 2017, it looked like a deal had been agreed; the UK had accepted that single market and customs union rules in Northern Ireland would not be changed. Then an intervention by DUP leader Arlene

---

[13] "David Davis warns Brexit timetable will be 'row of the summer'", *Financial Times*, 14.5.2017.

[14] "The significance of the Brexit sequencing U-turn", *Financial Times*, 20.6.2017.

[15] "11 Brexit promises the government quietly dropped", *op. cit.*

Foster stopped everything. Mrs Foster said that Northern Ireland must leave the EU on exactly the same terms as the rest of the UK.

> We will not accept any form of regulatory divergence which separates Northern Ireland economically or politically from the rest of the United Kingdom. The economic and constitutional integrity of the United Kingdom will not be compromised in any way. [...] The Republic of Ireland claim to be guarantors of the Belfast Agreement but they are clearly seeking to unilaterally change the Belfast Agreement without our input or consent.[16]

The Irish Government was "surprised and disappointed" that the deal had broken down. While the DUP's opinion was valued, the Taoiseach highlighted the fact that the majority of people in Northern Ireland had voted remain, and an even higher percentage voted in favour of the GFA.[17] Interestingly, although the DUP's objections related to regulatory divergence and the single market, the emphasis of public arguments by Brexiteers after the DUP intervention was on tariffs and the customs union. David Davis tried to redefine regulatory alignment: "regulatory alignment is not harmonisation: it's a question of ensuring similar outcomes in areas where you want to have trade relationships and free and frictionless trade." He also stressed that "… anything we agree for Northern Ireland in this respect, if we get our free trade area, will apply to the whole of the UK."[18]

Within days, just in time for the EU Council meeting on 14–15 December, a Joint Report on progress in phase 1 of the negotiations was published[19] without prejudging any adaptations that might be appropriate in case transitional arrangements were to be agreed in the second phase of the negotiations, and without prejudice to discussions on the framework of the future relationship: "Under the caveat that nothing is agreed until everything is agreed, the joint commitments set out in

---

[16] "How a phone-call from Arlene Foster in the middle of lunch ended Theresa May's hopes of an Irish border deal," *The Telegraph*, 4.12.2017.

[17] "Furious DUP 'sinks' Brexit deal: Arlene Foster DESTROYS May's negotiation with phone call", *The Express*, 5.12.2017.

[18] "Regulatory alignment could apply to whole of UK, Davis suggests", *Irish Times*, 5.12.2017.

[19] "Joint report from the negotiators of the European Union and the United Kingdom Government on progress during phase one of negotiations under Article 50 TEU on the United Kingdom's orderly withdrawal from the European Union", Brussels, European Commission, TF50 website, 8.12.2017.

this joint report shall be reflected in the Withdrawal Agreement in full detail." Issues relating to Ireland and Northern Ireland were contained in Paragraphs 42 to 56. The GFA was specifically referenced in paragraphs 42, 43, 44, 47, 49, 52, and 53.[20]

Following the Joint Report of 7 December 2017, the EU Commission (and later the EU Council) agreed that sufficient progress had been made on the three priority areas of citizens' rights, the dialogue on Ireland/Northern Ireland, and the financial settlement, allowing the negotiations to proceed to phase two.

> The Commission's negotiator has ensured that the life choices made by EU citizens living in the United Kingdom will be protected. The rights of EU citizens living in the United Kingdom and United Kingdom citizens in the EU 27 will remain the same after the United Kingdom has left the EU. The Commission has also made sure that any administrative procedures will be cheap and simple for EU citizens in the United Kingdom.
> As regards the financial settlement, the United Kingdom has agreed that commitments taken by the EU 28 will be honoured by the EU 28, including the United Kingdom.
> With regard to the border between Ireland and Northern Ireland, the United Kingdom acknowledges the unique situation on the island of Ireland and has made significant commitments to avoid a hard border.[21]

The UK side realised that winning the EU Council's acceptance of "sufficient progress" was required to allow the negotiations to proceed to the next phase. Almost immediately, however, British Cabinet ministers were told that promises made around full regulatory alignment were meaningless. David Davis suggested that the Withdrawal Agreement was just a "statement of intent," not legally enforceable. In a letter to Conservative MPs, Theresa May again asserted that "nothing is agreed until everything is agreed." Unsurprisingly, the Irish government was unhappy and warned that "Both Ireland and the EU will be holding the UK to the phase one agreement." Tánaiste Simon Coveney highlighted the part of the agreement that said commitments on Ireland would be

---

[20] *Ibid.*
[21] "Brexit: European Commission recommends sufficient progress to the European Council (Article 50)", Brussels, European Commission, Representation in Ireland, 8.12.2017.

"upheld in all circumstances, irrespective of the nature of any future agreement between the EU and the UK."[22]

With the EU warning that there was no question of accepting that sufficient progress had been made to allow moving on to discussions on the future relationship unless the agreement reached was respected in full, the British side was quick to insist that there was "no question of our commitment to the text of the Joint Report."[23] Nevertheless, the EU Commission warned regulatory divergence between Ireland and Northern Ireland was the single biggest risk to continued North-South cooperation. The intention to avoid a hard border was difficult to reconcile with the UK's "red lines" of leaving the single market and the customs union.[24]

Following publication of the Joint Report, Irish Taoiseach Leo Varadkar was able to announce that there had been a satisfactory conclusion on the issues relating to Ireland in phase one. Irish issues were one of three critical areas that needed to be dealt with in the talks, before the EU and the UK could proceed to phase two. Along with the issues related to Ireland, the other key elements of the first phase of negotiations related to reciprocal citizens' rights and the Financial Settlement of the UK's ongoing obligations to the EU. An Irish Government summary of what had been achieved noted that:

> First and foremost, the Good Friday Agreement in all its parts is protected. Everyone born in Northern Ireland will continue to have the right to Irish and therefore EU citizenship. So, a child born in Belfast or Derry today will have the right to study in Paris, buy property in Spain, work in Berlin or any other part of the European Union. All they have to do is exercise the right to Irish and therefore EU citizenship.
>
> The Common Travel Area will continue allowing free travel between Britain and Ireland. British and Irish citizens will continue to have the freedom to live, work, study, access housing, healthcare, pensions and welfare in each other's countries "as though we are citizens of both".
>
> Importantly, the UK committed to avoiding a hard border as an "over-arching requirement" with which "any future arrangements must be compatible". That is, there will be no physical infrastructure or related checks or control.[25]

---

[22] "David Davis clashes with Ireland over Brexit deal", *The Guardian*, 10.12.2017.
[23] *Ibid.*
[24] *Ibid.*
[25] Varadkar, L., "Statement on Brexit negotiations by Taoiseach Leo Varadkar", *Irish Government News Service*, 8.12.2017.

The government's statement explained that its preferred option was "a deep and comprehensive agreement between the EU and the UK in its entirety which will allow us to trade as we do now." However, if this were not to prove possible, the backstop arrangement in which Northern Ireland and perhaps all of the United Kingdom "will maintain full alignment with rules of the internal market and customs union which are relevant to the avoidance of a border, North-South cooperation and the all-island economy."

In its *White Paper on the Future Relationship between the UK and the EU*, published in July 2018, the UK government still insisted that: "The UK and the EU have been clear that the Withdrawal Agreement and the Future Framework form a package… nothing is agreed until everything is agreed, meaning that neither document can be considered final until this is true of both."[26] Therefore, it intended that a debate in the UK Parliament to give legal effect to the Withdrawal Agreement in the UK would take place only when agreement has been reached on both the Withdrawal Treaty and the Future Framework.[27]

The Withdrawal Agreement and the Ireland/Northern Ireland Protocol

The Withdrawal Agreement and the Political Declaration on the Future Relationship between the UK and the EU were endorsed by leaders at a special meeting of the European Council on 25 November 2018.

Addressing concerns expressed by Unionist politicians in particular, the Withdrawal Agreement included additional assurances for people and businesses in Northern Ireland that the UK government will ensure that Northern Ireland business will continue to have unfettered access to the whole of UK and that no new barriers will develop between Northern Ireland and Great Britain unless the Northern Ireland Executive and Assembly agree to it. Northern Ireland and Great Britain will not drift apart. It was also agreed that EU cross-border programmemes Peace and Interreg will continue until at least 2021. (Subsequently, the Irish

---

[26] May, T., *The Future Relationship between the United Kingdom and the European Union*, London, HM Stationery Office, CM9593, 2018.
[27] *Ibid.*, pp. 97–98.

government and the EU Commission have committed to a new Peace+ programme to follow the existing programmes.)

Significantly – particularly in light of the UK government's insistence that the EU Charter of Fundamental Rights will not be transposed into UK law after Brexit and repeated signals that the Conservative Party intends to withdraw from the European Convention on Human Rights (ECHR)[28] – the UK committed to ensuring that *in Northern Ireland* [our emphasis] there is "no diminution of human rights, safeguards and equality of opportunity set out in European Law". The Political Declaration asserts the UK's continued commitment to the ECHR, although it must be noted that the Conservative Party's Manifesto for the 2017 General Election committed to remaining a signatory only for the duration of the current parliament. Dominic Grieve MP, a former Attorney General for England and Wales and one of the Conservative Party's leading opponents of a no-deal Brexit, was one of the first voices to warn that withdrawal from the ECHR "calls into question" the devolution settlements for Wales, Scotland and Northern Ireland. Stating that the European Convention remains "arguably the single most important legal and political instrument for promoting human rights on our planet," the Conservative MP elaborated:

> In the case of Northern Ireland, it is also part of an international treaty involving Ireland. At a time when the peace settlement in Northern Ireland is still fragile and the future of the United Kingdom itself is in question, it opens up the prospect of new areas of political discord. While I appreciate that there may be some, including of course in this audience, who might welcome this as hastening their domestic political goals, I find this a very odd thing for a government committed to the Union to do.[29]

The Withdrawal Agreement contains special arrangements for Northern Ireland and the land border in the Ireland/Northern Ireland

---

[28] The Conservative Party Manifesto for the 2017 General Election contained a commitment to "We will not repeal or replace the Human Rights Act while the process of Brexit is underway but we will consider our human rights legal framework when the process of leaving the EU concludes. We will remain signatories to the European Convention on Human rights for the duration of the next parliament." The Human Rights Act is the legislation operationalizing the ECHR into UK law. The commitment to remain a signatory to the Convention for the duration of the next parliament indicates that withdrawal from the ECHR will be on the agenda after the next General Election should it result in a Conservative majority government.

[29] Grieve, D., "Speech to the Faculty of Advocates", Edinburgh, *Holyrood*, 23.9.2015.

Protocol. The Protocol provides for a single customs territory covering the EU and Northern Ireland, and provision for alignment of standards on company taxation, state aid and competition policy, labour regulations, public health and environmental protection. While upholding Northern Ireland's constitutional status as part of the UK, the Protocol comes closest to providing a legally binding framework that can "maintain the necessary conditions for continued North-South cooperation" and to "avoid a hard border" on the island of Ireland. No other existing proposal or agreement achieves this.

The EU Council and Commission have reiterated on numerous occasions that the (legally-binding) Withdrawal Agreement will not be reopened; although there is room for amendment to the (aspirational) Political Declaration on Future Relations between the EU and the UK. When he extended the deadline to 31 October (the UK would finally make an orderly exit only on 31 January 2020), EU Council President Donald Tusk made it clear that in the interim, it was up to the UK to decide whether it would ratify the Withdrawal Agreement, change its strategy, but not the Withdrawal Agreement, or decide to revoke the decision to withdraw. An explanatory document published by the UK government again made clear its view that the two should be considered together: "The documents have been settled together on the basis that nothing is agreed until everything is agreed... The future relationship between the UK and the EU will apply to the whole of the United Kingdom."[30]

While the UK government had promised a vote in Parliament on any negotiated deal, a requirement for a "meaningful vote" was enshrined in law during the passage of the EU Withdrawal Act, following negotiations with pro-EU Conservative MPs led by Dominic Grieve.[31] Since the conclusion of the Withdrawal Agreement negotiations, the world has watched – some with bemusement, some with horror – as the UK Parliament has been unable to achieve a majority for any version of Brexit – or indeed, no Brexit at all.

---

[30] "Explainer for the Political Declaration setting out the framework for the future relationship between the United Kingdom and the European Union", London, HM Stationery Office, HM Government, 25.11.2018.

[31] Thimont Jack, M., "Parliament's 'meaningful vote' on Brexit", Institute for Government, 29.3.2019.

After three attempts, UK Prime Minister Theresa May was unable to win a majority in Parliament for the Withdrawal Agreement; nor was there a majority for any of the options suggested by MPs. In fact, the only proposal that has achieved a majority has been to prevent a "No Deal" exit. With agreement by the EU Council, the date for exiting the EU has been three times postponed; first until 12 April, second to 31 October 2019 and again to 31 January 2020. There has been virtually no mention by British politicians or in the British media that any Withdrawal Agreement must also be ratified by the EU Parliament.

Mrs May resigned from her post as leader of the Conservative Party and was replaced by Boris Johnson through a vote by the party membership of approximately 160,000 people, as a result of which this leading Brexiteer is now Prime Minister. PM Boris Johnson continued for a long time to insist that he wanted to negotiate a new deal; despite having previously voted in favour of the Withdrawal Agreement negotiated by Theresa May, he insisted that the backstop must be removed in its entirety, stating: "I do not accept that all or part of the UK should remain in a customs union."[32] Thus, until the very last moment, the prospect of the UK "crashing out" of the EU without a deal looked increasingly unavoidable. Much government energy has been directed at shifting blame onto the perceived "intransigence" of the troublesome Irish and the EU. Brexit Secretary of State, Steven Barclay said, for example, that a no-deal exit would be attributed to the EU's "absolutism".[33] Interestingly, he indicated that the demand was solely for the removal of the backstop, "… distinct from the wider Northern Ireland Protocol, which covered other issues such as the single electricity market, the benefits of North-South co-operation and the Common Travel Area. So the Northern Ireland Protocol as a whole is not the same as the backstop which is around alignment."[34]

Within days, however, *The Guardian* was reporting that Johnson "wants to drive a coach and horses through other areas of the Brexit deal too, so even if the backstop was removed, support would not be guaranteed." The British demand was that the backstop should be

---

[32] "'UK will be greatest place on Earth after Brexit', says new PM Johnson", *Euronews*, 26.7.2019 (7.10.2019).

[33] "UK Brexit secretary accuses EU of clinging to 'absolutist' policy on backstop", *Irish Times*, 3.9.2019 (7.10.2019).

[34] *Ibid.*

removed from the Withdrawal Agreement and integrated into the Political Declaration. Johnson was also demanding revisions to the Political Declaration on promises for a "level playing field" allowing the UK to diverge on employment law and social policy and environmental protections and commitments to "close cooperation in union-led crisis management missions and operations, both civilian and military." The British also indicated that they wished to downgrade the commitment made in December 2017 to "frictionless trade" on the Irish border to "as frictionless as possible" and also that these commitments should not be legally operable. While Johnson indicated that he would be open to treating the island of Ireland as one unit for the agri-food industry, it has been speculated that he rather favoured regulatory alignment between Ireland and the UK on food. That is, Ireland would shift its food standards to align with those of the UK whenever it diverged from the EU's standards. Finally, there was a determination to win changes to the agreed dispute mechanisms although it was not always clear what exactly was proposed.[35]

However, as there still was no credible, legally-enforceable alternative proposal to the "backstop", it finally remained the solution adopted for Northern Ireland. This is an essential guarantee that protects the EU single market, the Irish peace process and the Belfast/Good Friday Agreement.

The View from Ireland

In contrast to the confusion and conflicts among and between UK political parties, the Irish government made its priorities clear from very early on. To its credit also, under the direction of the Taoiseach (Prime Minister) Enda Kenny and subsequently his successor, Leo Varadkar, it opened a comprehensive "All-Island Civic Dialogue" consultation process[36] in November 2016. At the fifth and final plenary session in February 2019, Tánaiste (Deputy Prime Minister) Simon Coveney provided an update on Irish government preparations for all possible

---

[35] "It's not just the backstop," *The Guardian*, 7.9.2019.

[36] The first of five plenary sessions took place on 2.11.2016. Over 20 sectoral dialogues subsequently took place across the country and concluded with the 5th Plenary on 15.2.2019. See https://bit.ly/2mne2kf (2.1.2020).

outcomes and to mitigate the "potentially profound political, social, economic and trade impacts of a no deal Brexit."[37]

Alongside the consultation process, a considerable effort across all government departments and the diplomatic service developed the Irish response over the intervening period. Its priorities as set out by Taoiseach Enda Kenny in November 2016 have remained constant: Northern Ireland, the peace process and the future of the border; the Common Travel Area; economic and trading relations with the UK and the future direction of the EU.[38] It is worth noting here, that there has never been any question that the Irish government's response – overwhelmingly supported across the political spectrum and public opinion – has been unequivocally embedded in its continued membership of the EU and a commitment to protect its shared interest with other Member States in protecting the single market and the customs union. From the time of Ireland's entry into the EC in 1973 until 2016, there had been a significant minority (consistently around 23 % to 29 %) supporting leaving the EU should the UK do so.

However, the public debate in the aftermath of the 2016 referendum, supported by a generally well-informed press, seems to have shifted Irish opinion. Only 9 % of those polled in July 2017 were in favour of following the UK out of the EU.[39] Reporting on this poll, an article in the *Irish Times* commented: "EU chiefs and national governments fear the result of the Brexit referendum will strengthen anti-EU groups in several Member States and weaken support for remaining in the EU. However, today's poll suggests that the Irish view is exactly the opposite."[40] Indeed, an EU Parliament survey in September 2018 found that only 7 % of Irish people would vote to leave the EU if a referendum were held "tomorrow"; joint lowest in the EU with Luxembourg. The survey also showed that 92 % of Irish people, the highest in the EU, agree that their country has benefited from EU membership.[41]

---

[37] See: All Island Civic Dialogue: 5th Plenary, 15.2.2019, https://bit.ly/2kEHJwN (2.1.2020).

[38] Kenny, E., "Irish Times Brexit Summit – Keynote address", *Irish Government News Service*, 7.11.2016.

[39] "Four out of five Irish voters say UK was wrong to leave EU", *The Irish Times*, 7.7.2016.

[40] *Ibid.*

[41] "Irish least likely to vote to leave the EU", *EU News You Can Use*, European Commission, 18.10.2018.

The Brexit debate has also included some self-serving arguments from Brexiteers – including some from Northern Ireland – in support of "Irexit". One of the most vocal proponents of this argument is DUP MP Ian Paisley Junior. In October 2017, he wrote in the *Belfast Telegraph*: "Unionists in general, whose very state is defined by partition, have been adamant that Brexit will protect the soft border between Northern Ireland and the Republic of Ireland." He argued that Irish politicians should be able to turn Brexit into a business advantage and "adopt a strategy to milk Brexit for all it is worth." Never a politician noted for his concern for the well-being of Irish citizens south of the border, Paisley's real objection was that by ensuring that the border was "centre stage of the negotiations", the issue was now "an albatross around the neck, choking progressive political conversation about the nature of the new relationship." It was time, he suggested, that "the Irish allowed a new national conversation to begin and that they at least considered what it would be like to exit the EU along with the UK."[42]

Paisley and some others for whom the GFA is an obstacle to Brexit have also come to see Brexit as a means through which they can amend, or dispense with the GFA in its entirety. An article in the *Belfast Telegraph* noted that: "In the space of barely 24 hours, there had been an unprecedented public broadside against the peace deal from the Brexit wing of British politics as a barrier to the type of UK exit that they desire."[43] In his column in the *Daily Telegraph*, Conservative MEP Daniel Hannan spent several paragraphs attacking the GFA, claiming he objected to it on "democratic grounds" and suggesting that Direct Rule [i.e. ending devolution for Northern Ireland] "seems inevitable – and that is no bad thing."[44] Former Secretary of State for Northern Ireland, Owen Patterson, tweeted: "The collapse of power-sharing in Northern Ireland shows the Good Friday Agreement has outlived its use".[45] And Labour Party MP Kate Hoey was quoted in the *Huffington Post* saying,

---

[42] "Ian Paisley: Ireland's in denial and should follow the UK's example," *Belfast Telegraph*, 25.10.2017.
[43] "Brexiteers launch broadside at Northern Ireland peace deal", *Politico*, 22.2.2018.
[44] "If Jeremy Corbyn dislikes his country so much, he isn't fit to lead it," *The Telegraph*, 17.2.2018.
[45] See https://bit.ly/2lRs0KR (2.2.2020).

"I think there is a need for a cold rational look at the Belfast agreement. Mandatory coalition is not sustainable in the long term…".[46]

The Brexiteer View of Ireland

As the *Financial Times* has pointed out, at least part of the problem has been the UK's underestimation of its opponents. This criticism was echoed by the *Irish Times*, which commented that "our shared history – and the responsibilities arising from it – appear to mean little to a Prime Minister intent on whatever political chicanery is necessary to exit the EU irrespective of the implications of the re-imposition of a border on this island."[47]

BBC presenter John Humphreys, in the course of an interview with Ireland's Europe Minister, Helen Mc Entee, queried, "that instead of Dublin telling this country that we have to stay in the single market etc. within the customs union, why doesn't Dublin, why doesn't the Republic of Ireland, leave the EU and throw in their lot with this country?"[48]

The *Irish Times* criticised Boris Johnson's "crude English exceptionalism" and reported that when he was Foreign Secretary, Johnson was reported to have questioned, in relation to Taoiseach Leo Varadkar (who is of Indian descent): "Why isn't he called Murphy like all the rest of them?" He was also heard to muse as to whether Chancellor Angela Merkel had served in East Germany's Stasi. French president Emmanuel Macron was a "jumped-up Napoleon."[49]

Johnson has been famously dismissive of concerns related to the Irish border. In February 2018, then Foreign Secretary, he claimed that these concerns were being exaggerated by those hoping to frustrate Britain's departure from the EU. He suggested that crossing the Irish border could be solved in the same way technology was deployed to collect congestion

---

[46] "Ireland condemns Kate Hoey's 'reckless' Good Friday agreement remarks", *The Guardian*, 20.2.2018.

[47] "The Irish Times view on Brexit politics: ignoring the Irish dimension", *Irish Times*, 3.9.2019.

[48] "Ireland dismisses suggestion it should quit EU and join UK", *The Guardian*, 26.1.2019.

[49] "Boris Johnson on Varadkar: " 'Why isn't he called Murphy like all the rest of them' " *Irish Times*, 18.7.2019.

charges between Camden and Westminster when he was London mayor: "… the issue of the Northern Irish border is being used quite a lot politically to try and keep the UK in the customs union – effectively the single market – so we cannot really leave the EU, that is what is going on."[50] In June 2018, he said the border is "… so small and there are so few firms that actually use that border regularly, [that] it's just beyond belief that we're allowing the tail to wag the dog in this way. We're allowing the whole of our agenda to be dictated by this folly."[51] Johnson described the Withdrawal Agreement as "vassal State stuff… utterly unacceptable to anyone who believes in democracy. For the first time since partition Dublin under these proposals will have more say in some aspects of the government of Northern Ireland than London…".[52]

While offering no specific proposals, there have been many assurances from others on the UK side dismissing concerns about the border in Ireland. For example, Jacob Rees-Mogg wrote in February 2018 that: "It would be wrong to pretend that the border forestalls Brexit and we would not expect the Prime Minister or the Cabinet to fall for such a weak argument. It is only put forward by people who have always opposed Brexit,"[53] He later commented:

> Ireland would not be a free for all… as we had during the Troubles, to have people inspected. It's not a border that everyone has to go through every day, but of course for security reasons during the Troubles, we kept a very close eye on the border, to try and stop gun-running and things like that.[54]

Tánaiste Simon Coveney spoke for the people of Ireland when he responded:

> It's hard to believe that a senior politician is so ill informed about Ireland **and** the politics of **the Brexit** Irish border issue that he could make comments like these. We have left 'the troubles' behind us, through the sincere efforts of many, **and** we intend on keeping it that way.[55]

---

[50] "Boris Johnson says Ireland border being used to frustrate Britain's departure from the EU", *The Irish News*, 28.2.2018.
[51] "Boris Johnson admits there may be a Brexit 'meltdown'", *The Guardian*, 7.6.2018.
[52] "May's Brexit Deal completely unacceptable: Boris Johnson", *Reuters World News*, 13.11.2018.
[53] "Brexiteers launch broadside at Northern Ireland peace deal", *Politico*, 22.2.2018.
[54] "Have people inspected at Irish Border after Brexit, says Rees-Mogg", *The Guardian*, 26.8.2018.
[55] *Ibid.*

Taoiseach Leo Varadkar would comment later in 2018 that:

> Brexit has undermined the Good Friday Agreement and is fraying the relationship between Britain and Ireland... Anything that pulls the communities apart in Northern Ireland undermines the Good Friday Agreement, and anything that pulls Britain and Ireland apart undermines that relationship.[56]

In March 2018, David Davis, then Brexit Secretary, dismissed what he referred to as "the backstop that the Commission has laid out." He insisted that, "the real likely outcome, overwhelmingly likely option, is... we get a free trade agreement, we get a customs agreement... all of those make the Northern Ireland issue much, much, easier to solve..."[57] It quickly became apparent, however, that delivering on the shared commitment to retaining an open border between Ireland and Northern Ireland is not so easily resolved. Not only is it the UK's only land border with the EU and therefore potentially a "back door" into the single market, but also because of the challenges it represents to political stability on the island and the GFA. The UK government nevertheless has persisted in defending its red lines – insisting that all of the UK, including Northern Ireland, must leave the customs union and the single market.

While we are focussed here on the "backstop", it is clear that many pro-Brexit politicians objected to the Withdrawal Agreement not only because in their view the backstop "threatens the integrity of our union", but also because "a vast quantity of UK taxpayers' money" was being handed over to the EU and the European Court of Justice would continue to have some jurisdiction. Britons had, after all, voted to "take back control over borders, laws and money."[58]

Of course, not all British politicians are so unconcerned about the impacts Brexit will have on Ireland and on Anglo-Irish relationships. Lord Alfred Dubs, perhaps best known as a champion of refugees, attempted to explain to his colleagues the complexity of border issues:

---

[56] "Leo Varadkar: Brexit has undermined Good Friday agreement", *The Guardian*, 3.11.2018.

[57] The Andrew Marr Show, BBC One, 25.3.2018.

[58] "Trade deals. Tax cuts. And taking time before triggering Article 50. A Brexit economic strategy for Britain", *Conservative Home*, 14.7.2016.

Let us remind ourselves that there is a 310-mile border between Northern Ireland and the Republic, with 257 crossing points. That compares with 137 crossing points on the EU's eastern border, which is much longer, yet has fewer crossing points. [...] 40 million vehicles move between Northern Ireland and the Republic every year.

If border restrictions are reintroduced, that will lead to a sense of disillusionment and the feeling that the Good Friday Agreement is being steadily dismantled. People who know more about these things than I do say that it will provide a boost for dissident republicans. The chief constable of the PSNI has warned of possible violence if border checks are reinstated and has said that many of the gains of the last 20 years will be lost.[59]

Conclusion

Only by protecting the 1998 Agreement, in all of its dimensions and the entirety of its territorial scope and relations, can a "hard" border be avoided. The invisible and frictionless UK-Ireland land border has had both symbolic and practical functions in supporting the peace process. Any form of physical infrastructure at the UK-Ireland land border risks disruption of the peace process and invites direct forms of sabotage. Failure to reach a legally binding agreement which includes a "backstop" guaranteeing these protections, would have made a "hard" UK-Ireland border inevitable and would have had severe consequences for UK-Irish relations. By disrupting the border's openness Brexit has threatened the ongoing peace and reconciliation process because it undermines economic prosperity, social cohesion and political stability on the island.

The conundrum, as pointed out by the *Belfast Telegraph*, is that, "... ultimately the 'backstop' was born out of a recognition that Mrs May's promises were contradictory – she had promised an invisible border, an independent trade policy and no border in the Irish Sea when, in truth, only two of these three promises could be true at any given moment".[60]

The Protocol on Ireland/Northern Ireland upholds Northern Ireland's constitutional status. The Protocol comes closest to providing a legally binding framework that can "maintain the necessary conditions for

---

[59] "Good Friday Agreement: Impact of Brexit – Motion to Take Note", London, House of Lords, C185, 11.10.2019.

[60] "Irish backstop explained: what does it mean for Brexit, and why is the Irish border so important?", *The Telegraph*, 4.7.2019.

continued North-South cooperation" and "avoid a hard border" on the island of Ireland. The Protocol does not, however, protect the totality of existing socio-economic relations within and between these islands, notably the East-West dimension of the 1998 Belfast/Good Friday Agreement.

So the Withdrawal Agreement with the "backstop" solution was the only deal ultimately possible. The revised version with a "backstop" for Northern Ireland was agreed upon on 17 October 2019, signed on 24 January and after the UK has officially left the EU on 31 January 2020, it finally came into force on 20 February 2020. Without the backstop, there would have been no Withdrawal Agreement and with no Withdrawal Agreement there can be no transition period to allow for an orderly exit.

Brexit's Territorial Externalities*

Jeremy Sacramento & Jaume Castan Pinos

The United Kingdom formally left the European Union on 31st January 2020, following the Brexit referendum of June 2016. It is becoming increasingly obvious that Brexit has unleashed various negative and unintended effects, which were not considered or acknowledged, at least not sufficiently, by the proponents of the British withdrawal from the EU during the referendum campaign. This article will focus on these consequences, referring to them as "externalities". Chief amongst these is the potential destabilisation of the UK's territorial interests in Scotland, Gibraltar and Northern Ireland.

Even though the British withdrawal has been effectuated, at the time of writing most details about the Future Agreement remain unclear, and of course this might have critical implications for the territorial consequences discussed here. We therefore acknowledge the difficulty of analysing a situation which is ongoing and susceptible to transformations. Despite these challenges, we are confident that our examination will be able to shed light on a dimension of Brexit which was largely neglected prior to the referendum.

Sovereignty, in the sense of "taking back control" and the restoration of decision-making powers, was one of the arguments of "Leave" supporters during the referendum campaign. Indeed, those advocating for Brexit argued that leaving the EU would "save" the UK's sovereignty, stressing that the UK would be able to gain control over crucial policies

---

* This article takes up large parts of a working paper published (open access) by the authors at the Danish Institute for International Studies: Castan Pinos, J., Sacramento, J., "The Sovereignty Paradox: Brexit's territorial consequences for Gibraltar, Scotland and Northern Ireland", *Working Paper* 2020, 02, Copenhagen, Danish Institute for International Studies, 2020.

such as the economy, migration and justice.[1] The paradox is that Brexit seems to have compromised, rather than saved, a fundamental aspect of sovereignty: territorial integrity. The central claim of this chapter is that the British withdrawal from the EU has reinvigorated territorial debates in the British peripheries that seemed to be settled prior to the referendum. Interestingly, in all these territories, the remaining option had won by considerable margins: in Northern Ireland 56 %, in Scotland 62 % and in Gibraltar, where the remaining option was supported by an astounding 96 % of the voters.[2]

We therefore agree with Bogdanor when he claims that "Brexit involves not just a new relationship between Britain and the Continent, but perhaps also a new relationship between the various components of the United Kingdom."[3] It is important to note that since the Acts of Union of 1707 and 1800, the UK's territorial composition has carried a varying precariousness amongst and between the constituent nations. This is particularly visible in the three territories analysed in this chapter. At its peak, this weak territorial equilibrium saw the partition of Ireland in 1921, the decades-long political violence that succeeded it and the resurgence of Scottish nationalism. In Gibraltar too, the Spanish sovereignty claim has persisted, albeit in peaks and troughs, since the territory's cession to the British Crown under the terms of the Treaty of Utrecht in 1713. These territorial questions only saw some closure in roughly the last two decades, with the 1998 Good Friday Agreement between the UK and the Republic of Ireland ending the so-called "troubles", the Gibraltar joint sovereignty referendum of 2002, where 98 % of Gibraltarians rejected the measure in favour of remaining British and blunted the Spanish claim, and, the independence referendum in Scotland in 2014, which dashed the ambitions of Scottish secessionists. In essence, the territorial status quo in the British peripheries had been settled, or at least it seemed to have been.

This territorial consensus is necessarily put in jeopardy by Brexit, which has triggered what we label territorial externalities. In effect,

---

[1] See for instance: "10 reasons why choosing Brexit on June 23 is a vote for a stronger, better Britain", *The Sun*, 22.6.2016.

[2] "Results", *BBC*, 2016, https://www.bbc.com/news/politics/eu_referendum/results (2.2.2020).

[3] Bogdanor, V., *Beyond Brexit. Towards a British Constitution*, London, Bloomsbury Publishing, 2019, p. xi.

the British withdrawal from the EU, enacted in early 2020, inevitably unravels this status quo by reanimating the respective actors to pursue their desired ends, namely the Scottish National Party's (SNP) ambitions for independence, Spain's sovereignty claim over Gibraltar, or the proponents of a politically united Ireland. This study claims that it does so because these territorial conflicts have been inextricably intertwined with membership of the EU. It could be argued that EU membership has invisible effects on Member States that only become apparent once they withdraw from it. In other words, membership of the EU prompts political stability and, as such, it perpetuates and reinforces the territorial status quo.

In that regard, it is worth remembering that during the Scottish independence referendum, the menace of having to reapply for EU membership was used by the "Better Together" campaign to argue against secession. This is in no way exceptional as it has also been used by other States challenged by secessionist movements. The scaremongering argument of a prospectively independent Catalonia being expelled from the EU – and therefore having to reapply for EU membership – has been used recurrently by successive Spanish governments to persuade Catalans to support Spanish unity. For Gibraltar, EU membership meant Spain having to comply with European obligations and freedoms, which in turn meant a curtailment to Madrid's sovereignty ambitions. In the case of Northern Ireland, the EU played a positive peace-making role during the "Troubles", which had ameliorating effects on this "deeply territorialized ethno-national conflict."[4] As Hayward and Murphy claim, common Irish and British membership triggered a myriad of positive developments in terms of conflict amelioration including the bilateral adjustments of policies, cross-border cooperation, the vision of a shared future and, perhaps most importantly, it "enabled Irish and British nationalisms to be entangled without either one being eroded."[5]

With the EU variable now removed from the equation, the proponents for territorial recalibration have been given the thumbs-up.

---

[4] O'Dowd, L., Mccall, C., "Escaping the Cage of Ethno-National Conflict in Northern Ireland? The Importance of Transnational Networks", *Ethnopolitics*, vol. 7/1, 2008, p. 81.

[5] Hayward, K., Murphy, M. C., "The EU's Influence on the Peace Process and Agreement in Northern Ireland in Light of Brexit", *Ethnopolitics*, vol. 17/3, 5.6.2018, p. 277.

To put it poetically, the territorial pandora box has been reopened. In fact, the popular Irish Republican dictum, "England's difficulty is Ireland's opportunity",[6] which dates back to the mid-19th century, suitably describes the essence of Brexit's territorial externalities. Replace Ireland with Scotland or Spain, and the essence remains the same. Brexit, a noticeably English (and Welsh) decision, therefore callously revives the territorial debates and actively creates the potential for possible territorial transformations in the UK. Yet despite this, the debate on territory was conspicuous by its absence in the main campaign leading up to the in/out referendum. It has been similarly absent, as a singular variable, in the otherwise abundant academic literature that has been produced in the wake of the vote.

Overwhelmingly, academic analyses have drawn focus on the potential impact of the UK's withdrawal on all pillars of the economy, such as trade, productivity, labour and foreign direct investment.[7] Similarly, there has been focus on immigration, both in the immediate impact following the vote, and in modelling the likely future impact.[8] There have also been a slew of studies on the question of parliamentary sovereignty, assessing the extent to which the UK Parliament stands to "take back control" in the post-Brexit era.[9] These analyses closely resonate with the main factors attributed to the vote's result, namely, movement of people

---

[6] The maxim is generally attributed to Irish revolutionary Daniel O'Connell (1775–1847). For further details see Speake, J., *Oxford Dictionary of Proverbs*, Oxford, Oxford University Press, 2015.

[7] See for instance Jafari, Y., Britz, W., "Brexit: an economy-wide impact assessment on trade, immigration, and foreign direct investment", *Empirica*, 15.9.2018; Ebell, M., Warren, J., "The Long-Term Economic Impact of Leaving the EU", *National Institute Economic Review*, 2016; Dhingra, S., Ottaviano, G., Sampson, T., Van Reenen, J., *The Consequences of Brexit for UK trade and Living Standards*, London, London School of Economics and Political Science, CEP, 2016.

[8] See Goodwin, M., Milazzo, C., "Taking back control? Investigating the role of immigration in the 2016 vote for Brexit", *The British Journal of Politics and International Relations*, vol. 13/1, 2017, pp. 450–464; Roots, L., "Impact of the Article 50 of TEU on Migration of the EU Workers in Case of Brexit", in Ramiro Troitiño, D., Kerikmäe, T., Chochia, A. (eds.), *Brexit: History, Reasoning and Perspectives*, Cham, Springer, 2018; Portes, J., Forte, G., "The economic impact of Brexit-induced reductions in migration", *Oxford Review of Economic Policy*, vol. 33/1, 2017, pp. 31–44.

[9] See for instance Bogdanor, V., *op. cit.*; Ewing, K., "Brexit and Parliamentary Sovereignty", *Modern Law Review*, vol. 80/4, 2017, pp. 711–726; Greer, A., "Brexit and Devolution", *The Political Quarterly*, vol. 89/1, 2018, pp. 135–138.

and migration, trade and financial contributions.[10] Yet, these factors have been overshadowed throughout the negotiation period by the territorial questions, arguably the "elephant in the room" during the referendum campaign. Perhaps the pro-Remain slant in Scotland, Gibraltar and Northern Ireland can be considered a harbinger for the prominence of territory in the post-withdrawal process.

The aim of this study is therefore to draw attention to the territorial externalities of the UK's withdrawal by examining how these territorial issues are inextricably intertwined with membership of the EU, and thus how the withdrawal serves to re-expose the cleavages between the different actors. Our analysis concentrates on three case studies: the UK's countries of Scotland and Northern Ireland, and the British Overseas Territory of Gibraltar. These three cases entail three different types of territorial challenges: secession in Scotland, annexation by Spain in the case of Gibraltar and reunification with the Republic of Ireland in Northern Ireland. Further, these three cases reflect the centrality of the EU in their respective territorial issues. In doing so, the studies reveal the inevitability of territorial externalities as a result of alterations to the status quo caused by Brexit.

It is important to bear in mind that borders are human creations and are therefore exposed to human transformations –they cannot be taken for granted. Brexit's territorial externalities illustrate the susceptibility of the notion of territory to political changes. It could be argued that ignoring this susceptibility may potentially come at a price, in this case a territorial price.

Scotland: A Door Open to a Second Referendum?

The first case of our empirical analysis is Scotland. The question of Scotland's territoriality centres on the ambitions of the Scottish pro-independence movement to secede from the UK. Consequently, in this case, the territorial externality emerges from an internal sovereignty challenge with no influence from external actors. The case here is that the

---

[10] See for instance http://www.voteleavetakecontrol.org/why_vote_leave.html (2.2.2020); Hobolt, S., "The Brexit vote: a divided nation, a divided continent", *Journal of European Public Policy*, vol. 21/9, 2016, pp. 1259–1277.

independence question was arguably settled "for a generation"[11] following the independence referendum, agreed with the British government, that took place just 21 months prior to the Brexit vote. The September 2014 plebiscite on possible Scottish secession from the UK was the product of a notable upsurge in Scottish nationalism and secessionism, manifested through electoral support for the pro-independence SNP, which has been the most voted party in the Scottish Parliament since 2007. Keating and McEwen argue that their spectacular results of 2011, when they obtained an absolute majority, were not due to their stand on independence but despite of it.[12] That is, their growth in popularity was connected to their popular progressive policies and public management rather than their, at least to that point, ill-defined independence project, which consistently enjoyed less support than the "devolution" option.

At any rate, the self-determination referendum had been a central electoral promise by the SNP, or more precisely, "independence subject to a referendum,"[13] stressing the Scottish people's right to decide. Shortly after the 2011 SNP's parliamentary majority, in October 2012, the British Prime Minister at the time, David Cameron, agreed with Scottish legislators to organise a Scottish independence referendum for 2014. The referendum results, in which 55 % of Scots voted against independence, were a clear defeat for Scottish nationalists in general and for the SNP in particular. Interestingly, the referendum result led to Alex Salmond's resignation as Scottish First Minister, for whom independence had become the *causa prima*, but not to the abandonment of the independence goal by the SNP as a party. In this context, Brexit presented a dilemma with a difficult solution, given especially that the Scottish electorate voted in favour of remaining in the EU (by 62 %). This effectively meant that the two results were in inevitable conflict with each other. In other words, Brexit's territorial externalities regarding Scotland rest in this antagonism between continuing to form part of the UK on the one hand and the wish to remain in the EU on the other.

---

[11] The main architect of the Scottish referendum, former leader of the SNP Alex Salmond, stressed that the referendum was "once in a lifetime opportunity". See Salmond, A., "Referendum is once in a generation opportunity", *BBC*, 14.9.2014.

[12] Keating, M., McEwen, N., *Debating Scotland: Issues of Independence and Union in the 2014 Referendum*, Oxford, Oxford University Press, 2017.

[13] Elias, A., "Making the economic case for independence: The Scottish National Party's electoral strategy in post-devolution Scotland", *Regional & Federal Studies*, 29:1, 2019, p. 11.

For the SNP, the decision by the British electorate to leave the EU was arguably a blessing in disguise, in so far as it presented the opportunity to revive the spectre of a second independence vote in defiance of the "for a generation" commitment. In this way, the pro-independence sections of the Scottish electorate fell squarely in line with O'Connell's dictum in that England's problems were now Scotland's opportunities. Nicola Sturgeon, the SNP's leader following Salmond's resignation, wasted no time in capitalising the window of opportunity offered by Brexit and a day after the referendum she warned that the context had fundamentally changed: "It is a significant material change in circumstances. It's a statement of the obvious that the option of a second independence referendum must be on the table, and it is on the table."[14] The "statement of the obvious" Sturgeon is alluding to corresponds to the aforementioned incongruity between Scottish voters' preference for remaining both in the UK and the EU, but also, to the role EU membership itself played in the independence referendum campaign. As mentioned above, one of the main pillars of the "Better Together" narrative during the Scottish independence referendum campaign was the need for Scotland to have to reapply for re-entry into EU in the event of independence,[15] a claim backed up by EU officials[16] and Member States' heads of government, most emphatically Spain.[17] In other words, a vote for continuing to be part of the UK, was a vote for remaining in the EU.

The EU's position similarly changed materially in the aftermath of the Brexit vote. This was clearly illustrated by the unprecedented reception that the Scottish First Minister received in Brussels on June 29th 2016, when she was given the red-carpet treatment and met the then President of the European Parliament, Martin Schulz, and the then President of the Commission, Jean-Claude Juncker. The content of these discussions was equally significant, with Juncker indicating his predisposition to discuss a potential permanence of Scotland in the EU in spite of the British

---

[14] Nicola Sturgeon cited in "Nicola Sturgeon: second Scottish independence poll highly likely", *The Guardian*, 24.6.2016.
[15] "Scottish independence: Better Together boss sets out Union case", *BBC News*, 1.2.2013.
[16] "Scottish independence: Barroso warning on EU membership", *BBC News*, 10.12.2012.
[17] "Scottish independence: Spain blocks Alex Salmond's hopes for EU transition", *The Guardian*, 27.11.2013.

withdrawal.[18] Spain too has moved away from its staunch opposition to the possible membership of an independent Scotland.[19] The reason behind this material change is crystal clear: Scotland was no longer a bothersome region challenging the territorial integrity of a Member state. In the post-Brexit era, Scotland had become, a legitimate interlocutor in the eyes of the EU. This is a historical and unprecedented achievement for a secessionist region in Europe, arguably the most successful day in Scottish para-diplomacy.[20] Nor would it be the last. Two days after the formal withdrawal of the UK from the EU, in an interview with the BBC, the former President of the European Council, Donald Tusk, stressed that if an independent Scotland applied for EU membership, "emotionally, I have no doubt that everyone will be enthusiastic here in Brussels, and more generally in Europe"[21]. Needless to say, any such statement implicitly supporting Scottish secession would have been unthinkable prior to Brexit.

Trying to capitalize on this momentum, from the outset the Scottish Government started exploring different roads to circumventing the current conundrum. For instance, along with the Gibraltarian authorities, it proposed a "reverse Greenland" model.[22] Using Greenland's departure in 1985 as the only pre-existing model for withdrawing from the bloc, the proposal suggested having only the Leave voting parts of the UK – England and Wales – withdraw from the EU, while keeping the Remain voting parts – Scotland, Northern Ireland and Gibraltar – inside the Union. This, however, cut no ice with the UK Government, which swiftly dismissed the proposal. Although it failed, the proposal reveals

---

[18] "European Commission president to 'listen' to Scotland's case to remain in EU", *The Independent*, 29.6.2016.

[19] "Spanish minister Josep Borrell says Scots could join EU", *The Times*, 21.11.2018.

[20] For further details on the concept of paradiplomacy in a secessionist context see Duchacek, I., *The Territorial Dimension of Politics: Within, Among, and Across Nations*, London, Westview Press, 1986; and McHugh, J., "Paradiplomacy, protodiplomacy and the foreign policy aspirations of Quebec and other Canadian provinces", *Canadian Foreign Policy Journal*, vol. 21/3, 2015, pp. 238–256; Tavares, R., *Paradiplomacy: Cities and States as Global Players*, Oxford, Oxford University Press, 2016; Castan Pinos, J., Sacramento, J., "L'État contre-attaque: un examen de la contra-paradiplomatie espagnole en Catalogne", *Relations internationales*, vol. 179/3, 2019, pp. 95–111.

[21] "'Empathy' for independent Scotland joining the EU says Tusk", *BBC News*, 2.2.2020.

[22] "'Reverse Greenland', anyone? Scots eye post-Brexit EU options", *Reuters*, 3.7.2016.

that, despite the rhetoric of a second independence referendum, the Scottish government was in practice paying heed to the electoral support for remaining in the EU while also accepting the still fresh results of the independence vote.

At any rate, no firm commitment was made to table a second independence referendum by the SNP until the end of April 2019, when Nicola Sturgeon announced her party's intention to hold a second vote by 2021. The content of her announcement closely resonates with the argument presented here: "I consider that a choice between Brexit and a future for Scotland as an independent European nation should be offered in the lifetime of this parliament." The stipulated date of 2021 is similarly telling and can be explained by the confusion and uncertainty that has tainted the Brexit negotiations, both at home and in Europe: "The political conditions are not right for another campaign to leave the UK amid so much unfolding uncertainty."[23] The push for a second referendum, and hence for independence, was reinvigorated by Sturgeon in the wake of the UK's formal withdrawal from the EU on January 31st 2020, on the grounds that "the UK that Scotland voted to be part of in 2014 ceases to exist"[24]. This push was accompanied by polls indicating that, for the first time since 2015, support for independence was once again in the lead (51/49) due to the fact that a considerable numbers of *remainers* had begun to back this option[25]. In light of the above, it seems evident that Brexit, by fundamentally altering the territorial status quo, has revived the territorial debate in Scotland, galvanising the possibility of a second referendum, and hence of secession. As Paddison and Rae put it, "the referendum has exposed and deepened pre-existing divisions in UK society, not least territorial cleavages, and in this respect it was to amplify the 'tyranny of the majority' as well as the 'brutalism' of the unconstrained referendum."[26] Furthermore, from the EU perspective, Scotland is not merely a potential new Member State, it is also a

---

[23] "Brexit breeds boredom, bafflement and frustration in Scotland", *The Guardian*, 28.11.2018.

[24] "Brexit will speed Scottish independence, says Nicola Sturgeon", *Financial Times*, 31.1.2020.

[25] "Scottish independence: Yes leads as Remainers increasingly back splitting with UK", *YouGov*, 31.1.2020.

[26] Paddison, R., Rae, N., "Brexit and Scotland: towards a political geography perspective", *Social Space Journal*, vol. 13, 2017, p. 1.

punishing mechanism – a deterrence to future rebel States – that leaving the club may trigger negative externalities in terms of compromising their territorial integrity.

Gibraltar and the Reignited Spanish Sovereignty Claim

The territorial dimension of the British Overseas Territory of Gibraltar emerges from Spain's well-known sovereignty claim over "the Rock". Spain has maintained an irredentist claim almost since the territory was ceded to the British Crown in perpetuity under the terms of the Treaty of Utrecht (1713). However, until Brexit the political realities of life inside the EU had, in the main, limited Spain's capacity to force a transfer of sovereignty over Gibraltar from the UK, and allowed the Rock to prosper economically. By extension, Brexit, in withdrawing the Overseas Territory from the EU, removes these limits and seemingly gives Spain's claim a new lease of life; thus, exposing an intrinsic territorial externality. However, unlike Scotland, in this case, with Spain as a third State, the externality is a fully external matter. The UK (and Gibraltar's) withdrawal from the EU reignites Spain's sovereignty aspirations in two important ways. First, it hands Spain a very convenient "carrot", in that it can use Gibraltar's pro-European sentiment, as expressed through its 96 % "remain" vote, to attempt to lure the Gibraltarians towards joint-sovereignty. Secondly, through the loss of the protections established by the European *acquis communautaire*, it also hands Spain a "stick". That is, it opens up the possibility to set the clock back to pre-accession, when Spain was free to impose stringent measures on Gibraltar in an attempt to coerce the Gibraltarian population.

The combination of being in a different time zone and the relatively small size of the electorate, meant that Gibraltar was the first constituency to reveal the results of the vote on the evening of the 23rd June 2016. The territory voted emphatically in favour of remaining in the EU, with 96 % of electors ticking the "remain" box on the ballot paper. Yet, this pro-EU sentiment was demonstrably at odds with the Brexit favouring electorate in the UK, specifically England and Wales. Gibraltar therefore faced the prospect of dividing its loyalties, which, since the UK's (and Gibraltar's) accession to the European Community (EC) in 1973, were one and the same. The referendum result bluntly separated these loyalties, and in so doing exposed Gibraltar's and the UK's divergent interests. It is in these

Gibraltar and the Reignited Spanish Sovereignty Claim 205

countervailing forces that Spain, to paraphrase O'Connell once again, has seen an opportunity.

Already in the lead up to the vote, Spain had made no secret of what it believed Brexit meant for its sovereignty claim. In a radio interview three months before the vote, then Foreign Minister Jose Manuel Garcia Margallo clearly stated that the British withdrawal from the EU would offer Spain an opportunity to advance its sovereignty ambitions over the Rock.[27] Given this context, it is little surprise that the territorial question featured prominently throughout referendum campaign in Gibraltar. A reality which contrasts with the absence of any consideration in the UK's central campaign. As mentioned above, Spain's territorial rhetoric has followed two interlinked paths: the carrot and the stick.

The carrot approach stems from Spain using its continued membership of the EU as a means to entice the people of Gibraltar; given that membership of the EU has in the most part proven beneficial to Gibraltar. The territory became a member of the EEC with the UK in 1973, under the terms of Article 227(4) of the Treaty of Rome (now Article 355(3) of the Lisbon Treaty).[28] This gave Gibraltar access to the single market and the freedom of movement of people, services and capital, while allowing it to opt out of certain aspects of EU law. Concretely, it did not form part of the customs union, the Common Agricultural Policy, the Common Fisheries Policy, or the Value Added Tax agreement.[29] Moreover, the border once opened in 1985[30], significantly boosted the scope for expansion of the tourism sector, as well as facilitated Gibraltar to make better use of the free movement of people to attract labour for its expanding economy.

In removing this access to the single market, departure has handed Spain, as continued member of the EU, an effective bargaining chip. Spain has extended an olive branch in the form of joint-sovereignty – as a

---

[27] Interview with Jose Manuel Garcia Margallo, Radio Nacional de España, 4.3.2016; HM Government of Gibraltar, "Margallo waiting to pounce if Gibraltar leaves the EU", HM Government of Gibraltar Press Release 100/2016, 4.3.2016.

[28] European Commission, Treaty of Rome, EUR-Lex, 1957.

[29] European Commission, Treaty concerning the accession of the Kingdom of Denmark, Ireland, the Kingdom of Norway and the United Kingdom of Great Britain and Northern Ireland to the European Economic Community and to the European Atomic Energy Community, Articles 28–30, *Official Journal*, 27.3.1972.

[30] Having been shut by the Spanish dictator General Franco in 1969.

means of offering Gibraltarians the best of both worlds, where Gibraltar remains (half) British and in the EU through Spanish membership[31]. This proposition which over the last four years since the in/out referendum has been extended by Spanish governments of differing colours, reinforces how Madrid sees the change in circumstances as a renewed opportunity on sovereignty.

Spain has complemented its "carrot" case set out above, with the threat of a "stick". This second approach centres on the *de jure* and *de facto* protections offered to Gibraltar through its membership of the EU. In fact, the many benefits became the cornerstone of the pre-referendum campaign for remaining in the EU. Most fundamentally, it was argued, EU membership has given Gibraltar a platform from where to advocate, and where necessary protect, its interests.[32] Indeed, the institutions themselves have facilitated the process. A clear example of this being the EU Commission's inspection visits to the border, following an increase in border checks by Spain in 2013. The visit culminated in a report by the Commission that assessed Spanish border measures as "disproportionate" – the result of which was a significant improvement in flow across the border.[33] Brexit therefore, very clearly removes this useful weapon from Gibraltar's arsenal when facing Spanish antagonism. In a post-Brexit scenario, Spain could freely impose restrictions on its border with a non-Member State, as an attempt to advance its position; a threat that is made credible when considering its behaviour throughout the period of negotiations.

That is, Spain's approach towards Gibraltar in the three years of withdrawal negotiations – since Art. 50 of the Lisbon Treaty was triggered by Theresa May – already conforms with the approaches set out above. For example, the EU's draft negotiating guidelines, i.e. its objectives and red lines, published just two days after Theresa May's letter, included a clause that stated "After the United Kingdom leaves the Union, no

---

[31] "Margallo, sobre Gibraltar: 'Pondré la bandera y mucho antes de lo que Picardo cree'", *El País*, 6.10.2016.

[32] See for instance, the joint appearance of Gibraltar's past and present Chief Ministers, for the Stronger in Europe, 2016, https://www.facebook.com/GibStrongerIN/videos/1761939984025467/ (2.2.2020).

[33] European Commission, *Commission reports on the border situation in La Línea (Spain) and Gibraltar (UK)*, Brussels, Presse Release, 15.11.2013; and HM Government of Gibraltar, *Government issues booklet explaining why Gibraltar should vote to REMAIN in the EU*, Gibraltar, Press Release 240/2016, 17.5.2016.

agreement between the EU and the United Kingdom may apply to the territory of Gibraltar without the agreement between the Kingdom of Spain and the United Kingdom."[34] This clause in effect granted Spain a double veto on the application of any future agreement on Gibraltar. In other words, any future agreement between the UK and the EU could exclude Gibraltar under this condition. Spain put this threat of a veto into practice at the eleventh hour of the Withdrawal Agreement being agreed by the EU 27 in November 2018.[35] Spain has similarly ensured that the de jure veto is re-emphasised in the EU's Future Agreement negotiating guidelines: "Any agreement between the Union and the United Kingdom negotiated on the basis of these negotiating directives will not include Gibraltar".[36]

It is clear that Spain's actions and rhetoric preceding the vote, during the withdrawal negotiations and since, have already illustrated the very real pressure on the UK and Gibraltar for matters of sovereignty to be opened for discussion. For its part, the British government has reconfirmed its commitment to the Rock. In his Greenwich speech 3rd February 2020, Prime Minister Boris Johnson underlined that despite the EU's negotiating posture, "the UK will be negotiating on behalf of the entire UK family, and that certainly includes Gibraltar; and the sovereignty of Gibraltar remains, as everybody knows, indivisible."[37] The Gibraltar Government has been similarly unequivocal in pronouncing where Gibraltar stands with respect to Spain's joint-sovereignty suggestion, "It's as dead as a dodo."[38] Nevertheless, it is absolutely clear that Brexit, through Spain's irredentist claim, presents very serious challenges for Gibraltar and, consequently, for the UK's territorial integrity. The Gibraltar question is therefore one of Brexit's negative externalities *par excellence*, and one which has become a cumbersome predicament to the UK's negotiation of the Future Agreement.

---

[34] European Council and Council of the European Union, European Council (Art. 50) guidelines for Brexit negotiations, Press Release, 29.4.2017.
[35] La Moncloa Gobierno de España, "España votará 'no' al Brexit si Bruselas no cambia los actuales términos sobre Gibraltar en el acuerdo de retirada", Madrid, 20.11.2018.
[36] European Commission (2020). "Directives for the Negotiation of a New Partnership with the United Kingdom of Great Britain and Northern Ireland", *Official Journal*, 3.2.2020.
[37] "Prime Minister reaffirms Gibraltar role in future relationship negotiations", *GBC*, 3.2.2020.
[38] Picardo, F., "Chief Minister's New Year's Message 2019", YourGibraltarTV, 7.1.2019.

Northern Ireland: The Return of Territoriality

It is important to note that in each of the cases analysed in this chapter we find different dynamics in terms of the types of actors that are challenging the territorial status quo. As we have seen above, in Scotland it is purely an internal matter of the pro-independence movement led by the SNP, whereas in Gibraltar the actor pushing for territorial transformation is external, namely Spain. In Northern Ireland (NI), where the territorial externality hinges on the reunification of the island, the dynamics are arguably less clear-cut. The reason for this is that Sinn Féin,[39] the main actor pushing for a reunification agenda and therefore for transforming the territorial status quo, is present both in Northern Ireland and in political institutions of the Republic of Ireland (RoI). Additionally, at least at a rhetorical level, the Republic of Ireland, through Art. 3 of its Constitution, maintains the goal of Irish reunification: "It is the firm will of the Irish Nation, in harmony and friendship, to unite all the people who share the territory of the island of Ireland [...] recognising that a united Ireland shall be brought about only by peaceful means with the consent of a majority of the people, democratically expressed, in both jurisdictions in the island."[40] The case of Northern Ireland could therefore be considered hybrid in terms of the nature of the actors that aim to transform the territorial status quo.

In this territory, Brexit has a few crucial particularities. Unlike the other cases analysed in this chapter, this contested territory was, as a result of partition, the centre of political violence throughout most of the 20th century. Possibly because of this, both British and EU negotiators treated this territory with particular caution, not least through the "backstop" clause, a sort of an insurance policy that would have prevented the hard border scenario in Ireland. Unsurprisingly, during the lengthy withdrawal negotiations the Irish border issue was one of the main points of friction. The "protocol on Ireland/Northern Ireland" attached to the revised withdrawal agreement recognizes the need "to address the unique

---

[39] The party, which could be considered the bedrock of Irish republicanism, is the second largest in NI, where they obtained 28 % of the ballots in the 2017 Assembly election. In the Republic of Ireland, they are the third largest party with nearly 14 % of the votes in the 2016 parliamentary elections. During the "troubles", Sinn Féin was the political wing of the Provisional Republican Army.

[40] Department of the Taoiseach, "Constitution of Ireland", 1.11.2018.

circumstances on the island of Ireland through a unique solution" and explicitly emphasizes the commitment of the UK, guaranteeing that there will be no "hard border"[41]. At the time of writing, however, the negotiations regarding the border issue between Ireland and Northern Ireland have still not been finalized. The various commitments to avoid a hard border have (thus far) prevented the worst-case scenario with regard to the Irish border issue, as the re-imposition of a border between north and south would have contravened the Belfast Agreement.

This agreement, which is popularly known as the Good Friday Agreement (GFA), is often praised for putting an end to three decades of political violence in Northern Ireland.[42] In brief, the GFA led to the disbandment and decommissioning of the Provisional Irish Republican Army (IRA) as well as of other Republican and British Loyalist paramilitary groups. This bilateral peace agreement between the Irish and the British governments, however, did not just terminate a violent conflict which had resulted in over 3,500 deaths,[43] it also had a tremendously significant territorial impact. Namely, it reinforced the British sovereignty over the territory in a paradoxical fashion. The acknowledgement of the right to the people of Northern Ireland to Irish (as well as British) citizenship, the recognition of the principle of self-determination over the future status of the territory[44] and the establishment of a power sharing agreement,[45] where both Irish Republicans and British Unionists shared control over

---

[41] British Government, "Agreement on the withdrawal of the United Kingdom of Great Britain and Northern Ireland from the European Union and the European Atomic Energy Community", 19.10.2019.

[42] With the exception of Irish Republican dissident groups that continue, to this day, using violence to pursue their goals. Their support and level of operations is, however, practically insignificant and in no way comparable to the Provisional Irish Republican Army and other paramilitary groups during *the Troubles*.

[43] For further details on deaths and casualties see: CAIN, "Information on Deaths During the Conflict", Ulster University, 2019.

[44] Northern Ireland Office, "The Belfast Agreement", Policy Paper, 10.4.1998.

[45] For more details on the power sharing agreement in NI see Taylor, R., "The Belfast Agreement and the Politics of Consociationalism: A Critique", *The Political Quarterly*, vol. 77/2, 2006, pp. 217–226; McGarry, J., O'Leary, B., "Power-Sharing Executives: Consociational and Centripetal Formulae and the Case of Northern Ireland", *Ethnopolitics*, vol. 15/5, 2016, pp. 497–519; White, T., "Consociation, Conditionality, and Commitment: Making Peace in Northern Ireland", in Jakala, M. *et al.* (eds.), *Consociationalism and Power-Sharing in Europe*, Cham, Palgrave Macmillan, 2018.

Northern Ireland's affairs, generated an erosion of the "territorial issue". In Hayward and Murphy's words, the GFA had the effect of redefining "relations across these islands in a way that [...] defused the border as a cause for political conflict and violence."[46]

It is not too far-fetched to claim that open discussions on territoriality in Ireland experienced a comeback in Northern Ireland, becoming strengthened in the aftermath of the Brexit referendum. The first, and perhaps most compelling, evidence for this is that, in the wake of the Brexit referendum, Sinn Féin called for a reunification referendum in Ireland.[47] The historical leader of the party, Gerry Adams, claimed in an op-ed in the *New York Times*, published shortly after the vote, that Brexit offered "a reason and an opportunity" for a referendum, where, he continued, Northern Irish citizens could decide whether they "wanted to be part of a Britain outside the European Union or belong to a unified Irish State in Europe"[48]. This was not too dissimilar to Spain's intimations on joint sovereignty discussed above. Equally, in close similarly to the Scottish nationalists, Irish Republicans built their case on the grounds of the different voting results of their territories compared to the rest of the UK. It should be noted that Northern Ireland (56 %), and particularly Irish Nationalists in this constituency (88 %), voted overwhelmingly in favour of the remaining option.[49]

The territorial debate that has been triggered by Brexit has also influenced developments in the Republic of Ireland. In the Irish general elections of February 2020, Sinn Féin, the quintessentially pro-reunification party that had been of marginal significance south of the border since the late 1920s, topped the polls with nearly a quarter of the votes[50]. In addition, according to a May 2019 survey, 77 % of Irish citizens (in the Republic of Ireland) support Irish reunification.[51] Support for a

---

[46] Hayward, K., Murphy, M. C., *op. cit.*, p. 276.
[47] Sinn Fein calls for border poll on united Ireland after Brexit win in EU referendum", *Belfast Telegraph*, 24.6.2016.
[48] "Brexit and Irish Unity", *The New York Times*, 12.7.2016.
[49] Garry, J., "The EU referendum Vote in Northern Ireland: Implications for our understanding of citizens' political views and behavior", Northern Ireland Assembly, Knowledge Exchange Seminar Series, 2017.
[50] "Irish general election: Sinn Féin tops first preference polls", *BBC News*, 10.2.2020.
[51] McMorrow, C., "Exit poll indicates strong support for Irish language", *RTE*, 2019, https://www.rte.ie/news/elections-2019/2019/0525/1051603-rte-tg4-exit-poll/ (2.3.2020).

united Ireland also came from an unsuspected actor: the EU Council. In a statement published in April 2017, this institution openly addressed the possibility of the political reunification of the island:

> "The European Council acknowledges that the Good Friday Agreement expressly provides for an agreed mechanism whereby a united Ireland may be brought about through peaceful and democratic means. In this regard, the European Council acknowledges that, in accordance with international law, the entire territory of such a united Ireland would thus be part of the European Union."[52]

In a similar way to both the Scottish and Gibraltarian cases examined above, it seems unlikely that the EU Council would have issued such a statement explicitly acknowledging the possibility of altering borders prior to the Brexit referendum.

The British withdrawal from the EU, has the potential to compromise political stability by aggravating the already fragile[53] institutional assemblage of Northern Ireland. It is indeed far from ideal that the parties of a power-sharing executive based on consociationalism become polarised. As explained above, Irish Nationalists led by Sinn Féin have stepped up their claims for a united Ireland referendum, whereas the Ulster Unionist Party (Northern Ireland's second largest Unionist party) has radicalised its positions by advocating for direct rule from Westminster.[54] Disagreements over a myriad of issues, including Brexit, led to the collapse of the NI power-sharing executive between 2017 and January 2020. Indeed, their view towards the future of the border is diametrically antagonistic: whereas Irish Nationalists categorically reject a hard border with the RoI, their Unionist counterparts irately oppose any differential treatment from the rest of the UK. The caveat is that in the event of a hard Brexit, one of the two possibilities will necessarily occur.

From the above, it is clear that the Irish border has not only become a point of friction between Unionists and Irish Republicans in NI, it has

---

[52] Drachenberg, R., "Outcome of the special European Council (Article 50) meeting of 29 April 2017", Brussels, European Parliamentary Research Service, 2017.

[53] The powersharing executive in Northern Ireland collapsed in January 2017, following a corruption scandal and disagreements over it between the two main parties, the unionist Democratic Unionist Party and Sinn Féin.

[54] "PM must introduce direct rule in Northern Ireland if no Brexit deal agreed – UUP", *Belfast Telegraph*, 6.2.2019.

also become a significantly contentious issue between the EU and UK negotiators. Interestingly, this territorial externality was utterly neglected during the Brexit referendum campaign.

Conclusion

Our study set out to draw attention to the territorial externalities inherent in the UK's withdrawal from the EU and their conspicuous absence during the referendum campaign. The three cases we have examined, Scotland, Gibraltar and Northern Ireland, illustrate how pre-existing (pre-accession) territorial issues had become inextricably intertwined with membership of the EU, meaning that exiting the bloc carries the very real possibility of re-exposing the cleavages between the different actors, and hence in effect reverting to the *status quo ante*.

In the case of Scotland, we found that the likelihood of a second independence referendum taking place within the next few years has gone from a distant possibility in the aftermath of the first vote in 2014, to an SNP policy commitment for this to happen in the immediate future. This emerges from the conflicting aspirations of the Scottish electorate, who voted to remain both in the UK in 2014 and the EU in 2016. The UK's extraction from the latter means that these aspirations are pitted against each other, producing the SNP's commitment, which is reinforced by the role EU membership played in the independence referendum.

The EU's role in Spain's sovereignty claim over Gibraltar has been similarly consequential. Gibraltar has benefited from the limitations imposed on Spain's approach towards the Rock provided by *acquis communautaire*, as well as from the economic benefits access to the single market. Leaving the EU, however, erodes these limitations and, for the first time since accession, gives Spain *carte blanche* to pursue its sovereignty claim in whichever manner it considers necessary. Specifically, based on the pre-accession *modus vivendi*, the nature of Gibraltar's EU membership, as well as the Spanish Government's narrative since the vote, this case study shows that Spain can now approach the claim with proverbial carrots and sticks. The former consists of offering Gibraltar the possibility of continued EU membership through joint sovereignty. The latter allows Spain to impose punitive measures on Gibraltar, in the same fashion as prior to Spain's accession in 1986.

Conclusion

The Northern Irish question was, similarly to the other territorial issues in the British peripheries analysed in this chapter, conspicuous by its absence during the Brexit referendum campaign (at least, outside of Northern Ireland). After the plebiscite, however, the status of Northern Ireland and the future of the Irish border has become one of the chief contentions and consequently one of the pivotal headaches for EU and British negotiators. In particular, the prospect of a hard Brexit threatened to destabilise the (already fragile) post-GFA political assemblage. One of the consequences of the unearthing of territoriality in Northern Ireland is that, following the O'Connell dictum, contemporary Irish Republicans are attempting to take political advantage of the current uncertain climate to push the agenda of a united Ireland. In contrast to the pre-Brexit scenario, this idea has now been institutionally (and explicitly) legitimised by the EU.

The cases therefore reveal an apparent inevitability of territorial externalities once the status quo of the UK vis-à-vis the EU changed. These cases also raise important questions regarding the main pre-referendum campaign, where very these issues received very little mention, despite the significance of the territorial externalities for the UK's territorial integrity. Michael Keating stresses that "although Brexit will leave behind fault lines in the territorial politics of the UK, it may not provoke fissures sufficiently deep as to break the UK itself apart."[55] Our analysis goes further and contends that, while Brexit might not necessarily lead to a change of the UK's territorial status quo (or that of its overseas territory), it has created the conditions for it, providing a fertile ground for multiple actors whose respective causes (secession, annexation or reunification) have been significantly strengthened as a result of the uncertainties generated by the withdrawal of the UK from the EU. After all, as we argued in the introduction, as human constructions borders are sensitive to political crises and vulnerable to human transformations.

---

[55] Keating, M., "Brexit and the nation", *op. cit.*, 2019, p. 175.

European Union-Japan Relations in the Shadow of Brexit

Ken Masujima

We are at a historical turning point in the development of the European Union (EU). The second largest economy of the EU, the UK, left the EU. This event is sure to have an impact on any foreign relations that the EU has in the world. This is more so with Asia, which had close historical ties with the UK. The relationship between Japan and the EU is no exception to this. This chapter therefore investigates first the role of the UK, and then the impact of Brexit that hinges upon that relationship.

The Role of the UK in Japan-EU Relations

Most analysts of the relations between the EU and Japan note the important role that the UK played in their development.[1] There are three specific roles that the UK played in EU-Japan Relations.

UK as a Gateway to Japanese Investment

The UK is often considered as a gateway for Japanese corporations interested in being present in the EU. The sheer fact of the concentration of most Japanese investment in the UK is a testimony to that gateway role. For Japan, the UK is the second largest destination of foreign investment after the US. As of 2017, about 1,000 Japanese corporations

---

[1] Masujima, K., "EU-Japan Relations", in Jørgensen, K. E., Aarstad, A. K., Drieskens, E., Laatikainen, K., Tonra, B. (eds.), *Sage Handbook of European Foreign Policy*, London, Sage, 2015, pp. 584–597.

operated in the UK, employing roughly 160,000 workers.[2] It is therefore natural that Japan relied on the UK for protecting its interests within the EU. Compared with China, which invested more in Eastern Europe and is said to be in relatively better shape to face challenges of Brexit, for Japan, this dependency is clearly a problem in the context of Brexit.

UK as an Agent of Mediation within the EU

This role was important from the time when the UK got admitted into the European Community (EC) in 1973. With the entry of the UK, the EC's relations with the outside world got wider, with the UK's former colonies (Commonwealth countries) joining the EC's outer circles (especially the Pacific and the Caribbean countries were to be treated favourably in terms of trade and aid as partners in the name of the ACP: African, Caribbean, and the Pacific). In Asia, it meant that the UK tried to ensure that its historical relations with such countries as Malaysia, Singapore, India, Pakistan, Sri Lanka, and Pakistan be maintained as part of the EC's foreign relations. Besides, it is in this context important to remember that English was not one of the official languages of the EC before the accession of the UK. It is no wonder that the EC with the UK as a Member State thus also facilitated in "linguistic" ways the links that other countries had in doing business with the EU.

Britain's role in the transition from the Tokugawa period (1603–1868) to the Meiji period (1868–1912) was significant, especially the personal role played by Sir Harry Smith Parkes, who stayed in Japan for 18 years during this period (1865–1883). Since then, Japan has not been colonized by the British, but it had close relations as an ally between 1902 and 1923. It is no wonder then that Bridges notes that "only the UK had a historical deep-seated relationship with Japan" among the European countries. This assertion needs to be nuanced, however, as since the conclusion of the Treaty of Amity and Commerce between France and Japan in 1868, France has also had deep relations with Japan (although unlike the UK, France took side with the losing Tokugawa side).

After the UK entered the EC, the UK's role in the relations between Japan and the EC became naturally preponderant but were ambiguous

---

[2] "Japan waves goodbye to U.K. As 'Gateway to Europe' Post-Brexit", *Bloomberg News*, 3.10.2018.

in nature. Indeed, during the heyday of trade frictions between the EC and Japan, at the end of the 1980s, the UK was "most vocal" against improving EC's relations with Japan.[3] It has also often been said that "the British had historically been among the most anti-Japanese."[4] The role of the UK in the development of EU-Japan relations was thus an ambiguous one.

However, since the end of the trade friction around 1990 up until the contemporary period, the UK has facilitated Japan's relations with the EU in many ways. Thus, Ueta notes that the "UK was the first country with which Japan developed politico-military cooperation in the 1990s."[5] In this context, the development of bilateral cooperation between the UK and Japan in political and military affairs was important in facilitating a similar development with the EU. This aspect is relevant to the policy affinity that the UK and Japan shared which we shall see next.

UK as an Agent of Policy Affinity

The UK occupied a special place in the development of Japan-EU relations not only because of historical connections, but of similar positions on many policy issues. This policy affinity has been important for the UK's mediating role within the EU, but also in their efforts to foster a desirable direction of the EU policies for both the UK and Japan, as they shared a similar policy outlook.

There are principally two areas where such policy affinity can be found between the UK and Japan. The first area of common agreement is economic policy. As is well known, within the EU, the UK (along with some other countries) advocates a liberal economic policy while France and southern Member States support more interventionist economic policies. Japan shared this liberal economic outlook and relied on the UK for pushing the EU in that direction.

---

[3] Nuttal, S., "The Reluctant Partnership", in *Euro-Japanese Relations in Respective Regional Developments, 1975–1995*, The JCIE Papers, Tokyo, Japan Center for International Exchange, vol. 19, 1997, p. 177.

[4] Nuttal, S., "Japan and the European Union: Reluctant Partners", *Survival*, vol. 38/2, 1996, p. 108.

[5] Ueta, T., "Evolution of Japan-Europe Relations since the End of the Cold War", in Ueta, T., Remacle, E. (eds.), *Japan and Enlarged Europe: Partners in Global Governance*, Brussels, P.I.E. Peter Lang, 2005, p. 22.

The second area of policy affinity is the political and military domain. Japan relies on US military protection (US-Japan Security Alliance) and therefore would like to see the security system guaranteed by the US intact. Within the EU, France, for a long time, has been advocating more independent EU policies both in political and military spheres. The UK for its part has been extremely prudent in this regard for fear of downgrading US security relations symbolized by the North Atlantic Treaty Organization (NATO). Japan thus favoured implicitly the "Atlantist" (in favour of NATO) positions advocated by the UK. It is in this context understandable that the UK was pushing for more cooperation in the politico-military field with Japan.

These important roles that the UK has been playing for Japan-EU relations will be compromised by Brexit if not completely.

Impact of Brexit on Japan's Relations with the EU

It is expected that with Brexit, the roles of the UK as gateway, mediator and policy advocate in Japan-EU relations will disappear from the scene. However, this chapter asserts that it is not simple as it first appears. Indeed, it will be shown that the UK will be expected to continue to play an important role for Japanese diplomacy in Europe. To see this, it is necessary to go into detail concerning various policy fields to analyse the effects that Brexit may have on the relations between Japan and the EU.

Trade and Investment

The perspective of Brexit precipitated the negotiation of a European Partnership Agreement (EPA) between Japan and the EU to a conclusion before the end of 2018 (It was signed on 17th July 2018). The strong desire on both sides to finish the negotiation (and eventual ratification) was manifest especially at the final stage of the negotiation. Both sides wanted to conclude the negotiation before Brexit, since it was thought that it would involve long and hard negotiations, sure to consume the energy of the EU trade officials. Japanese negotiators also wished to conclude while the UK's influence was still there before the UK is completely gone. It is therefore not surprising that the EPA entered into force on 1rst February 2020, the day after the official Brexit.

The EPA was considered also important by the Japanese side to set a model for an eventual future bilateral negotiation with the UK after Brexit. It was even hoped at the beginning that the EU and the UK could maintain more or less status quo (the "soft" Brexit option, with the UK remaining in the customs union). The Japanese Government sent a message pointing into this direction to both the EU and the UK on 26th September 2016. However, as the perspective for a "soft" Brexit became more and more remote, the discussions between the UK and Japan turned to a post-EPA solution. Both sides began to float the idea of the UK joining the Comprehensive and Progressive Agreement for Trans-Pacific Partnership (TPP11) that Japan and other 10 TPP Trans-Pacific Partnership Agreement (TPP) signatories hurriedly set up after the US under President Trump had withdrawn from the TPP. On the occasion of a Japan-UK Summit meeting held on 1rst December 2018, Prime Minister Shinzo Abe stated that "Japan and the United Kingdom are among the strongest champions of free trade, and in this regard, welcomed the United Kingdom's expression of its interest in joining the TPP11 Agreement". To this, then Prime Minister Theresa May responded that "she expects to discuss the UK's accession to the TPP11 agreement in the near future."[6]

Global Issues

The EU and Japan have started to discuss global issues since the beginning of the 1990s. But this discussion gained a new impetus with the signing of the Strategic Partnership Agreement (SPA) at the same moment as the signing of the EPA in 2018. In the SPA, some forty issues of global concern are mentioned for cooperation: promotion of world peace, innovation in economy and technology, climate change, environment, and cyber security, as well as terrorism and international crimes among others.

The UK, which occupies a permanent membership in the UN Security Council, has been important in its own right to Japanese diplomacy and as such both countries have continuously been discussing these global issues in their bilateral meetings. It is therefore expected that Japan and the UK will try to adapt their existing bilateral dialogues on global issues

---

[6] Ministry of Foreign Affairs of Japan, "Japan-U.K. Summit Meeting", Buenos Aires, 11.12.2018.

to the SPA. After Brexit, however, it remains to be seen whether these dialogues could become "trilateral" involving the EU.

International Cooperation for Development

The policy area of development cooperation within the EU is a hybrid one, involving both the European Commission and the Member States. It is therefore expected that the UK will concentrate its efforts on its own policy, taking resources away from the EU aid and policies pursued by the European Commission. Japan and the UK already have bilateral policy dialogue on development cooperation and therefore, this bilateral dialogue on development aid will be expected to continue. Since the EU may reduce its aid to the former Commonwealth countries (except for the countries which remain important for the interest for the EU like Nigeria and South Africa), Japan may be asked to cooperate with the UK to compensate for the eventual loss of the EU aid resources in these countries.[7]

Diplomacy and Defence

It is in this field that the departure of the UK from the EU will be most strongly felt. Japan was able to increase cooperation with the EU in security affairs as long as the basic posture of the EU was based on NATO. The EU without the UK will be expected to advance more independent defence positions (this seems in certain ways to be demanded by the US President Donald Trump as well). It will remain to be seen if Japan can be led to increase defence cooperation with more and more "independently minded" EU. Japan, however will certainly reach out to the UK to consolidate and eventually increase security dialogue and cooperation with the UK, which remains an important global ally as a bulwark of the Western Alliance in Europe led by the US[8] and as a permanent member of the UN Security Council.

---

[7] Kennes, W., "How Brexit May Affect ACP-EU Relations: An Historical Perspective", Discussion Paper 220, ECDPM, 2018.

[8] Ikemoto, D., "Is the Western Alliance Crumbling? A Japanese Perspective on Brexit", in Huang, D. W. F., Reilly, M. (eds.), *The Implications of Brexit for East Asia*, London, Palgrave, 2018, pp. 112–128.

Japan-EU Relations after Brexit

The roles assumed by the UK in the relations between Japan and the EU will certainly diminish after Brexit, in one way or another. The gateway role that the UK played in receiving major Japanese investment (both direct and indirect) in Europe will diminish to the benefit of the remaining EU Member States, especially France and Germany.[9] The mediating role that the UK has played in the EU for Japan will be reduced. In the field of regulation, trade, investment, research etc., the EU will continue to be a major actor trying to set global standard as the EU seems fit. Since the UK will not be able to exert influence in policy making of the EU after Brexit, the UK's role of bringing the EU closer to the ideological posture similar to that of Japan will be reduced if not completely lost. Japan will thus lose one of its strongest allies in the EU.[10]

Does Brexit then mean the end of any British role with regard to the EU for Japan? And will it cause the complete disappearance of the UK's role within the EU with regard to Japan?

As far as Japan's relations with the UK are concerned, it needs to be stressed that there is no alternative to a country like the UK with historical, linguistic, cultural and ideological connections. In this sense, France or Germany will not be able to completely fill the void left by Brexit in assuming the roles hitherto played by the UK. It is therefore to be expected that the UK will continue to be counted on by Japan, even for a reduced indirect influence from "outside" that the UK could have after Brexit. How much "outside" will depend on the final modality of the post-Brexit agreement still under negotiation between the EU and the UK (especially if the UK remains or exits from the customs union).

The EU, for its part, will see its global role diminished by Brexit. The economic size of the EU will be reduced by the departure of the second largest economy of the EU. The political importance of the EU will be reduced, with the loss of a permanent member of the UN Security Council with nuclear capability. It is also expected that the EU, with the

---

[9] Christiansen, T., Defraigne, J.-C., Kubo, H., "The Economic Security Dimension in EU-Japan Relations", in Kirchner, E., Dorussen, H. (eds.), *EU-Japan Security Cooperation: Trends and Prospects*, Abingdon-on-Thames, Routledge, 2019, pp. 163–182.

[10] Tsuruoka, M., "A New Japan-France Strategic Partnership: A View from Tokyo", *Lettre du Centre Asie*, IFRI, No. 75, 2018.

rise of populist anti-EU movements and governments in some Member States, will be obliged to be inward-looking for some time to come.

As for Japan, it is of primordial importance to protect its economic interests in Europe. However, Japan's preoccupation does not end here. Japan is also interested in preserving a peaceful and liberal order in the world on which the future of Japan also depends. Japan's position under these conditions is to maintain a secure and stable order in Europe as a whole, the EU, the UK, and other countries included. It is therefore this quest for order in Europe that will guide foreign policy of Japan in the aftermath of Brexit.

About the Authors

Stephanie Barczewski is Carol K. Brown Scholar in the Humanities and Professor of History at Clemson University. She is the author of five books, the most recent of which is *Heroic Failure and the British* (Yale University Press, 2016). Her current research projects include an exploration of Englishness and the country house and of the invocations of British history in the Brexit campaign.

Frédérique Berrod is Professor of Public Law at Sciences Po at the University of Strasbourg. Frédérique Berrod is teaching EU Law from an institutional and material perspective. She is also teaching EU Energy Law, EU health policy and the EU model of borders in the European integration process. She is invited Professor at the College of Europe in Bruges and invited by the ENA for vocational training sessions. She is the director of a Master 2 Degree on "EU health products" at the Law Faculty of Strasbourg. She is elected at the Conseil d'administration of the University of Strasbourg. Her fields of research are EU Energy Law and health policy. She is currently developing research on borders within the Internal market and cross-border cooperation in the context of EU integration.

Aude Bouveresse is Ph.D. in Law (University of Strasbourg 2007); Referendaire at European Court of Justice (2007–2008); Lecturer at University of Strasbourg (2008–2012), Professor of Public law and European Law, (University of La Réunion and Strasbourg, (since 2013); Director of Research Laboratory of International and EU law (EA 73 07) since 2016. Main Publications on Effectivity of EU law, in the area of Internal market and Judicial Review.

Emmanuel Brunet-Jailly (Ph.D. Western, 99) is a Professor of Public Policy at the University of Victoria, British Columbia, Canada, where he is Jean Monnet Chair in Innovative Governance (2016–2019). Currently, he is the principal investigator for Borders In Globalization a research programme that brings together 30 university research centres in 20 countries.

Jaume Castan Pinos works as an Associate Professor at the Department of Political Science and Public Management, University of

Southern Denmark. He holds a Ph.D. in International Politics (Queen's University Belfast, 2011). He is the Director of the European Studies Bachelor programme at the University of Southern Denmark. His academic interests are framed by ethno-territorial conflicts, sovereignty and political violence. He has conducted extensive research in Catalonia, North Africa and former Yugoslavia. He is the author of *Kosovo and the Collateral Effects of Humanitarian Intervention* (Routledge, 2019).

Catherine Haguenau-Moizard is professor of Public Law at the University of Strasbourg. She is responsible for the Master *Espace de liberté, de sécurité et de justice* and the joint Master in Law with the University of Freiburg (Germany). She has published books and articles about European Union Law and Comparative Law. She teaches in various Universities outside France.

Daisuke Ikemoto is Professor of International Relations in the Faculty of Law, Meiji Gakuin University, Japan. He obtained his DPhil in Politics from the University of Oxford. His work includes *European Monetary Integration 1970–79, British and French Experiences* (Palgrave Macmillan, 2011), for which he was awarded the Japan Society for Promotion of Science (JSPS) Prize in 2013. He is currently writing a biography of Margaret Thatcher.

Ken Masujima is Professor of international relations at Kobe University, Graduate School of Law. Publications in English include: (with Sebastian Harnisch) "Human Security-More Potential for Cooperation?", in Emil Kirchner and Han Dorussen, eds., *EU-Japan Security Cooperation* (London: Routledge, 2018); "EU-Japan Relations", in Knud Erik Jørgensen *et al.*, eds., *Sage Handbook of European Foreign Policy* (London: Sage, 2015).

Seiko Oyama is Associate Professor of International Studies at the School of Humanities and Culture at Tokai University, Japan. She obtained her PhD in Political Sciences from the University of Strasbourg. She works on migrant integration in the EU, and social inclusion through public education.

Jeremy Sacramento recently completed a Masters in International Law and Security at the University of Southern Denmark. Jeremy holds a Master in Public Policy from King's College London, where he was also elected an Associate of King's College, and a Bachelors in International Politics with First Class Honours from the University of Surrey. Jeremy presently authors a fortnightly column for Gibraltar's national newspaper, the Gibraltar Chronicle. His primary academic focus is on microstates, paradiplomacy, and self-determination.

Noriko Suzuki is Professor in Department of Social Sciences in Waseda University, in Japan. She obtained her PhD in Political Sciences from Keio University, in Japan. She is specialized in political sociology. She works on the European citizenship and political participation of European citizens living in the other EU States.

Ruth Taillon is former Director of the Centre for Cross Border Studies, based in Ireland/Northern Ireland. The Centre has a unique role in promoting and improving the quality of cross-border cooperation through research and provision of resources, tools and other practical support. Ruth has many years' experience working with public and civil society organizations in both jurisdictions as a researcher and evaluator specialising in gender, equality, and peace and conflict issues.

Birte Wassenberg is Professor of Contemporary History at Sciences Po at the University of Strasbourg. She holds a Jean Monnet Chair on the contribution of cross-border cooperation to the European Neighbourhood Policy and is Co-Director of the Franco-German Jean Monnet excellence Centre in Strasbourg, Member of the Research Unit UMR Dynamiques européennes and Director of the Master 2 Border Studies in International Relations. From 1993 to 2006 she was responsible for cross-border cooperation at the Région Alsace. She teaches on International Relations, Border studies, regionalism, the history of European Integration and Franco-German Relations. Her research fields are: border regions, Euroscepticism and the history of European organizations, especially the Council of Europe. She is also a former student from the College of Europe, promotion Charles IV (1992–1993).

Borders and European Integration

Edited by

Joachim Beck (Professor of Administrative Studies,
Hochschule Kehl)
Frédérique Berrod (Professor of Public Law, Université de Strasbourg)
Birte Wassenberg (Professor of History of International
Relations, Université de Strasbourg)

The Series « Borders and European Integration » fills in a gap in Social Sciences, as it connects two so far independent research strands: European Studies and Border Studies. Mainly initiated by geographers and originally hosted in the United States, Border Studies primarily deal with the study of borders and borderlands, whereas European Studies analyse the process of European Integration, its actors, institutions and policy fields. Although the idea of a Europe without borders was part of the project of the European Economic Community, the multidimensional role of the border has not been sufficiently taken into account by researchers in European Studies. Inversely, Border Studies have only rarely examined the specificity of borders and borderlands in Europe in comparison to other regions in the world.

At the crossroads between Area Studies and International Relations, this Series therefore offers a pluri-disciplinary approach to borders and their role in the European construction. Taking into account the perspective of different disciplines in Social Sciences, the diversity of actors of European Integration and borderlands (local, regional, national), it allows a new multi-level and decentred view on conflicts and cooperation at European borders. The Series addresses researchers and university scholars of all disciplines in Social Sciences and wishes to tackle the challenging contemporary questions on borders in Europe.

Scientific board

Joachim Beck (Professor of Administrative Sciences, Hochschule Kehl)

Frédérique Berrod (Professor of Public Law, Université de Strasbourg)

Emmanuel Brunet-Jailly (Professor of Public Policy at UVIC, Canada)

Hans-Jörg Drewello (Professor of Economic Sciences, Hochschule Kehl)

Christopher Huggins (Professor of Political Sciences, University of Suffolk)

Fabienne Leloup (Professor of Political Sciences, Université catholique de Louvain-la-Neuve)

Christian Mestre (Professor of Public Law, Université de Strasbourg)

Katarzyna Stoklosa (Professor of Contemporary History, University of Southern Denmark)

Bernard Reitel (Professor of Geography, Université d'Artois)

Birte Wassenberg (Professor of History of International Relations, Université de Strasbourg)

Series titles

Vol. 1. Birte Wassenberg & Bernard Reitel, in collaboration with Mission opérationnelle transfrontalière (Jean PEYRONY & Jean RUBIO), *Critical Dictionary on Borders, Cross-Border Cooperation and European Integration*, 2020.

Vol. 2. Birte Wassenberg & Noriko Suzuki (eds.), *Origins and Consequences of European Crises: Global Views on Brexit*, 2020.

www.ingramcontent.com/pod-product-compliance
Lightning Source LLC
LaVergne TN
LVHW012015060526
838201LV00061B/4312